OPIUM TEA

OPIUM TEA

BY

BIANCA TAM

WITH

Mim Eichler

TALE WEAVER
PUBLISHING

LOS ANGELES

Publisher's Note:

Due to the sensitive nature of this work, some of the names and circumstances have been altered to protect the privacy of persons, living or dead, who may or may not have had contact with the author during the time the events in this book took place.

However, aside from these instances the substance of this story is factual and true.

Library of Congress Cataloging in Publication Data

91-065503

ISBN: 0-942139-02-X

Printed in the United States of America

Tale Weaver Publishing, Los Angeles, CA 90069

In memory of Erwin

PROLOGUE

China. The summer of 1947. A Prisoner-of-War Camp on the Island of Hazelnuts, outside of Canton.

On the night before my scheduled execution, I did not sleep. Many weeks had passed since the conclusion of the trial, since the judge had uttered his irrevocable words: "We find the defendant, Bianca Tam, guilty as charged. She will be taken and shot to death in front of a firing squad, in punishment for her crimes."

All attempts to obtain a pardon had failed and by morning's light I would die.

Yet the night outside my prison cell seemed to pulse with life. The ocean's tide, lapping against the shore of the island, momentarily filled my senses with a strange serenity. Drifting in with fragrant smells from wooded groves surrounding the prison barracks, a warm wind blew through the small open window. The night birds sang, their melodies sweet and full of sorrow. I comforted myself in these last hours of life by thinking that the birds sang just for me, preparing me for the curtain of death soon to fall over the short span of my existence. I was twenty-seven years old.

I never planned on becoming a spy. Well, for that matter, I had never been one to give much thought whatsoever to the future. I was raised in the lap of luxury, in the upper echelons of Italian nobility. Certainly nothing in the education of a young Contessa could have prepared me for the ravages to come. But war changes everything. As does love.

Yes, I became a spy. That is as irrefutable as my guilt, which I never tried to deny. But I was not guilty of treason. I was guilty of youth and I was guilty of passion. It was passion that drove me to stop at nothing in providing for my four living children; the same passion to save them from the fate that took my two precious children who were now dead.

More than anything, I was guilty of passion for the man by whom I bore those children. It was this man who had once entered my secure and certain life, changing it forever. To him did I once swear undying devotion. He was the man I would have followed to the ends of the earth and practically did.

It was probably three in the morning, though I couldn't be sure, when I walked to the window of the cell. The lights of the port twinkled in the dark like stars, as the distant memories of childhood called to me. Or, I wondered, was it the seductive beckoning of death?

How would my life have been different had I never met Major Tam? What would have happened if he had never possessed me, had I never devoured his kisses, felt his caresses? Who would I have become had I never drunk from his cup, the cup of his own forbidden brew?

On my last night of life, my thoughts circled back to another night when I had just turned sixteen years old. it was the first night of married life, the night of my honeymoon. I recalled how Tam prepared it, its pungent smell, its dark and mysterious color. The initial taste was bitter, I was able to remember, but Tam added extra spoonfuls of sugar until finally I drank with desire and a powerful thirst. It was in these moments that a door to another place had been opened, a place in the mind where it was possible to communicate without words, to imagine the infinite galaxies of existence; to sense with heightened awareness the magic and mystery of life; to look down at our human plight with awakened eyes.

And as the panorama unfolded, I went through the opened door willingly, knowing that I journeyed with Tam, that somehow the tea had fused our souls. Whatever uncertainties were to come, I believed, they would be unable to sever us. No harm would come, I thought, not as long as the two of us were together.

For a long time we had remained silent in that place of total peace and in wonderous awe of the majesties of the universe. It was then, after Tam undressed me and we lay together naked on a fur rug in front of the fire, consumed with the most intense and seemingly endless pleasure, that I knew nothing would ever be the same.

Yes, love and war changed everything. And so did opium tea.

Part One:

OPIUM TEA

CHAPTER ONE

Italy. 1920 to 1930. La Spezia, a villa on the Italian Riviera.

"Bianca," my mother's melodic voice sang out, "would you like to help me select a dress for the party this evening?"

I was no more than eight years old and though Mama always allowed me to join her in her boudoir as she prepared for various social events, it never failed to fill me with a sense of excitement and pride.

And when we looked through what seemed to be the infinite number of dresses in her closets, it was always a challenge to pick one properly suited for whatever occasion was at hand. Finally, after debating over a pastel blue satin gown, I pointed emphatically to one of the treasures of her wardrobe — a burgundy velvet — hand embroidered with gold thread and pearls.

Mama laughed, her delicate features awash with delight. "Very well," she said to one of the maids in attendance, "can you put the other dresses away? I'll be wearing the burgundy velvet tonight. Bianca has made up her mind."

Even then my mother knew that once I'd decided upon something, it was impossible to think I could ever change my mind after that.

The closeness I shared with Mama colored the days of my childhood with a bounty of serenity and a happy anticipation of the many entertainments in which she included me. I also loved the quiet moments, sitting at her side in her boudoir when she put on her make-up or strolling together in the gardens of our villa.

Frequently, after Mama dismissed the chauffeur, the two of us would drive along the coast together, our 1925 black and yellow Lancia Augusta easing around the gentle hills of the Riviera. I accompanied her on her visits throughout La Spezia and observed how she was always treated with the utmost respect. And whenever she gave dinner parties for the officers of the nearby military port, I was never treated as a child or sent to bed. Instead, I would remain with the guests, listening to their polite conversations, sometimes noticing the more hidden sexual innuendo that passed between these ladies and gentlemen born to upperclass nobility.

"Maria," one of the officers commented on one such evening, first kissing Mama's hand with a chivalrous air, "you look exceptionally elegant tonight. May I compliment you on your exquisite taste?"

Mama accepted the familiar praise with a shy smile and a nod.

"And," the officer continued, "may I compliment the beauty of your daughter Bianca?"

Now Mama beamed with maternal pride, looking in my direction and responding, "Yes, she is rather extraordinary, isn't she?"

The officer went on, "Indeed, her face shines with an intelligence beyond her years. Her gaze is curious and challenging at the same time. I promise you, Maria, when she comes of age she will slay the hearts of many men."

Of course, these words weren't intended for my ears. But I heard them nevertheless, wondering at the time what possible good it could bring to be able to slay a man's heart! Yet, I suppose I was already aware that my looks were striking. My long wavy blond hair and pale green eyes, often referred to as aquamarine, were uncommon among our peers, young or old.

No matter how well-attired or intrinsically beautiful the female guests were, Mama made them pale by comparison. She was tiny, regal, reserved, her figure and face both perfect to the eyes of all beholders. She had a sweetness and an allure that gave her title of Countess added elements of respect and love. And she was very rich. Our villa, the Villa Lizza on the coast of La Spezia, in which I grew up, had belonged to her family, descendent of the royal Medicis and the noble lineage of the Ligurians.

It was a vast, two-story villa cloistered away in a grove of umbrella pines and eucalyptus trees. Year by year, the bougainvillea that grew along the walls of our estate inched its way toward the sea. A flight of steps carved into the rocks led to a small inlet where my father, Il Signor Conte, taught me to swim.

"Il Signor Conte" is what the local farmers who furnished us with the dry delicious wine and seasoned olive oil called him. But to his friends and colleagues he was Bernardo or Count Peritti and to me he was simply "Papa." A navy man, he would spend a few days with us at the villa between the voyages that sometimes kept him away for many months. He was energetic, a man well aware of his physical prowess. And his dark Mediterranean good looks, though sometimes intimidating, were greatly enhanced by his navy officer's uniform in the eyes of many women.

I eagerly awaited those rare appearances of his, looking forward to his adventurous tales of faraway lands. Papa, in turn, usually was forced to summon what little patience he had to satisfy my demands for attention. As soon as I would see him, striding in the door after an absence of many months, I would rush to him.

"Papa," I would tug at his sleeve almost without a hello, "show me the photographs of where you've been." And as we took a seat and he spread the pictures out in front of me, I had many more questions about the people and places they depicted. His unit frequently accompanied the ships going out to the African colonies and after a while I had collected an album full of pictures of Somalese, Ethiopians, Abyssinians. On other excursions, he was the Navy officer appointed to some of the most highly prestigious cruises of civilian fleets. The photos of these trips, in particular, captivated my young imagination. They portrayed a world of abundant luxury, even more lavish than the one I had come to know. This was my father's world — a privileged mingling of mysterious women and powerful men — a world he loved and kept separate from his family.

Over the years, after so many voyages, Mama came to know what my father expected of her and of our life. He desired many women, several lovers, but only one wife who happened also to be the mother of his child. This type of marital arrangement was perhaps common for men of his time and social class. It was generally accepted; the family had to stay together according to the rules of tradition, of religion, and of the regime. Ultimately, however, it would be an agreement my mother was unwilling to accept. She was much younger than he and resilient enough to overcome the disappointments of her marriage. With an independence unusual for the times, Mama would eventually rebel. In so doing, though probably not on purpose, she would instill a rebelliousness in me that would one day put me on trial for my life.

Of course, as a young child I didn't know that my parents' union was a failure. I accepted Papa's brief visits as parentheses which did not disturb the beauty and happiness of daily life in La Spezia that I shared with Mama.

While my mother spent a good deal of effort grooming me in the ways of the noble rich, she also was concerned that I gain a moral, spiritual upbringing. She tried to teach me what immense fortitude faith could bring, that it was possible to ask for help when one was alone or uncertain, from someone we call God. It was perhaps her greatest gift to me, a living philosophy that would be sorely tested in the not too distant future.

*   *   *

The Italy of my youth was filled with a fervor to create of itself an omnipotent empire. Both the desire to extend its borders through conquest abroad and the national support of Mussolini, were growing more and more widespread. In these early years of Fascism, my family adhered halfheartedly to the party line, hoping "Il Duce" would eliminate those who threatened to disturb our status quo.

When I was ten years old, Papa requested a transfer to land duty and was given a high post at the Ministry of the Navy. And so, I hurriedly said good-bye to La Spezia and along with my parents, made the auspicious move to Rome. I was prepared for the change, even then already aware of the advantages — respect, status, and security — that wealth brings. Little that lay immediately ahead would alter those notions.

*   *   *

Vatican City. 1932.

Quelling the nervousness I felt standing there in line with the other girls of my class, I took that first decisive step forward and readied to perform my well-rehearsed curtsy before Pope Pius XI. I had practiced it so many times in front of the critical, narrow-eyed Mother Superior of the English School in Rome, the most exclusive Catholic boarding school in Italy. It was there that Mama had enrolled me not long after our move to Rome and where I remained while she and Papa took up separate residences. The schooling offered me not only an opportunity to learn both English and French, but also, according to Mama's wishes, a strong religious foundation.

"Perfect, Bianca, perfect," the elderly nun had exclaimed after our last rehearsal. "Just remember: the same ease and grace and the same seriousness."

On this morning our graduating class was enjoying the most honored of the school's many privileges — a private audience with the Pope. We had entered the Vatican through the Arch of the Bells, filing past the Swiss guards in their orange and turquoise uniforms, down the long corridors and sumptuous rooms of the Pontifical Palace, through to the Royal Hall, where we had awaited the Pope's entrance.

The Pope had nodded with approval as trembling hands presented him with our handiwork. It was a fine linen tablecloth embroidered with edelweiss, chosen by the Mother Superior as an homage to the Pope's family origins. His father had been a magnate of the textile industry and the Pope himself, even at his seventy years of age, was known to be an avid Alpine mountain climber.

I swallowed and cast my eyes down, as I had been instructed, and curtsied. At the same moment,

one of the younger priests in attendance leaned close
to the Pope and spoke softly. "This is Bianca, the
daughter and only child of your niece Maria."

I was standing in a child's pose, my feet
together, hands behind my back. My eyes were
lowered as I gazed at my uniform — flat-heeled,
black patent leather shoes and a short, white,
embroidered dress. It was the uniform worn by all
the girls. But already, I had subtly broken rank.
Instead of the braids and ribbons worn by the rest of
my classmates, I had chosen to let my blonde waves
cascade freely down around my shoulders.

It is hard to imagine what prompted the High
Pontiff to draw me close and speak words meant
only for my ears. Perhaps in his wisdom he could see
that I was quite different from my classmates,
already becoming restless and headstrong, and he
offered his words in what would later become a
prophetic note. As he spoke, talking just above a
whisper, my eyes filled with moisture and my face
flushed with pride. Moved as I was, I did not then
grasp the full meaning of what he had said and in
response bowed again quickly.

With a stern glance, the Mother Superior urged
me back to my place in line.

That evening the other girls in the dormitory
gathered in anticipation around my bed. "Bianca,"
one said, "tell us exactly what the High Pontiff
said to you."

"Yes, yes," the others clamored, jumping up
and down.

"Oh," I pretended, "I don't really remember."

They continued to insist I tell them, but the
truth was that I had no intention of sharing the
special recognition I'd received with anyone. After a
while they gave up and still animated by the day's
events, my classmates broke into a youthful chatter,
daydreaming aloud of their futures among the
Roman aristocracy or nouveau riche. Their hopes

were rather predictable as they talked of romance, boyfriends, well-made marriages and the vast fortunes they would one day inherit.

Their visions seemed to have little to do with mine. And when I fell asleep that night, I didn't dream of handsome suitors or material luxuries. Rather, my dreams were wild and dangerous, set in strange and exotic places. I wondered how what the Pope had said to me would affect me in years to come, if it was in fact true that I wasn't headed for a common destiny.

But certainly I would never forget the impact of his words.

"You are very pretty," he had first said. Then the Pope had peered deeply into my eyes and added, "You are very pretty indeed. You must not waste this beauty the Lord has bestowed upon you."

CHAPTER 2

Rome. 1935.

While Il Duce danced the mazurka and the waltz in the arms of robust country girls across the farmhouse floors of central Italy, his sons Bruno and Vittorio took to the syncopated rhythms of the *St. Louis Blues,* played by the likes of Louis Armstrong or the *Hot Five.* In the mid '30s, jazz wasn't yet branded "degenerate music" and English was not yet a prohibited language.

Il Duce's sons gave their parties on the ground floor of the Villa Torlonia where many of the stylish adolescents of Rome's upper class would gather. These young men—their hair slicked back with brilliantine, one curl dangling on their foreheads, long jackets tight around the hips, and shirts open to the waist— were trying to imitate the most fashionable movie idol of the day, Vittorio De Sica, whom we all adored for his role in *What Scoundrels, Men.*

Satchmo's piercing notes and the driving rhythms of Duke Ellington alternated with the languor of songs like "Speak to Me of Love, Mariu" as the early mating rituals got underway. Bruno and Vittorio were a year apart in age, both in the same class with me at the Tasso Lycee in Rome. I had transferred there from the parochial boarding school when Mama decided that an overly-long stay with the nuns might limit me from getting the most well-rounded education possible.

"Bianca," she had said, "you have learned to speak English and French and the nuns have instructed you to be a proper young Italian woman, one day a mother. But now it is time to come into the world and mingle with society."

She reasoned that if the head of state sent his own children to a public school, there was no reason why her daughter—of noble lineage—shouldn't attend as well.

I spent many an afternoon in the official residence of Mussolini, but I never met Il Duce himself or was able to catch a glimpse of Rachel, his wife. It was common knowledge, even to her, that her husband was entangled in several extra-marital affairs, most notably his scandalous trysts with the infamous Claretta, a woman who had certainly become Italy's most talked about personage. Over the years, Rachel Mussolini's recourse seemed to be the same. She was Il Duce's wife and the mother of his five children. She refused to relinquish either role, appearing rarely in public except on official occasions and then closely at her husband's side. As for Bruno and Vittorio, both parents indulged them and allowed them to hold their soirees without chaperones.

It was on one such afternoon that Vittorio Mussolini strode over to me with an invitation to go horseback riding with him the following day. Unlike the other teenage girls who were part of our crowd, I didn't regard our male classmates as possible boyfriends or future husbands. To me, they were more like pals in assorted games—the more adventurous the better! So I gladly accepted, anticipating our date as a challenge to my horsemanship, rather than a romantic encounter.

* * *

It was October. The Roman summer had come alive again, a warm and sunny day, when Vittorio and I took off on horseback into the woods near Lake Bracciano. His horse was a few paces ahead of mine, leading the way up the hill through a thick grove of chestnut trees. Every now and then he turned back to smile at me, but my focus was only on the sunny autumn afternoon and the lush setting surrounding us.

Suddenly, without warning, we found ourselves immersed in a dense fog that completely covered the trail.

Instinctively, I continued up the hill and tried to calm my horse.

"Bianca, wait," Vittorio called out, his voice echoing from behind me at some distance. "We should go back. The fog might last for hours."

I disagreed, reminding him of how he'd boasted that he was familiar with all the trails in the area.

"Yes, I know this trail," he countered, "but this is your first time here."

"Well, then," I exclaimed and spurred my horse, "I suppose I've got a lot to learn!" And off I galloped to the crest of the hill, calling back to him above the pounding of hooves, "Ciao, Vittorio, I'll see you back at the stable."

Just barely, I could hear his panicked voice telling me, "It's a big forest and it'll be dark in a couple of hours. No one will come looking for you!"

"Good," I said out loud to myself, laughing in delight. I was on my own and liked it that way.

Vittorio found his way back along his tracks and I, thanks mostly to luck as I galloped blindly along, managed to head straight down the hill towards a road that encircled the woods.

He eventually caught up with me, dismounted, and took hold of my horse's halter.

"Bianca, are you always so crazy?" he asked, his eyes wide and impressed.

I was out of breath, panting. I told him, "Only when I'm having fun."

Poor Vittorio's face fell, as he muttered sarcastically, "Then I amuse you like a clown. Thanks for the compliment."

"Oh," I shrugged, "what's wrong with that? It's so easy to be bored nowadays."

His eyebrows raised as he pressed in closely to the horse, his eyes riveted to the swell of my bosom and his voice full of young lust. "You know, Bianca, I could never be bored when you're around." Used to getting what he wanted, he didn't wait for a response and firmly placed his hands on my breast, attempting to pull me down off the horse. "Oh," he moaned, "I'm ready to explode for wanting you."

Without a second's hesitation, I pushed his hands away and responded with a cool smile, telling him, "Good. Let's keep it that way." Again, I spurred my horse and with an expression of complete surprise, Vittorio let go of the halter.

* * *

Later, I said nothing to my friends about the outing, much to their disappointment. Though most of the young contessas I knew would have given anything to have captured the heart of so eligible a suitor, the idea simply didn't occur to me that Vittorio could have been my future fiancé. But before I was even in a position to slay his heart, as had once been predicted, Vittorio and his brother Bruno had departed for East Africa to join the Italian troops then engaged in a sinister war.

Perhaps my lack of interest in romantic overtures, which so frequently occupy the concerns of most fifteen year olds, was due to my family situation. Though my parents' separation had been amicable, and though Papa continued to maintain contact during holidays and special occasions by showering me with generous gifts, I suppose I had developed a precocious kind of cynicism about the opposite sex.

It wasn't that I felt personally wounded by my father's lifestyle or by his choices. If anything, I only begrudged him his initial dishonesty which had been such a blatant betrayal—the sacrificing of my mother's love for his unbridled desires. Yet, I could also see that, at least, my father was true to himself, to what he believed. Somehow, despite a lack of experience, I had already come to the conclusion that human passions—those we cannot control or even foresee—can determine our lives much more than those relationships that are sanctified by law or convention.

What I did not know at the time, as the world stood poised on the brink of war, was to what extent my own passions would very soon carry me and to what degree I would ultimately challenge both convention and the law.

CHAPTER 3

Salsomaggiore. 1936.

"Bianca, this just isn't like you," my mother called from her adjoining hotel room. It was the summer of 1936 and as an annual excursion, I'd come with Mama to bathe in the spa's waters at Salsomaggiore. We were staying in our favorite suite at the Grand Hotel des Bains. It had two adjoining rooms that both opened onto the same salon and terrace. In addition to the water's curative affects for her chronic rheumatism, my mother had also been able to spend some time with Captain Ferrari, a dashing Florentine nobleman she had been seeing for several months.

But on the evening that lay ahead, she and I had planned to dine alone on the hotel terrace and Mama was growing impatient at the inordinate amount of time I was taking to dress. It was true, as she said, that it wasn't like me. Though perhaps I'd already inherited a fondness for haute couture, I almost never bothered to primp before an event. Yet something was different about the evening, I thought to myself, as I slipped into the low cut ebony silk dress, its belt cinching in tight at my waist. I felt a sense of impending excitement in the warm summer air, as if something magical was in store for me.

When I finally stepped through the door into Mama's room, she quickly drew in a breath. "Bianca..." she began with a serious tone and paused to study my choice of attire. Then her voice trailed off.

"What is it?" I inquired, thinking maybe I was overdressed—my hair pinned up in loose blonde ringlets and Papa's gift of an expensive strand of pearls looped around my neck, somewhat enhancing the gown's low cut.

"Oh, it's nothing," she laughed, composing herself. "It's just that you look very beautiful. And, I might add, very sophisticated for a sixteen-year- old."

I certainly wasn't consciously planning on impressing anyone. If anything about me that night was calculated, it was merely to find a diversion in a routine that was starting to bore me. I had to admit, however, as we took our seats in the center of the hotel terrace, I couldn't help noticing the stolen glances thrown at me by many of the hotel patrons— from both men and women. Nor did these reactions escape my mother's observant eyes. But just as she opened her mouth to say something, our attention was drawn to the entrance of the dining area where we spotted an unexpected yet familiar face. It was Antonio, my cousin and childhood playmate. He strode gallantly in our direction and a group of young men in uniforms followed close behind him.

"Aunt Maria, Cousin Bianca," Antonio sang out, kissing Mama's hand and my cheek, "I was given a few hours leave from the military academy in

Modena where I've been studying and decided, on the spur of the moment, to pay you a visit."

I could see that my cousin was in high spirits, no doubt a result of the comraderie so characteristic of the military academy. His severe blue officer's uniform, complete with a cutlass and gold braid, seemed to me to be rather incongruous with the childish expression of his eyes and his actual age. It occurred to me that his stance more befitted a little boy playing soldier than a young officer studying the art of war. I didn't comment, of course, since in those days—as the prospect of a world-wide war had begun to turn real—one didn't dare criticize the seriousness of the Italian military academies. Instead, I asked him whether he was going to let his friends continue to look so awkward standing off in a huddle by themselves.

Antonio laughed, gesturing to the young officers to approach, and apologized to Mama for not coming alone.

"Don't be silly," my mother insisted. Recognizing that the young men were very hungry after their long drive, she asked the waiter to prepare a table that could accommodate all of us.

Mama and I rose as Antonio began a round of introductions. Each of the cadets, in turn, made sweeping bows, greeting the Countess Maria with gratitude for her hospitality. Most of the young men were familiar to us from various social events in Rome. Only one of the faces was new. And it was a face that had me entirely tongue-tied.

In fact, I wasn't hearing a word of what Antonio and his friends were saying. Rather, I was aware of a strange beating in my chest, a pulsing of my blood that I'd never felt before. It happened every time I looked at the mysterious stranger.

His face and skin were smooth like marble and he had the most intense black eyes. His physique was also striking—tall, sinewy, with a broad chest and square shoulders. He exuded a calm but powerful determination.

"This is Tam Gian Ciau," Antonio introduced him at last, "but everyone calls him Tam. He was born in Canton, China, and is here in Italy for military studies." Then Antonio laughed, explaining, "Our professors are highly regarded abroad."

"I will leave your country," said Tam, in a clear, almost solemn voice, "as soon as I have earned my degree. My country is at war and needs me."

One of the other cadets pointed out, "As you can hear, he has already mastered Italian."

"Excellent, really," my mother agreed, visibly impressed.

Antonio held my chair as we sat down again. "Tam, or rather Prince Tam," he murmured in my ear, "is a true gentleman and a remarkable fellow. You'll see what I mean."

Once again I saw of flicker of concern mixed with maternal pride in my mother's expression as she could hardly overlook the affect I was having on the five young men at the table.

Thankfully, though, by the time dinner was served the conversation turned to talk of the war. The young cadets were eager to join their fellow officers who had already embarked for the sands of East Africa. Their bravado and outspoken opinions were articulated with raised voices. Perhaps they behaved so on purpose, as a way to bait any possible opposition to the war from nearby hotel guests. All the while, however, Tam remained silent.

"Don't you share the enthusiasm of your friends?" I asked, speaking directly to him for the first time.

He said without apology, "My classmates want to conquer a country that their government has declared war on. I am six thousand miles from my home which has been attacked by the Japanese. And every day my people are dying in an attempt to defend themselves from this domination. None of you can even imagine what it is like to live under foreign occupation."

Tam's Italian was correct but not yet fluent, and he spoke these words resolutely, syllable by syllable. Everything about his demeanor was utterly different from the fatuous and exaggerated airs of Antonio and the other young Italian cadets.

"Couldn't you already be there helping your country?" I asked.

"No, Signorina, we have many soldiers but few officers who know how to combat the Japanese. They are a race of warriors and they consider us inferior because they have defeated us many times. I will be more useful when I have finished my studies."

"Be patient," Antonio butted in. "In three years you will be the youngest officer in the Chinese army. And the best, I'm sure."

Tam smiled at Antonio's compliment and then put his dessert spoon down in the empty dish. He was silent again, his eyes lowered as if in deep concentration, as if he was about to do something that required great effort and that he decidedly wanted to succeed.

Finally, he lifted his face and spoke his words all in one breath, "I believe that the ladies are sufficiently informed as to our plans and that we shouldn't annoy them any longer. The orchestra has begun to play and," he nodded to my mother, "I would like to ask the Countess if I may have the honor of the first dance with Bianca."

Mama responded nonchalantly, "Of course. That is, if Bianca wishes." But the look on her face, as I eagerly accompanied Tam to the dance floor, was far from nonchalant.

I was smitten. To the sounds of the soaring violins, Tam moved with a commanding grace. Like a stalking tiger, he was sure of his steps, never tiring. There was something awesome and enthralling in the way he carried himself—that power I had first recognized which he kept hidden beneath a veneer of civility. I was sure, by the fact that no one even attempted to break in, that everyone could see how taken I was. But I didn't care. I had never felt so at ease in the arms of a man. Tam was a real man, despite his smooth, beardless chin and flushed cheeks. His eyes shone with depth and focus, a quality that sent new, strange flutters of desire throughout my body. And there was something more. While we twirled in perfect rhythm with one another, I had the eeriest feeling that our meeting had been somehow ordained, planned, that this Tam was in some way a chosen person in my destiny. I knew already that he was about to change my destiny.

As the music continued to resound, Tam came to a stop and our dancing ceased. "I have very little time before I go back to the barracks," he said, fixing me with those purposeful eyes. "I do not want to waste a single moment."

Still, he didn't try to take me aside, or as many other young men had tried without success, to lure me outdoors for a private walk in the lamp-lit gardens. Yet even so, from these moments forward, I knew I would follow him anywhere.

Just before we returned to the table, he said in what seemed to be an offhand way, "Signorina Bianca, I would love someday to show you my country."

"When?" I replied instantly, but was cut short by Antonio's voice calling to his friends that it was time to go back to the academy.

Quickly, Tam asked, "Can I see you next Sunday? I mean, if I were to come alone?"

Our words overlapped and my heart pounded with happiness. "Yes," I sang, "that will be fine. We'll still be here on Sunday."

He whispered solemnly, "I would have come to you wherever you were."

Tam turned to my mother and kissed her hand. "Bianca has occupied me all evening. You must be proud to have such a lovely daughter."

Her own beauty and elegance evident as always, Mama said, "Yes, Bianca is a delightful girl."

"Woman, you mean," Tam objected. "In China girls may marry at fifteen."

There was a slight combative edge to my mother's voice as she explained that in Italy our customs were altogether different.

Tam was unscathed in stating his philosophy. "But, regardless of culture, love knows no age." His eyes darted for a second to mine as he added, "As long as both the husband and wife agree."

At the same moment, Antonio took my arm and gestured toward Tam. "What did I tell you," he asked, "isn't he extraordinary? You never took your eyes off him."

For once my matchmaking cousin had been right.

Mama and I accompanied the young men to the stairs and watched as they descended down from the terrace to the park, she and I waving to them while the five took their seats in a shiny new Balilla and drove speedily away.

I floated back across the hotel's dance floor as if in a trance, heading up to my room without a word. Later, when Mama came to say goodnight, she sat down at my bedside, took my hand and stroked my hair. "Did you enjoy yourself this evening?"

Seeing only my subtle smile, she must have understood that, indeed, her daughter had fallen in love for the very first time.

The next morning, after I'd ordered a breakfast to be sent up to my room, I was surprised to see the entrance of not one but two maids. One carried the breakfast tray, while the other held a huge basket of yellow roses. They were exquisite, brilliantly

hued yellow buds, not a simple bouquet but dozens
of the most fragrant roses I'd ever smelled. As soon
as the maids left, I jumped out of bed and tore open
the card that was pinned to the roses. There on the
note, I read only his name, the name I knew I would
find: "TAM."

*   *   *

The days that followed loomed like centuries.
When, oh when, I kept wondering, was it going to
be Sunday?

Finally, the afternoon had arrived and there it
was, the Balilla approaching in the distance and
turning toward the hotel. From where I sat, below a
willow tree by one of the spa's many pools, I could
see Tam before he spotted me; this, for some reason,
being a matter of importance.

I was dressed very simply, with no make-up, no
pearls, my hair casually falling around my shoulders
and had carefully chosen the tranquil setting in
which to wait for him. Luckily, the area happened to
be deserted for a change, affording me the
opportunity to be alone with my thoughts. I had
pondered whether perhaps the intoxication I felt
over Tam had been a fleeting illusion of that magical
night when we'd met. Maybe, I had wondered, I
would feel differently by the light of day.

But just as the car came to a stop, I knew
otherwise. Seeing Tam emerge from it, I thought I
was going to faint. My chest palpitated with
excitement as I saw him walking toward the hotel.
For a second, he stopped to put some small package
into his pocket and then he ran up the steps and
disappeared inside the hotel. Moments later, as I'd
hoped, he reappeared at the back side of the hotel
and headed in my direction. True to his word, Tam
would search for me and find me wherever I was. I
stood up, unsteady as my legs were, to greet him.

His face was flushed from the drive. Under the heat of the afternoon summer sun, his skin glistened through a veil of masculine perspiration. Once more I saw his dark eyes sparkling with life. Above them, beads of sweat had gathered along his hairline. He seemed wrought with emotion when he spoke, "I rushed all the way here to see you."

Tam was sensual like a young animal and I was overwhelmed by his beauty.

Quietly, I suggested that we remain in the park under the shade of the willow trees to escape some of the summer heat. I swallowed and found the courage to say, "Why don't you loosen your collar?"

"If you don't mind." Tam did so, taking a seat next to me on the grass.

Everything that was happening seemed to be moving in slow motion, like in a dream or a pastoral painting. My words and actions were in no way premeditated, but appearing to happen of their own accord.

"Here," I said softly and handed him my scented handkerchief. He inhaled its sweet fragrance, wiped his face, then tucked the handkerchief away in his jacket.

"Oh, Tam," I remembered, "the roses have bloomed, every one of them. They are so lovely."

A cool gentle breeze blew a few strands of hair into my face. With a light, instinctual touch, Tam brushed them back into place. I smiled at him, lowering my eyes when he next took my hand in his. The sensation was that of silk upon silk.

"I have been thinking about you every hour of every day for the last week," he said. "Ever since we met. I've never met anyone like you before and I know I'll never meet anyone like you in the future."

Before I could say anything, he took me in his arms and kissed me. His lips explored mine at length and his taste was even sweeter than I'd imagined. It was a long, deep kiss, only a hint of the incredible hunger for one another that was to come. In the meantime, he held me against him firmly for several minutes, both of us unable to speak. Despite the coolness of the shade under the tree, the contact of our bodies created a heat inside us that was even more enhanced by the hot weather.

The world surrounding us grew still and silent. Clouds gathered overhead, obscuring the sun. The wind picked up again and the landscape darkened. I knew we were in for a storm, but I only pressed closer to Tam and was uncertain anymore whose pulse was whose. A few drops of warm rain fell from the willow branches as Tam released from our embrace and removed the small wrapped box from his pocket. "A gift," he explained.

I opened it slowly, wanting to savor every second, and found myself gazing at a dainty gold ring that held a magnificent sapphire. I looked back at Tam, speechless.

He placed it on my finger, saying, "This was a gift from my mother, to be given in turn to the first woman I fell in love with."

Suddenly there was a violent crack of thunder and a jagged flash of lightning across the sky. All at once, the rain pounded on us in a heavy downpour. But instead of running, Tam took me again in his arms and kissed me more ardently than before. This time our lips parted and our tongues drank each other in, the taste of the falling raindrops on our mouths as well. He ran his hands closely down the curves of my body, revealed so boldly to him by the tightness with which my wet clothes were clinging. I had never experienced such a state of arousal and I wanted more. I wanted to touch his manhood, to feel his taut musculature through his soaking wet uniform, to see how far the extent of our mutual desire could go. The fact that our little corner of the park was about to be flooded thrilled me even more.

It was the danger of it I loved. And perhaps, on an unconscious level, it was the potential danger of Tam that I loved. In any event, had I been in any way prescient, I might have realized that the storm was an ill omen—nature's warning that the road ahead with him would be full of peril.

Before giving in to the aims of our libidos, we came almost simultaneously to our senses, leapt to our feet, joined hands and ran together through the blinding rain. By the time we reached the entrance of the hotel, we were both completely drenched and shivering from the sudden cold.

"Let's go and dry off in my room," I said as we stepped inside.

Seeing us so—like two bedraggled urchins—the startled doorkeeper's jaw dropped. No doubt that we had certainly shaken up the tedium of his afternoon.

Laughing outright, Tam and I ran up two flights of steps and down the corridor to my room. There, waiting for us by the door, was Mama, her arms folded and her tone strained. "Bianca, I was just coming to look for you. No one knew where you were. You're soaking wet, you know, and you'll have to change immediately."

"In a moment," I said, gesturing to my companion, "Mama, you remember Tam, don't you?"

"Yes, of course," she nodded, "Hello, Tam." And to me she added only a bit sternly, "You didn't tell me we were expecting him."

Not sure exactly why I'd refrained from informing her, I shrugged, offering no excuse as I said, "Well, he came to see me."

"Yes, Countess," Tam interjected, "I had something urgent to say to Bianca."

My mother turned to him, mildly taken aback and said with a laugh, "Am I allowed to know what was so urgent or is it a secret?"

Tam smiled, a smile both mysterious and open. When he answered her, I didn't know who was more surprised—Mama or myself.

"No secret at all," he said. "I came to ask Bianca to marry me."

CHAPTER 4

Rome. 1936.

My mother was totally up in arms, but during the first few weeks she tried to reason with me.

"Look," she said, taking my hand and sitting down next to me, "I know you, Bianca. I raised you. Believe me, I know that you were born to love a man with all your heart and soul. But darling, you have no earthly idea of what it means to be a wife in China. Tam will be away fighting, you'll be at home waiting, with no friends and no one to keep you company, and God knows how many children."

"I love Tam, Mama, and if I don't marry him, what will I do with myself?" I tried to use reason as well, reminding her that I'd finished my schooling and asking whether she expected me to play countess for several more years, hoping someone more acceptable might come along. I rose up, pulling my hands from hers, imploring, "Mama, do you want me to be like all the other frivolous Italian girls, is that it?"

So our conversations would usually begin, leading directly to her plaintive question, "Bianca, I just don't understand, why are the two of you in such a hurry?"

"And I don't understand why we should wait," I would insist, my voice raising. "After all, he comes from an excellent family."

She would momentarily agree, "Yes, a rich and a united family. But in China a woman is considered nothing. The man marries her, gets her pregnant numerous times, runs off with a concubine, and then comes back just to get her pregnant again. And she waits, and waits, and isn't even allowed to throw a fit of jealousy, because they don't even know what jealousy is!"

I would counter sharply, "That's nonsense! Tam was educated in Europe and has grown up with our ways."

By this point Mother and I would reach a full-blown argument. I would accuse her of being provincial, a racist, that her superior attitude suggested she believed our culture was more civilized than China's.

Very nearly in tears, Mama would beg me to think of Papa and what our life had been like during his long absences. She truly believed that Tam would revert to the ways of his world once he was back in it and that I would be the one forced to adapt to him. "Just remember," she warned, "it is very difficult for a woman to maintain her independence. In any culture."

The arguments continued incessantly for two months until the end of summer, when, as I'd promised, I was to give Tam my final answer. Since our return to Rome, I hadn't even been able to see him and my only comfort had been from his long, passionate letters that arrived at least once a day.

In my heart, I was certain that my mother's worries were unfounded, that she didn't know the Tam I knew. Her biggest concern, however, had little to do with him or his nationality. It was the fact that because Tam and I would be married in a Catholic ceremony—his family was also Catholic—I would be unable to obtain a divorce should things not work out.

At her wit's end and unbeknownst to me, Mama appealed to my father for help. I was understandably surprised when he appeared for dinner one evening, after not having seen us in many months, accompanied by an old friend who had been the military attaché of the Italian Embassy in China for many years. This gentleman, now retired from the army, presented me with his opinion on the matter.

An attractive older man, he began by saying that his feelings were formed not by a superficial reaction but by many, many years of experience in the East. He seemed to speak with wisdom and compassion and for once I tried to at least consider an opposing point of view.

"You see, Bianca, the Chinese are a very proud people who do not care for foreigners. You may win favor with Tam's family, but you will never be accepted by others. Europeans who live in China keep exclusively to their own company and do not mix with the Chinese. They have no contact with the local population and would neither appreciate nor understand a young and beautiful Italian girl like yourself who marries a Chinese. If you decide to go through with it, keep in mind that you will soon find yourself completely alone, and remember that everything your mother has told you about the customs of Chinese husbands is perfectly true."

"Yes," Papa echoed, "and please understand that we are not trying to control you, because we know that would be impossible. We're only afraid for you."

I looked around at the three adults, fear plainly revealed in their eyes, and shook off a sudden chill. I rose from the table, defiance and fearlessness emblazoned on my face, and ran up to my room.

It was their last attempt to dissuade me. Later that night, Mama came to my room. From the resigned look on her face, it appeared that she had given up the fight to hold me back from my plans. I glanced up from my desk, where I sat in my nightgown with all of Tam's letters spread out in front of me.

"One last question," she began, her voice unsteady. "From everything that has been said, do you really understand what sort of life awaits you?"

"Yes, I do," I answered emphatically. "And I'm not afraid. I know that Tam would never be untrue to me and I am prepared to stake that knowledge against everything that's been predicted."

"That's your decision?" She muffled a deep sigh.

"Yes."

Mama hurried from the room, true despair plainly written in her eyes. It occurred to me that in a strange way I was stronger than my own parents. In breaking down their resistance, I had never before been so unyielding and in the process came to see them in a new light. Perhaps it was a false light, but I saw them as small-minded and attached to the mundane security of playing everything safe, unable to take risks. In contrast, I saw myself as the one with real daring, the risk-taker, the lover of danger. I knew without question that Tam would bring me a new way of life—one that was more fascinating and more unpredictable. In this, I would not be wrong.

*   *   *

The wedding was celebrated in Rome in October 1936 at Saint Peter's Cathedral. Pope Ratti was still head of the Catholic Church and my mother had been able to arrange for us to be married there. She wanted to exalt the traditions of our family and to remind everyone in attendance that Tam was Catholic too. But unfortunately, I realized as I walked down the aisle on Papa's arm, the small number of guests on hand was proof of the hostility and disapproval that the news of our marriage had stirred publicly.

As I approached my handsome beloved who waited nervously for me at the altar, I noted that very few of my father's friends—officials, important men from the Ministry of Defense and the Diplomatic Corps—were present at the ceremony. Nor had any of my friends from the Tasso Lycee deigned to come. These were the years of the "racial superiority" of Fascism. I found it ironic that little distinction was made between the black slaves that the regime was supposedly trying to liberate in Africa and the "impenetrable yellow devils." That was what the Chinese were called by westerners who knew nothing about them, except their passion for opium and the savagery they had demonstrated during the Boxer Rebellion of 1900—a brutal uprising that had been targeted against foreign influence in China.

In defiance of such stereotypical thinking and in homage to Tam, I had chosen to wear a wedding dress that had been designed to evoke a Chinese influence. It was a floor-length gown of priceless white crêpe de Chine that was fitted tightly around the bodice, waist and ankles, with a hood that left only my face and a few strands of hair showing. More than one person had commented that, attired as I was, I resembled the stylized art nouveau prints of Oriental women which had recently become so popular in Europe.

As I reached Tam's side, he nodded with a poignant expression, acknowledging how much the dress meant to him. We knelt together before the

Priest, both of us gladdened in the knowledge that all of his classmates from the military academy were there to share in our nuptials. It was also heartening to have the Chinese ambassador to Rome join with us to serve as Tam's witness. Even more meaningful was the fact that a few years earlier, in this very same chapel, Pope Pius XI had consecrated the first Chinese bishops. So I took the Papal benediction we were receiving as a reproach to all who were absent.

And certainly nothing could surpass or detract from the pure happiness I felt when I gazed at my groom. The joy that shone in Tam's face gave him the most endearing, boyish look. Truly, after all, he was little more than a boy, so obviously and deeply in love, victorious in being able to declare his love in the eyes of God and the congregation. In that moment, of course, I didn't reflect on my own youth. As naive and sheltered as I was, it simply wasn't within my sphere of experience to realize how drastically life could possibly change as a result of our hurry to be married.

I couldn't help but notice that Mama was beaming at the two of us. Maybe, I hoped, she was finally giving us a vote of approval. Or maybe, the intense happiness that Tam and I exuded was just contagious.

Having been pronounced "man and wife," my new husband and I turned triumphantly to one another. As we left the church, the cadets formed an arch with their upraised swords for us to pass through. When we emerged from it, a sharp gust of wind suddenly cut through the fine silk of my dress. I drew closer to Tam and he in turn took me under his officer's cloak, the both of us laughing openly that we had thwarted the attempts of the photographer who was standing by to take the official wedding photos.

The reception was held in the salon of the exclusive Casina Valadier. Although Tam's mother, an elderly widow, had been unable to journey to Rome, it was her gift that became the centerpiece of the party. At considerable expense, she had sent us an eighteenth century kimono—originally made for the concubine of Hung-li, the Fourth Emperor of the Ch'ing Dynasty which had ruled China for three centuries. On its sky blue silk background were red and gold embroidered dragons crisscrossed with inlaid stripes of green and royal blue silk. To acknowledge its beauty and display it properly, Mama had special ordered a large mannequin. As we had intended, the kimono drew nothing but awed praise from all the guests.

In addition to the kimono, Tam's mother would continue to give her blessings to our marriage by sending us a generous check from Canton every month for the next three years. Mama, too, contributed to our well-being by furnishing the house in Turin where we planned to live while Tam completed his military studies there.

And Papa's gift was a brand new six-cylinder Alfa Romeo Spider, the first touring car ever produced by an Italian maker.

It was in this flaming red convertible sports car that we departed for our honeymoon immediately following the reception. Because Tam's leave was almost over, we had planned to take a brief five day getaway to an inn many miles north of Rome. But as we sped up the Via Cassia, our mutual desires prevented us from continuing much past the outskirts of town. The autumn wind pounded in our faces almost as powerfully as we hungered for one another and we pulled off near the medieval walls of Viterbo, hurriedly checking into a local hotel. For the first time I signed my new name, "Bianca Tam," in the register and just for a few seconds lovingly ran my fingers over the signature. Then, Tam and I literally raced to our suite. To anyone seeing us, there could have been no doubt as to why we were in such a rush and even as he carried me over the threshold, our breathing had already become measured and husky. At long last, we were finally alone.

Looking out the window of our room, we could actually see the tall spire of the Church where we had just been wed. In the twilight, it was breathtaking to gaze at the Piazza of the Popes and the Ducal Palace. And beyond the arches of Viterbo, a few house lights flickered along the hillside.

We turned from the glorious view to drink one another in. Since we had driven the whole way with the roof open, my cheeks were tinged a deep red from the cool evening air and my eyes still stung with tears from the wind. Tam removed my hat, loosened my hair down upon my shoulders and kissed away the moisture on my face. Then he put his hands on my waist, almost encircling it. Slowly, he kissed my eyes, my cheeks, my chin, my mouth. He kissed me for a long time until the room was dark, then eased the fur coat off my shoulders so that it dropped to the floor. Slowly, surely, he began to undress me. When I was naked he pressed me against the wall near the window, took off his clothes, and went down on his knees in front of me. He kissed my belly, my thighs, caressing me with his tongue, then exploring between my legs. He licked me tenderly at first, then more deeply, insistently. I clutched at his hair, breathing heavily, gasping, and moaning softly. But Tam kept on and on, the wetness and rhythm of his mouth causing a great fluid sensation all through me as my body undulated of its own volition. Finally, I forced a whisper of my desire, "Tam, I beg you, possess me completely, take me now!"

He lifted me in his long muscular arms, placed me gently onto the bed, and separated my legs. Then he took me for the first time—all of me—until together we convulsed in exquisite spasms of ecstasy. All through the night, he took me again and again.

The first rays of dawn were streaking across the night sky when Tam got up to stir the coals of the dying fire. He closed the shutters and returned to bed. I fell asleep cradled in his arms and we didn't awaken until the afternoon. When we opened our eyes to the sound of a thick, steady rain outside, we were both filled with a cozy sense of contentment.

"Hungry?" he asked.

"They won't bring us anything to eat at this hour," I said sleepily.

"They will bring us a cup of tea. That will do fine." He smiled mysteriously and rose to re-ignite the fire.

There was a knock at the door. Tam hastily put on his yellow silk robe and I, still nude, slipped quickly into the bathroom while he opened the door.

"Everything all right, sir?"

I heard Tam respond, "Yes, fine, thank you. We were about to order some tea. Bring an extra pot of hot water, please. We are very thirsty."

"Yes, sir, right away. Would you care for some pastries?"

"Yes, thank you," Tam replied. I came out of the bathroom just as Tam closed the door, then saw him jerk it open again and call down the corridor, "And lots of sugar, please."

After the two pots and the pastries had been delivered, I curled up in the armchair, loving the fact that I was dressed in the shirt of my husband's uniform. I watched him with curiosity as he opened a silver tobacco case.

"It's from India. There are some things they do better than we Chinese do." He warmed a small ball of black-green paste over the fire. "It's better to smoke it, but I don't believe that my superiors would be very pleased to see me with an opium pipe. Besides, pipes are a real bother." He felt the side of the teapot and seemed satisfied with its temperature. Then, stepping into the bathroom, he poured the tea down the sink, dropped the ball of opium into the teapot, filled the pot with all the hot water from the second pot, and added a few spoonfuls of sugar. He placed the tea tray near the fire.

"Don't think that I will fix you a cup of opium tea every time you're hungry," Tam warned with a laugh. A dreamy look came into his eyes and he added, "But there's nothing better when you are feeling tired and you still want to make love."

My curiosity had changed to agitation. This was a side of Tam I'd known nothing about and I didn't think myself so totally naive. I'd heard of the addictions, the madness that opium could bring. "How... how often," I stammered, "do you do this?" I pointed to the steaming cup, referring also to the smoking of the opium as well.

Tam responded cryptically, "Only on special occasions." Then he added that the partaking of opium's pleasures was prevalent among most of the upperclasses throughout the East. He started to say something about his family, "You know we..." but apparently changed his mind about what he wanted to say, smiled again and said briefly, "...we respect its powers and use it with discretion."

"But Tam," I murmured, "I've heard that, well, doesn't it make you lose your mind?"

He gave me a fond, teasing look, as if to say I was talking like a foolish adolescent.

"No," he said, shaking his head, "you do not lose your mind. And you do not find it. It is quite natural, the opium relaxes you completely. You have no idea how good it feels." With this, his eyes compelled me to draw near and I realized that, no matter what, I would follow him in whatever dark adventure he initiated.

He checked to make sure the opium had dissolved, poured me a large cup of it and told me to drink it slowly. It was very bitter at first, but after he had added some more sugar, I had no more objections. Tam lay down on the fur skins carpeting the floor and propped his back against a pillow, waiting for the opium to take effect. I stretched out on the floor as well, not far from him, experiencing the beginnings of a blissful state. It seemed that the distance separating me from various objects in the room had vanished, and that I could touch anything merely by thinking about it.

"Do not worry," he said, "if your words do not come as quickly as your thoughts." A blanket of serenity hovered around us and magical visions danced before me. It was neither hallucinatory nor sedating, but rather, everything I thought seemed to crystalize and become purer and clearer and more alive. Not in the wildest dreams of the child that I really was—or that I had been up until this moment—had I imagined such oneness with another, without even touching, and such oneness with the universe.

Tam was breathing deeply when he spoke again, promising, "Whatever you wish, whatever you desire, I will feel before you tell me." He turned on his side, facing me, loosening his silk robe, and he guided my hand between his legs. I caressed him at length, then covered his naked smooth body with kisses. As I took him fully in my mouth, he swelled with excitement and at just the split-second before the very height of his pleasure, I straddled his hips and let him release, his body shuddering and his seed flowing inside of me. Never had I imagined such heaven, such a merging of two bodies as one, but I held back on my own pleasure. I wanted to devote myself totally to his every wish, to serve him in this most fundamental way. Seeing the effect of his fulfillment, which I had given him, made me feel all the more aroused and desirous.

"Now you," he whispered and I abandoned myself to him, my body quivering as he stroked the insides of my thighs, his lips kissing and tongue licking between my legs, the ripples of pleasure growing more and more intense inside of me. When he entered me again, his entire body stroking up into me, I gave in completely to continual waves of pleasure that seemed as though they would never end.

Later, as we lay naked still, our energies completely spent, Tam saw the goosebumps on my skin and reached for my fur coat, covering me with it.

His eyes glistened with moisture as he spoke. "Today I have learned something new about our love. When I saw you come into the Pauline Chapel, and later by the way you looked at the city while we were driving through it, I saw that Rome is something that belongs to you; something ancient which lives in you, it is yours. In the same way, I belong to what is left of the most ancient Chinese civilization. We are different, we come from distant worlds, but we both have our deep love in common."

"No, Tam," I said softly, "I don't feel you are different. Our wedding confirmed to me that I have always been waiting for you. I said yes to you immediately because it was as if I had always known you and I had always been waiting for you to arrive and to take me away with you."

On some level, though I didn't say so, the opened doors to experince that had come with the drinking of the tea had also been exactly what I had been waiting for—as much a part of my destiny as Tam himself was.

*   *   *

After we left Viterbo, we continued our honeymoon northwards without set plans or fixed destinations. All the while we indulged our passions and appetites as our awareness of time and place was suspended. Our love was so vast, like the mighty oceans, pulsing with a vital power and continually changing to reveal new and different features. With or without the drinking of opium tea, sometimes smoking it instead, or forgetting about it altogether, the moments with Tam ebbed and flowed as he proposed a million different ways to love me. He possessed me each time with both force and tenderness, never once neglecting my needs and desires.

It seemed to me that I had lived unaware, until him, that this kind of pleasure could exist. Rather than becoming exhausted, it was one that constantly grew. And as our pleasure grew more and more satisfying, it too became more and more intense. This perfect melding of two souls and two bodies into one, I knew, was rare for my young age. What I didn't know was that it was rare at any age. But as only fate would bear out, I still had much more to learn about love.

CHAPTER 5

Turin. 1936-1939.

Tam began his studies at the School of War in Turin and I began my new life as a housewife and soon-to-be mother. Yes, it was no surprise when a few months after our wedding I discovered I was pregnant with our first child.

Life was simple and sublime, I acknowledged to myself, bringing dinner to the table and announcing to Tam, "Chicken with almonds in a sweet and sour sauce. It's a recipe from Shanghai. At least that's what it says in the cookbook! And you have a choice of jasmine tea or Barbera wine to drink."

"Tea for me and wine for you," he answered, giving me a quick approving smile. "This is delicious," he commented upon tasting my culinary efforts. "But I know this dish takes a long time to prepare."

I could only sigh, reminding him that since he was rarely at home, my days spent waiting for him to return from school were long and that I didn't much care for going out alone.

His face registered concern as he took my hands and asked, "Is it boring to be the wife of a military man?"

"Not at all," I shook my head, telling him, "because I'm so in with love you."

It was true, as I said to him, that I preferred waiting for him at home over going out and developing superficial friendships. I relished our precious time together and the fact that I was several months pregnant did nothing to diminish Tam's healthy sexual appetite for me; nor mine for him. I also loved just sitting down with him after a long day and listening to him talk about everything—about strategic ideology, about the exciting life we would soon be leading in China, and about the immense countryside. Tam talked and talked and I dreamed along with him, envisioning our little growing family cloistered away waiting for him in some tiny village near the front. I was still obstinately convinced that I'd made the right choice by discarding the comfortable, conventional life promised to me as the daughter of a good Italian family to instead follow Tam.

Realistically speaking, it was hard to imagine that the world waiting for us in China would be anything but difficult. The waiting itself took its toll as the continual news of the success of the Japanese army dampened Tam's spirits. I comforted him by repeatedly pointing out what a difference he would be able to make once he had returned and reported for duty. At the same time, I tried to learn everything I could about the recent brutal history of his beloved land.

Tam described how, after conquering Manchuria, the Japanese troops had arrived in Hong Kong and had systematically begun to surround the Republic of China. Not even the Chinese destruction of the dams on the Yellow River and the flooding of the plains to the south of Shantung had been able to keep the Japanese from advancing.

Peking had fallen and after a cruel battle, so had Shanghai. Nanking—where Chiang Kai-shek's government was based, Canton—where Tam's family lived, and Hankau were all abandoned to the Japanese who proclaimed a New Order for East Asia. The intent, Tam explained, was for all the occupied territories to be united in one single state including Japan, China, and Indochina, and all to be ruled from Tokyo.

With one defeat after another, the Nationalist Army continued to retreat inland, establishing its new capital in Chungking, a city in the province of Szechwan on the banks of the Yangtze River, thousands of miles from the sea.

Meanwhile, Tam related, in the province of Yunan, Mao Tse-tung gathered what was left of his troops. Mao ruled over a small but well-organized infantry, well-defended in a secure region of the Soviet Republic. Knowing that his troops were much too weak to face the Japanese, he preferred to avoid a clash and to consolidate his position. There was great hostility between the Nationalist and Communist armies, incited particularly by the memory of the 1927 Shanghai massacre. It was there that Nationalist troops wiped out thousands of militant Communists and the wound was ever fresh.

Worse, Tam complained, European and American politics had complicated his country's plight. In November of 1936 the Tokyo government signed an anti-Communist treaty with the Axis forces. In Italy and Germany, the Japanese conquests in China were viewed as victories over communism.

"Even my classmates are rooting for the Japanese," Tam said woefully, leaning his head into his hands. "They put up with me, but as each day passes, I feel they are more and more resentful. To them I am an enemy."

"But don't forget," I told him, "our life here will soon come to an end."

"Yes, I know," he sighed. "Until then, I feel I must keep out of sight and not tell anyone what I really think."

I swept my husband into my arms, embracing him heartily while still being careful of the life growing inside of me. "You can always talk to me, Tam. I'll never get tired of listening to you."

He admitted that during his lessons he would daydream incessantly about coming home to me. Only with me, he declared, did he feel truly free.

With the expressions of such profound love, I believed we would be unharmed by any war. Undoubtedly, however, I still had a lot to learn about war.

* * *

It was during one of our nightly discussions that I had a sudden inspiration. Tam had looked at me questioningly, sensing that I had something up my sleeve.

"Darling," I had begun, "I don't want to feel like an outsider when we finally go to China. I couldn't bear not feeling a part of things. So I've come to an important decision. I want you to teach me Chinese."

"Me? Impossible!" He stood up with a laugh, then softened and said, "You can't imagine how difficult and tedious it is. And besides, I have no patience."

"Then find me a teacher."

"A Chinese in Turin? That's even more impossible."

Typically, however, once I'd made up my mind there was no swaying me otherwise. And Tam knew it.

Sure enough, he did locate a young man from Peking who was living in Turin and working as a shipping clerk. From then on every evening my tutor guided me through the mysterious and crowded universe of the Mandarin Chinese ideograms, that language being more widespread than Tam's native Cantonese.

Tam, the quintessential military man, who was born to plan and strategize in all areas of his life, now dedicated himself—with the same intensity that had enticed me so quickly to marry him—to procreation. Our darling baby daughter, Lylongo, was born during our first year of marriage. Three months later I was pregnant again, awaiting what would be our first son, Jonathan.

Unlike other young mothers who despair of exhaustion in the caretaking of babies, I felt that my children completely vitalized me. Lylongo, talkative and outgoing, and the more sensitive, thoughtful Jonathan, were both living, breathing little human beings, unique unto themselves, and at the same time the greater sum of Tam and me as parts; the combined fruit of our love. Even in infancy, our children bore the distinctive look that sets apart children born of mixed racial heritage. Their slanted eyes, a dominant trait, testified to their father's origins, as did Lylongo's straight jet black hair; by contrast, the lightness of my daughter's eyes and my son's blonde curls hinted at their European descent. They were Chinese by nationality since I had assumed Chinese citizenship when I married Tam. But just as Tam had never been accepted in Italy, I knew that my children, wherever they were destined to grow up, would never be easily accepted by others—not in a conventional world that shuns with mediocre certainty whatever might disturb its complacency. This challenge only strengthened my determination. The family was my whole world and I decided early in motherhood that, come what may,

I would devote myself utterly to my children's well-being and growth. I couldn't imagine a more doting father than Tam and so I looked forward blissfully to the prospect of more children.

In addition to continuing my study of Mandarin Chinese, which was coming along amazingly well—much to the surprise of Tam and my tutor—I endeavored to learn other aspects of my husband's culture. It was at the Regio Theater where he and I had gone to see the opera of Turandot that I asked him whether all Chinese women were like Liu, the tragic heroine who sacrifices her life for her love. I'd noted the dramatic difference between the selfless slave girl Liu and the cruel bloodthirstiness of Princess Turandot who is protected by wealth and beauty.

Tam answered my question by saying, "Well, they're certainly not like Turandot. Turandot is not a Chinese woman and no Chinese man would ever humiliate himself as Calaf did, though I certainly admire his audacity." He pointed out that the opera wasn't an authentic representation of China and quipped, "One should never speak about things one does not understand."

"But, darling," I asked seriously, "wouldn't you sacrifice your life for me?"

"For you, yes, but not to solve a riddle." Artfully, Tam changed the subject by asking me who I had identified with in the opera.

"Heavens, with no one."

I was about to add, "not even Butterfly," but I kept silent because I knew that this had been Tam's first time to an opera and he wouldn't have understood the reference.

Tam whistled as we strolled to our car, his arm gently sloped around my shoulder. I recalled for a small second all the warnings given to me by my mother and others, thinking at the same time how wrong I'd proven them all. Tam treated me as a perfect equal. In return, I asked for little more than to serve him, give in to him, to follow him unfailingly in everything. Yet his needs in no way limited me; his desires were my own. I was discovering a new side of myself as a result of having been catapulted from adolescence to womanhood. But I also was aware that I retained the impulsiveness of my youth, a tendency to confront or accept events without thoughts of the future. One thing was already certain: I was definitely a woman who would act on the strongest demands of the moment.

It is widely known that the soldier who follows such a canon of behavior becomes a hero; certainly the ability to react speedily to challenges would spell life or death for Tam in the coming years. What I didn't know was that this particular trait is not so frequently indulged in women and that it would fatefully one day be my very undoing.

*   *   *

The world was about to succumb to a full-blown global war, the likes of which it had never known. There was no escaping this. Even so, just as willingly as I drank Tam's opium tea, I was internally intoxicated that we were going into the heart of it. There was almost a physical thrill that accompanied thoughts of making my way through the battle zones together with the man who had come so boldly into my life and with the children we both had chosen to bring into this difficult world.

In February of 1939 Tam finished his studies, graduating at the head of his class and with the rank of Captain. It wasn't many weeks later that my cousin Antonio and my parents gathered at the boarding dock to see us off. Papa had booked us the very best cabin aboard the "Green Count," the Orient Express of the Italian fleet that would be reaching the Sea of China in three weeks time.

Tam and I couldn't help laughing as the weight of our baggage suddenly doubled, what with Mama's gifts to Tam's family and with all the items she had brought for my journey.

"Here," she said, holding back her tears, and handed me the several extra valises. She took her grandchildren in her arms and explained to two-and-half year old Lylongo and Jonathan, a year younger, "These are things your Mama loves, memories from her childhood." To me she said, "I hope it will be a comfort for you to have them near." Then Mama broke down and wept silently as she embraced me one last time.

It wasn't until several months later, when the memory of parting with both my parents would begin to haunt me, would I regret not savoring these precious moments of our being together. Later, I would weep many tears from missing them and from missing my lost childhood. But I was infused with my hunger for adventure and my desire to share in everything that my husband was feeling.

He himself couldn't contain his joy. He embraced his old friend Antonio, not bothering to hide his eagerness to leave. Finally, his face seemed to say, he was going home, back to where he'd longed to be for so many years.

"Don't worry," Tam joked with my parents, trying to make our break with Europe seem less final, "China is not that far away. After all, it is only a few days voyage aboard a splendid and comfortable ship." He pointed at our ocean liner as we all watched the last of the baggage and the Alfa Romeo being loaded onto the lower deck. Not even Mama and Papa's mournful faces could penetrate Tam's and my exuberance.

Tam held Lylongo by the hand and I carried Jonathan as we walked up the plank, the last passengers to board. The Captain gave his orders to the machine room and the steamship slowly left the harbor and headed out towards the open sea.

I never once looked back.

Part Two:

WHITE FLOWERS

CHAPTER 6

A Prisoner-of-War Camp on the Isle of Hazelnuts. 1947.

The night outside my cell's window had grown even darker. I turned from the window and went again to the cot that had served as my bed for almost two years.

That old expression came to mind, the one about how the darkest hour is always just before the dawn. How ironic, I thought, knowing that my dawn would bring first rosy streaks against a sunlit sky and then infinite, permanent darkness.

I had taken some comfort in reliving my early years with Tam. For a condemned woman, I was oddly resigned. I had no regrets, no apologies; not for what might have been called a blind optimism, nor for having turned a deaf ear to the foreboding murmurs of fate.

When did it all change, I asked myself. And at what point had I changed? What was it exactly that first altered my sensibilities—from a free and adventurous spirit to a woman tainted by the scourge of tragedy? What monstrous events had led ultimately to my being labelled a spy and traitor and used by many nations as a political scapegoat?

I knew one of the answers well, as would any mother or any woman who had loved as unconditionally as I had, but this was an unkind memory, painful to recall and illusive to grasp. I tried pushing the horror of the image away, trying instead to remember the grander pictures of our arrival in China in 1939. In my mind I could vaguely see the dim outline of the port's black granite wharf. Then, I recalled it had become more and more visible through the fog and how the Captain at last had given orders to hoist the flag.

How could I forget—Tam and I standing on the bridge, looking towards the shore. With a wistful adoration, like one about to embrace an old lover, Tam had surveyed the gentle hills that flattened out along the plain by the Si-kiang River, the many branches of which encircled the British island of Hong Kong.

"Bianca," he had murmured, "I cannot help but compare this moment to my last view of China, seven years ago. "Now, look," he had said and pointed to the disturbing sight that met our eyes. It was an unfurled Japanese flag, flying from the high mast of the "Kyoto," the heaviest cruiser of the Japanese fleet. Beyond it was a row of British warships anchored in the harbor.

The moor lines of the "Green Count" had been tossed down from the bow between the sampans that made their way towards the shore. Above the roaring of our engine, we had heard the shouts of the Chinese men and women crowded along the railing, already offering their services as porters and guides to the passengers on board.

Tam had said goodbye to the ship's officers and then had stood silently for a few moments, perhaps meditating on those long years spent in Italy that were about to slip forever into the past. I had taken his arm to encourage him and we'd gone ashore— Tam holding a sleepy Jonathan in his arms and I leading an awe-struck Lylongo by the hand.

Even in my cell these eight years later, I could still envision those first exotic sights and still hear the foreign sounds and smell the strange, potent odors of the new land. Tam's older brother Lin had been waiting for us on the wharf and had pushed his way through the crowd to greet us. As Tam introduced me and the children, I had understood nothing of what was being said. It appeared that my studies of Chinese had gone for naught, since Tam's family—like most other inhabitants of Kwang-tung and of Southern China—spoke Cantonese. Although Mandarin was the official language of China, it was spoken primarily in the central areas and in the North. I had felt an odd ripple of doubt, a precursor of the ultimate shattering of the calm certainty with which I had previously accepted all of Tam's wishes. Instinctively, I had squeezed Lylongo's hand tighter and looked into her deep, wise eyes.

As we piled into the two rickshaws which had been hired by Lin and began to ride off, we had heard sudden shouts of wild surprise from the wharf. Turning to look, we had seen the astonished crowd on the wharf gaping at the sight of Tam's Alfa Romeo that dangled precariously from a crane and was being lowered to the ground. Tam had told me not to worry, that Lin, who lived in Hong Kong, would take care of the car and that one of the family's servants would be transporting our baggage to Canton for us.

In the starkness of my cell, I remembered that some of the trunks actually hadn't made it to Canton and that those lost had been the ones containing the good luck momentos that Mama had sent along with me. If I had been more attuned to such things at the time, I would have known that the loss was a bad omen.

I recalled vividly that all around us there had been a hustle and bustle together with an eerie undercurrent of suspense. It was a feeling that at any moment what appeared to me to be a beautiful sight could give way to peril. From a wide luxurious palm-lined street that led through the center of Hong Kong, we had gone as far as the banks of the Si-kiang, where rows and rows of junks had extended for miles along the river. More than 100,000 Chinese, I had been told, lived at that time on the water there, their existence a measure of the hardest survival.

I remembered well the ferry we had taken for the peninsula of Kowloon. After we'd crossed the river, we had our first direct exposure to the Japanese military—who patrolled the border between China and Hong Kong. At the checkpoint the guard had warily studied my passport for a long time.

"Is this your wife?" the guard had asked Tam.

My husband had replied tersely, "Yes, just like it says."

"And the children?"

"Mine," Tam had said, adding proudly with emphasis, "Chinese children."

The Japanese soldier had given us a last once-over. For caution's sake, Tam had worn civilian clothes. But in that tense split-second, I had worried that his innate powerful demeanor might have given his true purpose away.

Luckily, the moment had passed and finally the bar had been lifted so that we could board the train to Canton. Practically incognito, Tam had officially re-entered China after an absence of seven years.

I began to pace in my barracks cell. Like a caged animal, stalking the memories that I held dear, I was also being stalked by those I preferred to forget. The unbearable images of the two children of mine that would die in the course of time haunted me. "No," I said out loud to myself and forced my thoughts back to our train ride to Canton—where I had been given a ringside seat to the sweeping spectacle of the lush, varied Chinese topography.

In those years the British-built railway had run a regular service between Hong Kong and Canton. Our train, driven by Chinese, had crossed the fertile plain of the Si-kiang River, the most densely populated area of China, where all the roads to the south converged.

I had peered through the closed window, kept shut because of the steam engine's soot, as a succession of cultivated fields passed by—sugar cane, flax, rice, kaoling. Nestled among the rolling hills were bamboo groves mixed in with a few sparse palms. It had been a bright, clear day, too early in the year for the sultry summer mist I would later come to know. But though we had obtained reserved seats in the first class car, the compartment had been very hot. To cool us, a waiter had come after a while with refreshments: water, mint tea, and honey cake. I recalled these many years later, how simultaneously sweet and strange the cake had tasted.

Before this night of remembrance, I had thought frequently about that day, my first in China. What had most often come to mind were the disapproving stares that Lylongo and Jonathan got from the Chinese porters in Hong Kong and from the Japanese soldiers at the border—looks that betrayed suspicion and hostility; not at all the kind of reaction that two innocent children normally instill. As much as I wanted to remember only the good, I could not forget Tam's brother's polite but distant attitude, a silent reproach it seemed toward Tam for having strayed so far from the traditions of their family. Nor could I forget the fact that Tam had appeared to have a modicum of embarrassment.

A passing wave of self-pity swept through me, leaving as rapidly as it arrived. No, I didn't feel sorry for myself. My sadness was only what any mother would feel, had she—through unpreventable circumstances—suffered the loss of a child. Try as I might, I could not erase the vision etched inextricably in my mind—a tiny cross of white blossoms placed beside the baby's corpse.

Like much of the trouble that was to come, that memory contained events that had taken place in Canton.

CHAPTER 7

Canton. 1939.

Tam's mother was standing in the courtyard in front of the large house. The garden was shaded by magnolia trees and in the center grew a gingko, the sacred tree of China, surrounded by a circle of slightly larger trees.

Tam leapt down from the rickshaw, bowed to his mother and kissed her. Placing his hand on her cheek, he stood looking into her face with an immovable expression of tenderness and joy, savoring his long-awaited moment. She was quite short and, as is sometimes common among the upper classes, she had gained a good deal of weight in her old age. The baggy kimono she wore accentuated her roundness, but her most striking characteristic was the traditional mask of white powder she wore. As was probably intended, the ghostly coloring of the mask brought forth feelings of both respect and fear. It also hid her wrinkles and accentuated her fiery dark eyes.

She too spoke Cantonese and Tam translated her greeting. "My mother says she wishes that her home will become a place of happiness for the new family who are about to enter it."

Tam took the children and went to greet the servants of the household, many still familiar to him, as I followed his mother inside. She gestured to a beautiful teenage girl, two or three years younger than my nineteen years. The girl stepped forward shyly and spoke in English. "I am Tanya, your amah."

My look of uncertainty prompted her to explain, "I am your servant. I will take care of the children and all your personal needs." I was to discover later that since Tam's family knew I spoke English, they had required Tanya to study it and become quite conversant in it.

Tam's mother led me next to a sliding screen door that was painted with a landscape scene of rolling hills and served to guard the privacy of the room designated to be Tam's and mine. Outside the door, she turned away, taking her leave of me. Although the Chinese customarily sleep on straw mats stretched on brick platforms—during the day using them as sofas—Tam's mother had been mindful of my western ways and left two mattresses in the bedroom for us, instead of mats. In the children's adjoining room, however, straw mats had been prepared for them to sleep on.

A few minutes later Tanya entered and announced, "A hot bath is ready if you wish."

"But where are Tam and the children?" I asked.

"They are bathing," she said, "and later you will go to meet your husband alone in the courtyard of the ancestors."

There were orange blossoms floating in the blue porcelain tub which had been filled for my bath.

After the long journey, the fragrant and steamy water was certainly a welcoming sight. But seeing Tanya and another young woman servant standing nearby, I hesitated before undressing.

Tanya asked, "Is something wrong?"

"No," I laughed, realizing that their presence was quite natural in this new culture, and nonchalantly removed my silk robe and stepped into the bath. The two girls smiled, studying my body with keen curiosity.

"We have never seen a white woman naked before," said Tanya. "You are very beautiful."

When I finished my bath it was she who dried me with the hot white towel, her movements impeccably gentle and careful.

All at once the door suddenly slid open and the white mask of Tam's mother's face appeared. She said nothing, but in her eyes I read distinct disapproval for such an act of intimacy with a servant. I was allowing myself to be dried by Tanya and acknowledging how well it pleased me. This was behavior, I would later learn, that was far removed from the rigid attitude of detached authority with which the Chinese treated their servants.

On my way out to meet Tam, I spotted him through a window that looked onto a courtyard which was shaded and enclosed by wisteria vine. He was kneeling in front of a tomb formed by a large white rock, and dressed in a long regal blue robe that buttoned up the side. When he saw me approaching, he rose and came towards me.

"This is where my father began his day," Tam said in a solemn voice. "This is the side of the house which faces the rising sun and it is here that we honor the memory of the dead. There is also a courtyard which faces west where we can watch the sunset. The western courtyard is traditionally dedicated to the god of the earth who protects our crops." He wore an ominous expression as he said this, as though he was preparing to tell me something important that had somehow been previously withheld.

Instead, Tam took my hand and led me towards the fields of his family where areas of the bushy white cotton plants were alternated with red flaming opium poppies.

He explained, "It's illegal to grow opium, but the British buy it and resell it for ten times the price they paid. The Japanese smoke it and so they allow us to smoke it." He reflected, letting out a small sarcastic laugh, "A fondness for opium is the only thing we agree on."

This was new information, new insight as to how Tam's family had managed to retain their wealth despite the invasions. It wasn't for me to judge, but the revelation bothered me nonetheless. There was something sinister in the bright red of the poppy petals waving in the warm wind.

"And your mother..." I began to ask, unable to shake the chill her implacable white mask had engendered in me, "your mother takes care of everything?"

"Yes, ever since my father died. She gives the orders to the peasants, follows the harvest, and pays the workers. Lin takes care of selling the crop in Hong Kong."

Along the way we encountered a few peasants who took off their straw hats and bowed to Tam.

"You are a powerful family," I commented.

"We are a powerful and respected family and so it will continue unless the Japanese requisition our fields. But I doubt that will happen. They are not completely unreasonable."

We returned right before sunset. The children's dinner was already prepared and Tam could tell I was unhappy that we weren't going to be eating with Lylongo and Jonathan.

Sensitive to my well-being, he assured me that they would be fine with the amah. "Besides," he said, "tonight mother is giving a party for us and it will be much too late for the children to attend." Then Tam urged me to go and dress for our celebration.

Some of the trunks from Turin that held my wardrobe had been carried into our room, but there was another chest beside them which I did not recognize.

"What's this?" I asked Tanya, who was helping me dress.

The amah lowered her eyes, not responding.

"Oh well," I said, "I'll have a look," and lifted up the lid of the chest. Inside were piles of Chinese clothes, uncannily just my size. I slammed the lid shut, my cheeks burning hot with resentment. Tam's mother, I knew, was the one who had so discreetly left the chest there. "With all due respect to the customs here," I exclaimed, "no one, not even my own mother would think of trying to dictate to me what I should wear!"

Tanya said nothing.

"Besides," I said as my temper continued to flare, "I am not Chinese and I have no desire to look Chinese." But after a few minutes, my irritation diminished and I struck upon a solution to the situation.

Having deliberately delayed my appearance at dinner, I stepped into the room wearing one of the dresses Tam's mother had left for me—an elegant blue silk. Contrary to Chinese custom, however, I had let my hair down and it fell freely around the high collar of the dress. Aside from a touch of rouge, I wore no make-up and I hadn't plucked my eyebrows the way Chinese women do. All of the guests, excluding Tam's mother, let out audible gasps of admiration.

Tam stood up, a secret glint of desire in his eyes, and began to introduce me in Cantonese.

I interrupted him. "Good evening," I said in Mandarin, "what an honor it is to meet all of you." I could see that most of the guests had understood and that I'd taken them by surprise—especially my mother-in-law, who, only as I spoke, finally lifted her eyes to look directly at me.

The room was warmed by an oak log fire burning on two bronze braziers. Off in a corner, three musicians played traditional festive music and meanwhile a magnificent, sumptuous feast was served. I sat to the right of the mistress of the house, following her lead in the tasting of a long succession of dishes set out in the center of the salon's large round table. Attentive servants continually refilled each guest's gold enameled cup with a musky jasmine tea.

Tam, of course, was the center of attention. Now at last, in the security of his home, among his friends, he felt free to speak his mind and the subject of war dominated the discussion. The conversation included the cruelty of the Japanese and their oppression of the Chinese people, already being felt in Canton. Now and then, Tam paused to translate some of what was being said. His eyebrows raised in hearing something and he related to me that there was talk that the Nationalist Army was receiving more substantial aid from the United States. There was also a debate as to why Mao was holding out in the Yunan territory, which all the dinner guests hoped would soon be occupied by Chiang Kai-shek's troops.

It occurred to me, based on the attitudes I perceived when Tam was able to translate, that there were a great many references to good and bad signs, to fortunate and evil omens. More than anything so far, it was this philosophy that was so wholly foreign to me.

But Tam, in his way, believed in luck and in the power of various symbols. Around his neck, in fact, he always wore a thin gold chain that held a small luminous opal. Fingering it with a passionate optimism, Tam conveyed an impetuous and bold confidence as he spoke.

I decided then and there to learn Cantonese and promised myself that I would grow to love and respect my mother-in-law. I even chose to try to understand the Eastern concept of destiny, to try to put away for awhile my old notions that we, as individuals, could control the future. Whatever fate held for me, I silently swore, I would accept.

Perhaps Tam sensed my inner resolve in those moments, but in any event he signalled to the servants to pour a round of kau-pah, similar to saké, for the guests. And then he proposed a toast to me— his lovely bride and new Chinese citizen.

Later that night in the darkness of our bedroom, we made private toasts to one another by sharing a pot of opium tea and by making love for hours on end. Tam took me with a newly heightened desire and an overwhelming dominance. Each time he entered me, bolts of electricity seemed to be triggered through my body as I heaved and shook with an inestimable pleasure. Finally, as the light of dawn filtered into the room, I began to drift into a welcomed sleep.

"Bianca, my love," Tam whispered, shaking me lightly out of sleep, "I have news." His were words I had been dreading, "I'll be leaving for Chungking in two days."

I sat up abruptly. "How long will you be away?"

"Until I know where they're going to send me. As soon as I know, I'll come back to get you and we'll leave for the front."

CHAPTER 8

Canton. 1940.

Jula, my second girl and third child, was born in the French hospital in Hong Kong. Because it was run by French nuns and under European medical standards, I had insisted on making the trip to give birth there.

When the baby was a few days old, I returned to Canton to resume the life I had been living ever since Tam had left. Lylongo, almost four, and two-and-a-half year old Jonathan were being given a traditional Chinese education and spent most of their time with their amah Tanya. She fed them, washed them, dressed them in their Chinese clothing, played with them, and saw to their every need. I had frequently been informed that household chores and caring for children were considered far too burdensome for the wife of an important officer such as Tam.

Tam's mother and I saw each other only at lunch and dinner. Often, it was just the two of us at the table. We would exchange a few words in Cantonese, which I had begun to learn, and afterwards I would withdraw to my room.

During this time, I had found an outlet by sitting down and writing long letters to Mama in Italy. The extensive correspondence strengthened our bond that over the years and throughout all the coming difficulties would become more and more precious to me. But I lied in those letters on several accounts. In the process, I lied to myself about the happy days spent with my children and about how kindly everyone treated us. I was actually describing to Mama how I wanted things to be. So while I wrote, it all seemed temporarily real. I was careful not to let my true feelings out—the welling anxiety I felt for having left everything to follow a man whom I hadn't seen or heard from for almost a year.

Jula's arrival, however, helped to console me. I dedicated myself completely to my new baby and breast fed her for many months. A happy, healthy and pretty baby, she distracted me, absorbed me, made me feel I was not alone. And when she slept, I spent time playing with Lylongo and Jonathan, allowing myself to laugh and frolic in their presence.

But without the company of my children, I simply couldn't shake my loneliness and often found myself crying quietly in the solitude of my room. It was on one such evening that Tanya entered and was dismayed to see me—sobbing almost uncontrollably into the pillow on the bed. She uttered a little sigh of concern and darted out. A moment later, she returned with a small clay pot that she placed on the floor. Then she drew the curtains and kneeled in the dark beside the mattress where I lay weeping. Smiling, her lovely face warm with compassion, she slipped off my silk dressing gown and gently turned me over on my stomach. I did not refuse these gestures of kindness and watched as she dipped her fingers into a delicately scented lotion that had been heated in the clay pot. As she began to massage my shoulders, I could feel my muscles relaxing in her expert hands. She continued massaging me, humming softly all the while, and slid her hands from my neck and shoulders down to my back, to my hips and buttocks, and over my thighs. Then she guided me slowly onto my back.

"Shall I massage you too?" I whispered, eager to return her expression of comfort.

Tanya shook her head and blushed, probably embarrassed at the notion of a madame asking an amah such a thing. This was her duty—to give to the needs of those she served—physically as well as emotionally. Such were the ways of an amah. Saying nothing, Tanya removed her cotton robe and stood naked before me, her petite alabaster body and small rose-colored breasts and slender legs all pleasing to my eyes. She sat down beside me on the bed and leaned down to brush my lips with hers. Ever so sensuously, she kissed my eyes still wet from tears and then my ears and neck. I could smell the sweet fragrance of her perfumed hair as she pressed herself against me, kissing my breasts, moving her mouth down across my belly and then rubbing the lotion between my parted thighs. She began to kiss me there, her tongue lapping first lightly and slowly with more and more intensity. As the ripples of pleasure started to accelerate inside me, I ran my fingers through her long silky hair and finally clutched desperately at it while spasms of wild joy gripped me.

Afterwards, Tanya covered me with a quilt and lay down beside me, caressing me until I fell asleep. Later I awoke to Jula's crying and saw that Tanya had gone.

*   *   *

Spring wore on to summer. The countryside was alive with colors, but in my heart, with still no word from Tam, all was cloudy. I took happiness where I could find it—in the growth of my children and the nightly visits of Tanya. Though I had been amply warned, nothing could quell the disappointment I had that my little ones were growing up with an absentee father. It pained me deeply that Tam probably knew nothing of Jula, the latest addition to our family.

Seeing me preoccupied with these thoughts, Tanya asked one night, "Are you sad again?"

I noticed that she had brought in a tea tray and without being told realized that she had prepared a pot of opium tea, hoping it would provide me with a temporary antidote to my pervasive melancholy. I began to protest, having promised myself to only share the special delights of the opium with Tam. But then I changed my mind and agreed to drink one cup of it with her. The room darkened as she blew out the candles, undressed me and then herself before she came to kneel beside me in the bed. The serenity of the opium overtook me and I arched up to enjoy Tanya's fingers moving like butterflies over my back. Her hands rubbed and explored my body, massaged my buttocks and reached around to caress up and down the front of me. She kissed my shoulders, with little delicate bites at the back of my neck and began to turn me over as was her usual manner. Instead of merely allowing her to serve me in my pleasure, I wanted this night to be different. With the freeing affects of the opium, I put aside the restraints of her role as servant and turned on my side to face her—for the first time touching her pretty body—exploring it with the same generosity she had always shown me.

Tanya's breathing quickened and her eyelids fluttered. "It is not necessary," she tried to object.

"Please let me," I begged, continuing to kiss and caress her. She could not refuse and yielded to my mouth by separating her legs, her hands now entangled in the curls of my hair. It aroused me greatly to see her pleasure, to give fully for the mere sensual experience and soon both us were gasping and convulsing simultaneously, pressing wet against each other. For these intoxicated moments, the troubles of the world went away and we were no longer servant and madame—but instead just two young, alive women, really just girls still. Until my intimacies with Tanya, I had only known the intensity of coupling with the man I loved, the man I married. I was only beginning to learn of the many forms of lovemaking that existed in the world. Pleasure for pleasure's sake—and for other more dangerous purposes—outside the bounds of marriage was a new concept, something I would eventually come to understand extensively.

*   *   *

One day at lunch, Tam's mother broke our usual mealtime silence by asking, "Does your amah take good care of you?"

"Why," I responded, "has she complained about me?" I looked at her curiously, unfazed by her impassive white mask and suspicious eyes.

"No," she said, "they do not think they have the right to complain for any reason."

I insisted that Tanya was an excellent amah.

Casually, Tam's mother said, "I've noticed that you and Tanya spend a lot of time together. A good companion should be helpful when one is waiting for one's man."

I understood finally how common private intimacy with one's amah was to most Chinese women of the upperclass. And though she was right about Tanya's being a nice distraction, there was nothing she could say to lessen the anguish I had over Tam's long absence.

*   *   *

"Hello, Jula," I crooned to my youngest, reaching to pick her up from her cradle for feeding time and expecting to hear her usual happy gurgle or peal of laughter.

It was in the afternoon, just after my lunch. As I held her in my arms, I saw immediately that something was wrong. Jula's face was red and she was sweating and breathing with difficulty. I wrapped her in a blanket and ran out of the room, calling desperately for Tanya.

"We're on the veranda," I heard her call. Clutching the baby, whose condition seemed to worsen with every second, I rushed to the veranda where Tanya was playing with Jonathan and Lylongo. Suddenly, in the midst of my terror for Jula, we all heard echoed shouts of joy from the front courtyard.

I knew exactly the cause of the tumultuous celebration. Immediately, I placed Jula in Tanya's arms, and raced through the pavilions of the house toward the first courtyard. I saw him—it was Tam! He had just dismounted and was handing the reins to a servant. Without a word, I went to him and threw my arms around his neck and sobbed. Then, still unable to speak, I grabbed his hand and pulled him speedily through the house towards the children. Lylongo and Jonathan both recognized their father at once and began to jump up and down in excitement. Taking each one in each of his arms, Tam kissed them both and then put them down as he strode to take the baby from Tanya.

I found my voice finally and my words spilled out hurriedly. "Her name is Jula, she was born five months ago. But she's just taken ill and I don't know what's the matter with her. We must go right now and take her to the French hospital in Hong Kong."

"Relax," he said, "There's a hospital in Canton that is much closer."

"No, Tam," I stated, the commanding tone of my voice startling him, "she was born in the French hospital and I want her to be treated there. It's only a few hours drive. Please get the car and let's go."

He was stalling and suggested that perhaps it was only a fever that would pass.

In turn, I cried out that I refused to take the chance that it was something worse.

Tam explained coolly that he'd just received his assignment and our priority was to leave the following day for the front.

Even more icily than him, I bit my words out. "One thing at a time. Jula must get well. Then we will leave together."

"But Bianca, our ship sails tomorrow night. There won't be another one until a month from now. In any event, the children won't be coming with us because we're going where the fighting is."

His words had a staggering effect on me. I felt wholly exhausted, drained from having spent a year without him, having been driven to the brink of despair from not being able to have him take me in his arms. Now I could only stare at him dully before turning away to go look out at the garden. For a few seconds, I silently gathered my thoughts and then, without emotion, turned back to ask him how long we were to be away from Canton.

"I have no way of knowing that," he replied impatiently. In military form he marched to my side and said, "The war seems very long and we will not be able to travel back and forth between the front and Canton."

"Do you mean years perhaps?"

"It's possible."

"Perhaps we'll never come back. That's possible too, isn't it?" My anger came unleashed with the momentum of my words. "We may never come back, isn't that so?" I struck his chest with my fists. "You're asking me to go away with you, after waiting for you all these months, and leave behind my children that I may never see again. That's what you're asking me to do isn't it?"

Tam's eyes narrowed to mere slits. He recoiled his hand and then slapped me with the back of it, knocking me to the ground.

"We're taking the boat tomorrow night," he snapped.

Tanya quietly led the children away from the veranda. I remained on the ground, glaring at Tam and speaking softly but surely, "I'm going to go say goodbye to your mother and we're going to leave for Hong Kong. When Jula is better we will all come to live with you. We'll be no trouble to you at all, I assure you."

It was not yet dark by the time Tam parked the Alfa Romeo in front of the French hospital in Hong Kong. I rushed ahead of him, Jula bundled in my arms, and finally located the head physician.

"Madame Tam," the wizened doctor said after thoroughly examining the baby, "Jula has pleurisy. We must hospitalize her right now."

"All right," I murmured, "as long as I can stay here with her."

"I'm sorry, you can stay with her until she falls asleep but I cannot allow you to remain here overnight."

Despite my repeated insistence that I stay longer, he continually reassured me that Jula would be fine—treated with the utmost care and attention. When at last I saw that she was sleeping easily, I left to join Tam at the hotel in the European quarter where he'd taken a room for us.

Over the dinner that had been sent up from the dining room, Tam dared not say a word to me. He was understandably tired after his three-day journey from Chungking—so many hundreds of miles northwest of Canton—and though I could not sleep, I quietly suggested he try to rest.

Watching his face as he slept, I put aside my earlier anger and felt I recognized once more the thoughtful, caring man I loved. As long as we had each other, I believed, everything would ultimately be fine. And so, as I sat in an armchair by the window, looking out at the long line of warships in the harbor, I resolved that Jula was under expert care and would be her happy, healthy little self in no time.

At that very instant of calm, the phone rang abruptly. It was the doctor, asking us to hurry to the hospital.

He was waiting for us at the entrance to the ward, his face drawn. He spoke in a low tone, saying, "A few hours ago, Jula's condition took a sudden turn for the worse..." he paused, "...and just before I called you, she died very suddenly. It was painless."

He opened the door to her room and I saw our little girl laid out on the bed. Next to her was a small cross of white anemones. I sat with her, weeping silently for a long, long time.

Meanwhile, Tam had gone to ask his brother to arrange the funeral. Upon his return, he said, "Bianca, we need to go home now so that you can get the children ready."

I rose, my knees unsteady and my voice barely audible. "Tanya will take care of everything." In a hushed murmur, I added, "Ask her to come say goodbye to me and then we'll all go to your ship."

I made no further effort to convince him to delay the departure, but asked only to be given a few more hours to grieve alone. Gazing at the serene expression on Jula's face, I took off the ring which had been my mother's first gift to me as a child. At first, I placed it among the white blossoms, those stark flowers I would never forget, wanting to leave some tangible part of myself with Jula. After a second thought, I took the ring and placed it in the hand of the nun who had attended to my child and been with her until the end.

Lin arrived not many hours later and without knowing where Jula was to be buried, I let him lead me to the wharf. At the port, Tam, Tanya, Lylongo, and Jonathan were waiting for me.

Seeing my two children, still very much alive, with concern clearly showing in their faces, I found a modicum of strength. I held them both, forcing back the tears, and told them, "Your little sister has gone to a beautiful place full of peace and white light. She is with the angels now." Jonathan and Lylongo looked at me solemnly, their eyes brightening slightly as we talked of Heaven.

Then I went to Tanya, whose sadness was great. She bowed to me, saying, "If you ever need me, wherever you are, if you send for me I will come." I thanked her, promising that I would indeed call upon her in the future, but somehow I knew that we would never see one another again. And I would be right.

I left in a state of complete emotional and physical shock, not even knowing where we were headed. Nor did I ask to know. Numb and desolate, it didn't matter—one place or another, it was all the same to me. I went on board and fell asleep next to my children, whose unusual silence that evening seemed to me an acknowledgment of my most profound sorrow.

CHAPTER 9

Tuyun. 1940.

Major Tam was assigned to Kwei-chow, an inland region to the northwest, and one of the poorest territories in China. The Japanese had concentrated their efforts on destroying the nationalist resistance there in order to march towards Chungking, the new capital of the nationalist Kuomingtang government. Fighting along the Kwei-chow dragged on.

The Japanese presence throughout the Kwang-tung, the region surrounding Canton, kept us from taking a direct route from Hong Kong to the war zone in Kwei-chow. Instead, we took a ship a great distance south until we arrived at the Vietnamese port of Haiphong in French Indochina. From there we began the long, arduous truck ride that finally brought us into Chinese territory and to our destination of Tuyun. It was a small rustic village that had been hastily made to serve as the local headquarters for the Nationalist forces. The front was only a few miles from the village and the officers had constructed their barracks in a valley sheltered from the nearby Japanese cannons.

Even so, the constant thunder of explosives had become a daily way of life. But over the many weeks that passed after our arrival, I had, out of necessity, gone through a virtual transformation.

Our initial residence had been in a house which was requisitioned by the military. On the first night there, Tam had informed me that because we would be in Tuyun for quite a while, I would be given a squad of soldiers to help me build a house. He'd cautioned me, "You'll have to make all the decisions yourself and manage on your own. I'll be away most of the time."

I had still been in mourning for Jula, and at the time, had done little more than stare up at the ceiling, listening to the guns and rockets screaming in the distance. The only thing I had been able to ask was how often he would make it home to visit us, given the fact that the front wasn't that far away. But Tam had been unable to answer.

What he had said, however, taking my hand in his, was this: "I never tried to hide the truth from you. I told you what to expect and now we are in the middle of it."

In that moment something powerful had turned inside of me. It was then that I decided to make the best of the existence I had chosen and throw myself entirely into the task of building a house. After all, I liked a challenge and that certainly had been one. I had even smiled for the first time in many weeks, teasing Tam by saying, "You know, I must be the only woman here among all these soldiers. I haven't even seen any other officers' wives."

"Then," he had promised, "I will have to come home as much as I can to keep an eye on you."

Tam had laughed and we'd fallen together on the bed, making love after that with a tender abandon.

All in all, the difficulties we faced in this period had reinforced my combative spirit. I had felt obliterated and numb during the journey, my mind unable to grasp the simplest of conversations or remember the names of people we'd met. Nothing could have eased the pain over the loss of my daughter and Tam's apparent insensitivity. At first, I had judged him to be cruel and allowed myself to be carried along by the course of events. But over the subsequent weeks, a new survival instinct was born inside. As ironic as it was, our station in the primitive village of Tuyun reminded me of those visions I once had when I was back in Italy. I had foreseen our little family as a formidable unit living at the front, impervious to harm and the harsh elements—because of our monumental love for one another. Here we were at the front in that very state and, oddly enough, as I began to settle in, I confronted the reality that Tuyun was exactly what I had somehow asked for.

So everything had been left to me—the spot in which to build, the materials, and the design of the house. On his few visits, Tam would beg to see the work in progress.

"No," I would routinely object, "not until it's completely done."

Because it doesn't rot easily, we used poles of alder wood, first to form a foundation and then to build the frame. A thatched straw roof was fastened on top. There was a room for the children, a room for Tam and me, and a central room heated by a large fireplace. There was also a small room for the two military attachés, Chen and Low, who had been assigned to Tam as cook and house servant. I even had doors made, instead of curtains, to separate the rooms. A ditch was dug around the base of the fireplace, lined with bricks, and filled with water to serve two purposes—to provide water for household use and to isolate the fire from the wooden floor. My last chore was to have the willow branches cut down that hid the house from view so that visitors could reach the site on foot or on horseback.

Right before dusk, on what was to be my first night with the children in our new home, I heard Lylongo calling excitedly from outside.

"Mama," she cried, "come look!"

With our proximity to the battlezone, I panicked and rushed out to find her and Jonathan gazing down the path. There, way down the hillside was Tam, riding alone on horseback.

"Sssh," I put my finger over my mouth, quieting the two little ones and leading them over to a high clump of bushes nestled on the hill. From our hiding place we watched as Tam dismounted, ran up the steps, pushed open the door and called out our names with happy anticipation. Upon not finding us, a look of disappointment came over his face.

The children and I jumped out from behind the bushes. "Surprise!" we all shouted and ran to embrace him. He was amazed by what I'd accomplished and all through dinner refused to let go of my hand, kissing it or reaching over to whisper his potent desire in my ear. And when he finally possessed me, the two of us clutching at one another with an unparalleled ecstasy, our bodies undulating with animal heat, I felt a total release of the sadness that had plagued me for several months. I knew instantly that it had been replaced with a new life and wasn't the least bit surprised to later confirm that I was pregnant again.

*   *   *

The war was part of the daily life of the village of Tuyun. But in our little wooden house, I tried to create a haven, a separate world that would provide us with a refuge from the horrors so close at hand. It was, no doubt, a vain and impossible attempt to think I was invincible over powers far greater than myself, but it was all I could muster to defend my family from the atrocity that was slowly tightening its grip on us and was about to appear in its full fury.

As a brutal winter was on its way, I needed to find a reliable source of firewood and the soldiers had suggested I talk to a peasant who lived outside the village. I put on a heavy padded jacket, mounted my horse, and made my way along the muddy trail in the direction of the peasant's hut. Coming around a bend in the road, I saw a thin, weathered old man bending over a dung heap where he had just placed an infant's naked body. My stomach contracted and I gripped the reins to keep my balance.

Hearing the sound of the hooves, the old man straightened up and looked at me, his eyes wide with fear. Obviously, he wasn't used to seeing a fair-haired Caucasian woman on horseback; much less while he was performing so heinous an act.

I dismounted and rushed to pick up the baby. Its body was blue with cold.

Waves of nausea rose in my throat as I held the tiny thing. I looked up at him and asked, "Is she dead?"

Hearing me speak in his language, he heaved a garbled sigh of relief as if he had convinced himself that the blond woman who stood before him was not a ghostly apparition.

"She died this morning," he explained at last. "I am her grandfather."

"And what about her mother?"

He shook his head sorrowfully. "She doesn't know yet. I have walked a long time to find a place for her where my daughter won't come looking for her. I will tell her that I sold the baby, so at least she will believe that her baby is still alive."

I pointed out to him that his daughter would want to see the money.

"No," he muttered, shivering from the cold, dressed as he was in only a shabby wool shirt. "Women never ask anything. Never. She is in the forest gathering wood and when she comes home she won't find her little girl. She will understand that we had to do it because we don't have enough food to feed Sue. The war has taken all my fields away and my sons are fighting."

I was stunned by this hardship, not knowing what to say or do. Desperately looking around for a spot, I begged him, "Let me bury Sue, please."

"It won't help," the old man said. "We won't be able to dig a hole deep enough to keep her from the dogs. They are even hungrier than we are."

I at least wanted to wrap the baby in something, but only had the blouse underneath my jacket and asked quickly that he turn around so I could slip it off. I bundled Sue's body in the blouse and gently placed her in a hollow niche in the frozen ground.

"That doesn't change anything," he said. "The dogs will get to Sue and eat her, but it's better this way. My daughter, if she does come looking for the baby, will never find a trace of her."

I was still reeling from the horror as I asked him to take me to his daughter immediately.

"What do you want her mother for?"

"I may have work for her and I will pay you if you agree. And if you have wood to sell, I will buy that too."

The old man insisted on walking, but after a while agreed to climb onto the saddle behind me. We arrived at a straw hut where several members of his family had silently gathered at a table for a meal of sorghum soup. I recognized Sue's mother by her anxious stance. Without a word, her eyes implored her father to tell her what had happened to the baby.

I lied to her, hoping to spare her the anguish of the truth, saying, "I had your daughter sold to an army officer and his wife who were unable to have children. They live in a large house with many servants. Little Sue will have a good life."

The mother paled, got up and ran out to the field behind the house. I caught up with her, telling her I had more to say. At first, she could not look at me, but I spoke as gently as possible, explaining that I too once had lost a child. "We must be strong and go on living the best we can."

As she turned to me, I saw the numbness in her expression and remembered again that cross of white flowers that had accompanied my Jula to her grave. This poor girl's baby had not even been granted that last honor. I repeated my story about Sue being fine with her new family. "In the meantime," I said, "I have two young children and another one on the way. Will you come live with us and be my children's amah?"

We rode away before dark as I headed back on a different route so that we would not pass the place where I'd left the baby's body. It hadn't taken long to convince the old man. In one day he had eliminated two mouths from his meager table and had been paid well for both his daughter's services to me and the firewood we brought with us. Once her watching family had faded from sight, the young mother leaned her head against my back and began to sob.

Her name was Lynn and though uneducated, she would prove herself quick to learn in all respects. Lynn would remain in my service for many years. In the same sense that I had saved her life—since so many of the peasants unharmed by the bloodshed of the war would nevertheless die of starvation and cold—one day Lynn would be called upon to save mine. And when, a few months later, my time to deliver came, it was she who ran through the village in the middle of the night in search of a doctor, begging him to come and help the wife of Major Tam who had just gone into labor.

"Madam, I have never seen a baby being born," the middle-aged, stocky doctor said nervously when he saw me. "I've been living here for years with the soldiers and I haven't even had the chance to get married."

"Don't worry," I gasped between the rapidly progressing contractions, "I've already given birth three times. Do what I say and everything will be fine. I'm sure you've seen enough blood in the military hospital."

The doctor stayed fairly calm, even when I told him it was time to cut the umbilical cord. There on the dining table of our little wooden house, a baby girl was born. I named her Jula, in memory of her departed sister. Lynn took her from the doctor's trembling hands, washed her in a basin, and wrapped her in a cloth cut from sheets of my wedding trousseau. I looked in wonder at my new baby, conceived and born in the heart of a gruesome war, and laughed with pure joy. Out of all of us, it was the doctor who was the most worn out by the ordeal.

*   *   *

We lived with war from day to day, as those who are survivors must do. My husband was away most of the time fighting at the front, but a few months after Jula's birth, I became pregnant for the fifth time. It was what Tam wanted—a big family—which in China traditionally symbolized great power and opulence. Despite some of the bad omens that I'd chosen to ignore, I wanted to fulfill this desire of Tam's and to bring him what happiness I could. Up until this point, loving him unconditionally was all I'd known.

But there were even more important lessons soon to be forced upon me. In a very short while, events would unfold that would drastically alter my destiny.

CHAPTER 10

Tuyun. 1941.

"The Japanese want to proclaim their own Republic of China with the capital in Nanking," Tam began angrily. He had spent a few hurried minutes with the children, much less time than usual, eaten a brisk dinner and not until we were alone did he start to express what was on his mind.

Since morning, when he had come riding down to the shallow pool at the bottom of the hill where I had taken the children swimming, I had sensed that something was different. This had been a particularly long absence, without any news of him, and I had run to embrace him with great exuberance. In return, he'd barely said a word and had seemed almost stiff or awkward when he kissed me. Of course, I knew better than to ask how long he'd be staying with us or to raise other questions about his distant attitude.

So I listened carefully as he made his thoughts known. "This new Japanese Republic will have a Chinese government with a Chinese president. This is their way of trying to render their occupation legitimate while they go on conquering new territories. We are managing to hold out here, but I don't know for how much longer. It's as though we are fighting in complete isolation. We have received no orders and no help from Chungking in over two months. And yet we know that America is sending money. All the arms are American, except for a few old Russian guns and some British cannons. Our only hope is to learn to fight in the air."

"How will you do that?" I asked quietly, not wanting to interrupt his flow of words.

His mood brightened somewhat. "There is an American pilot," Tam answered as he paced over to his jacket which hung on a nearby chair. "Chennault is his name. He and his patrol, the Flying Tigers, have arrived to train our men. They have inspected the surrounding area. Here, have a look at this..." he said, removing a military map of Kwei-chow from his jacket and rolling it out in front of me on the bed.

"They have chosen excellent spots," he said, pointing to the future sites of the landing strips. "They are hidden in the forest. To handle them, we'll need good pilots, but if it works, it will be of great importance. Chennault is a remarkable pilot—capable of doing wonders with our men."

Although Tam often gave me a general idea of his strategic concerns, this was the most specific he had ever been about military maneuvers. I was happy to provide him with an open ear, but somewhat disappointed that he had so little to say about personal matters—about how these latest developments might affect me and the children. Without allowing myself to become too hopeful, I asked him whether he had received orders to remain in the village.

"No, I will lead a company of heavy artillery from the hills north of Tuyun. We're going to bombard the Japanese installations until we run out of ammunition."

"Will we have to retreat afterwards?"

Tam stretched out on the bed again, continuing with a defiant air. "The orders are not to retreat under any circumstances. Three divisions are our only line of defense. It's very weak, but the only good thing is that the Japanese don't know that." He folded his arms and gazed up at the ceiling. "They think we have reserve troops in the north. But there's no one left in Chungking except for Chiang Kai-shek's personal guard." He turned to look at me, saying, "By the way, there's been a rumor that he might come here soon to inspect the troops."

"When?" I asked, knowing how excited Tam would be to finally meet Chiang Kai-shek. I reached over and began to massage the tired muscles of my husband's legs.

Perhaps it was my imagination but it seemed that he flinched under my touch. Almost imperceptibly, Tam rolled out of arm's reach as he told me that they would have no way of knowing the date and time of the arrival until the last minute. "We couldn't risk earlier notification, since there's always the possibility that the Japanese would intercept the convoy."

"Will you be there or do you have to stay at your post in the hills?"

"I must be there," he declared.

Tam had fallen asleep just after that, without even any overtures at making love to me. Naturally, my feelings were hurt. It was our first night together after such a long separation and never before had he failed at making all that waiting so worthwhile. I sat up awake for nearly an hour trying to shake the sensation that a bad omen was about to reveal itself until, slowly but surely, I came to a rationalization about his behavior—after all, poor Tam was exhausted. And I chastised myself for being so selfish.

As soon as I went to lay down next to him, however, there was a violent explosion, a ferocious roaring of bombs that vibrated throughout the house. I looked to the window to see the night sky streaked with rocket fire.

"Wake the children," Tam said with urgency, scrambling from the bed and dressing all in an instant. "Take them to the shelter in the woods."

I shouted above the tumult, "What about you?"

Strapping up his boots, he said quickly, "I'm going to Tuyun."

"But Tam," I implored him, "the bombing isn't over yet!"

"Bianca," his voice rose over mine as he spoke with clipped military timing. "I am in command of a company. I don't want them to have to come looking for me. If you hurry, you'll get to the shelter in no time."

Seeing the panic in my eyes, his tone softened and he came to take my face in his hands. "Don't be afraid. It won't last long, and here there is no real danger." He kissed me briefly and rushed out.

"You haven't said goodbye to your children!" I called out after him. But he had gone and in response, I heard only the unkind reverberations of the door slamming shut.

Lynn carried baby Jula and I held four-and-half year old Lylongo and three-and-half year old Jonathan as we headed out to the woods where we had constructed our shelter. It was no more than a hole dug a few feet in the ground. Cramped and uncomfortable quarters, to say the least, but I thanked God that we were safe there. We left at dawn, after the Japanese cannons had been silent for awhile.

They opened fire on Tuyun the next day and when they continued to bombard the area for several days, we all became accustomed to our retreats into the shelter. Then, thankfully, came a week without an attack. It appeared that the worst was over. But for me, the worst was about to begin.

*   *   *

"What's wrong?" I had asked the two soldiers in our service, who were regularly in good spirits, but who this morning had seemed to be entirely out of sorts.

Chen, chubby and balding, had been preparing vegetables for our lunch and Low, a tall muscular fellow, had been in the middle of helping Lynn heat water for the bath.

"Chiang Kai-shek and David Kung are coming," Chen had grumbled. "Everyone will be there to greet them and we have to stay here in the kitchen doing women's work."

Low had added despondently, "If we don't see them today, we may never get the chance again."

"But you'll be there," I had proposed, "and so will I. You have the day off so we can all go to Tuyun."

It wasn't many hours later that the three of us stood and watched the extraordinary geometric elegance and charismatic composure—learned as a youth at the Tokyo Military College—of the commander-in-chief of the Kuomintang riding amidst the troops of the southwest. His second-in-command, David Kung, rode a few paces behind him.

I searched the legions looking for Tam and saw him standing alongside the officers in front of the many rows of soldiers. At first sight, my heart began to beat passionately, as it had from the beginning some five years before, every time I looked at Tam. But then, it was as if my heart stopped with a chilling realization—Tam had come back from the battlefield, but not to me.

The company commanders filed past the head of the government and I watched as David Kung introduced my husband, the youngest officer in the army, to Chiang Kai-shek. In Tam's face I could read the joy he had imagined years ago in Italy when he spoke about his country, and about the man who was now shaking his hand. It was a dream made real, but without my participation.

In these swift seconds my powers of awareness seemed to swell and time slowed to an eerie snail's pace—almost as if I was under the influence of opium. Yet this was not an experience of pleasure. On the contrary, it was as though I had been stabbed by a horrifying revelation. While there were very few women on the field, it hadn't taken me long to observe that I wasn't the only woman watching Tam with such fierce pride and intensity as he triumphantly received his honors. I looked up and, as if drawn by the same magnetic force, met the eyes of a Chinese nurse sitting beside the tent that served as the military hospital. Suddenly I knew everything. She was Tam's lover!

I felt paralyzed. Everything around me clouded over. Tam, oblivious to my inner rage, had spotted me but kept himself at attention. Then the officers filed into the tent and the nurse disappeared inside along with them.

"Why don't you join us? We have heard so much about you," said a voice beside me, jangling my nerves even more. "You do speak English, don't you? Aren't you Major Tam's Italian wife?"

"Yes," I replied distractedly.

"I am Meilin Soong, the wife of General Kung."

I managed a nod to her and a few muttered words. "Yes, Tam has told me about you."

"Come, then. We'll go inside where it's warmer and wait for them there."

As we walked towards the officer's quarters, I forced myself to think straight, to remember more about her. With her short hair and khaki jacket, her pants tucked into her boots, Madam Kung often accompanied her husband to inspect the troops at the front.

Thanks to their well-calculated marriages, Meilin Soong and her two sisters, daughters of a Methodist minister who had studied in the United States, were the leading ladies of China. Their husbands were the most important men in the land: Chiang Kai-shek, baptized in the Methodist Church; David Kung, descendant of Confucius, Protestant convert, and ex-West Point cadet; and Sun Yat-sen, hero of the first Chinese Republic, founder of the Kuomintang.

The sisters, along with their brother, T.V. Soong, the Minister of the Kuomintang's Foreign Affairs, were envied by many for the wealth they had accumulated during their rise to the top of the Chinese political and military hierarchy. Yet it was also suspected that their reign of power was corrupt to the core—that a large percentage of the money sent by the United States to supply arms for the poorly equipped and badly organized troops was being swallowed up by the expenses of what was then called "the new Chinese court."

The ever-growing, generous amounts of dollars sent to the Kuomintang government made a quick round trip; out of the safes of the United States Treasury, into the Chinese banks, and back to America, where they were deposited into the savings accounts of these powerful few Chinese who would collect them when the war was over.

These facts collided in my brain, but for the life of me I was unable to utter a proper acknowledgement to this woman of social prominence.

Instead Meilin Soong spoke—both to me and to some officers standing by—"When the Major told us about his wife, he failed to boast of her rare beauty."

A round of further compliments came from the men. I stood in my riding outfit that did a good job at hiding five months of pregnancy and felt all the praise was unfounded. How could I be truly beautiful when the man to whom I'd given all had betrayed me?

The hair on the back of my neck bristled as Tam and David Kung joined the entourage. So many times, my husband had daydreamed aloud about the meeting that was now taking place. But for me it was unbelievable and unreal, like watching the proceedings on a screen from afar. I could barely catch my breath—as if the shock from the discovery of Tam's unfaithfulness had submerged me in freezing water and that I was about to drown.

"Your husband is very selfish to keep you hidden," said David Kung, bowing to kiss my hand. "But what made you follow him to this dismal place?"

I answered in numb monosyllables, "Your Excellency, I wanted to come."

"Well, you are far too beautiful to stay in a place like Tuyun."

"Yes," interjected Meilin Soong. "It's certainly no place for a mother with small children. You have been too generous in following Major Tam to such a dangerous place. China is a wonderful country and you must absolutely get to know it better. You can start with Chungking, where your presence will be helpful to the war."

"No," said the General. "Chungking is a small town where we are forced to live for the moment. Bianca must go to Nanking or Shanghai to see how the Chinese really live—to see how they entertain themselves." He smiled and glanced at Tam. "But a woman like her cannot go alone to Shanghai." How little I suspected here the prophetic nature of David Kung's words.

For the meantime, however, I had other concerns in my mind. When I finally stole a minute alone with

Tam, I made a few pressing questions known. My tone had been learned from him—a clipped military demand—as I asked, "Why didn't you tell me that Chiang Kai-shek was coming today?"

He smiled and shrugged. "It happened so suddenly."

"The soldiers knew," I said.

Growing irritated, Tam replied, "I was away on a mission until yesterday."

Aware that we could be overheard, even though we spoke in Italian, I quietly told him that I had something important to say to him when he got home, that I would be waiting. With no emotion whatsoever I said, "I'm going now," and turned to leave.

Tam grabbed my elbow, pulling me back. "You can't just go off like that. You must stay for lunch."

I didn't look at him as I said diffidently, "I wasn't invited."

"You are now," he exclaimed, smiling with hospitality.

"No thank you," my words bit back at him. "Get your concubine to stay for lunch."

With that, I strode from the tent, located my horse and galloped at top speed the entire way home. When I got back, I told Lynn to make sure the children stayed in their room when Tam returned. Then I shut myself in my room.

Hurt and rage co-mingled, filling every cell of my being and building to what could only be a violent crescendo. Not wanting to appear weak when it came time to face him, I wept alone in my room so that I could get the crying done before Tam returned. His betrayal had shattered my whole world. I felt a monstrous disbelief—how could it have happened? In the midst of that war, in the midst of the anxiety and uncertainty of our daily lives, Tam's love had been the only sure thing, the only fixed point. Or so I had deluded myself from the start.

Just as I was once warned, Tam had obviously acquired the life of his contemporaries—a wife, a concubine, many concubines, all ready to accept their condition, happy to welcome him whenever he desired them. This I could never accept. For the first time in our marriage, I refused to bow to his way; I would rebel and lash out at him; cause him to suffer as deeply as I did.

Having wiped away any trace of tears, I tore off my riding clothes, perfumed myself, brushed out my hair and put on one of my prized possessions—a shimmering gold silk dress, sewn with real gold thread.

That day so many of the officers had admired me and though never before had praise of my physical charms mattered, I now believed they were correct in asserting that my beauty was wasted on the village of Tuyun. I studied myself in the mirror and saw that I was still attractive, still supple—even with a child on the way. Until this day, my body had been a gift to my husband. But now I was rediscovering that it was something that belonged to me alone, not to Tam and not to my children. I was twenty-one years old and my body was as shapely and youthful as it had been when I met Tam. I was going to own it again, to feel it in its full vitality, to touch it and be touched—my high rounded breasts, tight buttocks and smooth slender legs—to live by it and fulfill its every desire. Yes, my body was alive and so was I! I would recapture the sensuality that only Tam had received and give it where I saw fit.

I shirked off my humiliation, took a deep swallow of wine, and realized how infinitely desirable and truly powerful I was. No, not after giving birth four times—and soon a fifth, I would not be made world-weary; not in body, not in mind. I knew the drink helped my confidence, but I needed it to face Tam without buckling under. After several glasses, when I felt the warmth of the alcohol spreading through me,

I put the bottle back in the cupboard and took a seat in an armchair in the dark room.

"I couldn't come earlier," he said, upon entering.

Though I hadn't planned my words at all, they were surprisingly calm and resolved. "I won't stay in Tuyun any longer," I told him. "I won't have another baby on the kitchen table. It's too dangerous."

"But it was all right the last time." He approached me, waving off the issue, and studying me with a desire he didn't try to hide.

"I won't go through that again. Besides, the doctor who assisted me died in the bombing. Or did you forget that?"

"Well, then, when the time comes, I'll take you to Kweilin. It's the capital of Wangsi and there's a hospital there. But that's months from now."

I turned my face from his, saying, "No. Kwelin is in the heart of the fighting. I've made up my mind, I'm leaving immediately."

"And when did you realize this?"

I turned my face back and looked him straight in the eyes. "Today, when I saw that I am not your only woman."

Tam took the accusation in silence, his face impassive. Perhaps I'd had the smallest hope that my suspicions were wrong. But such was not the case.

I watched him remove his coat and drape it over the back of a chair. Then he sat down on the edge of the bed a few feet from me as he stated acidly, "You are still my wife and the mother of my children. You still have your rights."

"Tam," I said, cocking my head to look closely at the man for whom I would have died many times over, "rights mean nothing to me from a man who doesn't love me."

Now he became plaintive. "I love you Bianca and you know that."

"Then what do you need a lover for?"

"I was away, she was a nurse tending the soldiers..." he began slowly.

I interrupted, "So it is her—the nurse in the field."

Tam stood defensively as he continued, "... and that's how things are in China."

I stood as well, proclaiming, "But I'm not Chinese. I don't give a damn about your Chinese customs. I don't want you to have a concubine and I don't want the rights of a Chinese wife. Believe me, Tam, I will not raise another woman's children. You've made a terrible mistake. I gave you everything and you shouldn't have done this, because now I'm going to take the children and leave. You can go ahead and have children by other women, but I'm not going to take care of them. And I'm not going to Kweilin, to some dirty village two feet from the front." I was making my decisions as rapidly as my words were flowing. Hadn't I earlier that day heard about the wonders of Shanghai? Wasn't that where Tam's superiors said I belonged? So I announced on the spur of the moment, "I'm going to the only place where I can live a decent life, to Shanghai. You've made an irrevocable mistake and I won't accept what you have done."

"You're upset, Bianca. You don't know what you're saying. We can talk about it tomorrow."

"There'll be no need to talk about it tomorrow." I could hear my voice trembling and tried to control it by breathing deeply. "There'll be no need to talk any further about it. I'm leaving tomorrow for Shanghai and in the morning you will organize a trip for me. You're a major in Chiang Kai-shek's army and you have that capability."

He started to protest, but I interrupted him again. "You know, everyone is amazed that I followed you here to this filthy place. You're the only one who doesn't know why I did, and that's a shame, Tam." I watched the face I'd once adored, already asking myself whether he had been worthy of my love.

Not even addressing what I'd said, he reminded me that Shanghai was completely cut off—thousands of miles away and across fortified enemy lines.

"There are airplanes, you know."

"Only military ones."

"The wife of an officer and his children will have no difficulty finding a plane, you can be sure of that."

"If you really want to leave, the only logistical solution is for you to go back to Canton to my family."

I spat words at him, "Take your logistics to hell. You will locate a plane and I will go where you'll never find me. I'm young and beautiful and I'm not going to rot here in Tuyun for a man who treats me like dirt."

He shook his fist, shouting, "You can't leave me, I forbid you to go! What you are asking is impossible."

Tam grabbed his coat and made for the door. I knew that if I didn't hold firm, my courage would dissolve and I would never have another chance for independence.

"It is possible and it is going to happen. If you want to keep me in this place, you'll have to kill me first. You don't have to tell anyone I'm going to Shanghai if you are afraid they'll laugh at you. You can tell them whatever you like, I don't care, but the children and I are leaving."

His face snarled in disbelief, Tam stormed out the door. That night he did not sleep in our little house on the hill. And that was another grave mistake because it showed that he didn't fully grasp the change that was taking place in me. Until that day my only happiness was in knowing that I was his and he was mine, wherever, in whatever condition. But no more.

He probably thought that no woman would dare set out across a war-torn country with three small children, but he was wrong. For me, it was the only way out. What else could I have done? Stay there? Return to Italy in failure? Go live at his mother's house while he went on betraying me? No, not one of the alternatives was acceptable.

I swallowed deeply with a somber finality, and went to look in on Lylongo, Jonathan, and Jula who were asleep in their room. Lynn, whose loyalty was unshakeable, slept beside them on her mat. In the morning, we would pack and all leave together.

I needed some air and went outside, noticing that the sky was strangely clear, the moon nearly full. Before it reached its completion, I would be far away. For many nights previously, the sky had been covered with low clouds that had kept the Japanese from attacking the village. This night was ideal for a bombardment, but evidently the spirit of war had been calmed by the beauty and quiet of the moonlight, disguising the destruction so visible in daylight. Tomorrow it would begin again.

I spotted the kindly Chen off to the side of the house, he too staring up at the night sky.

Chen bowed when I approached him, explaining, "I heard the dog bark and came out to see what was wrong. I couldn't sleep. It's such a beautiful night."

"Isn't it a good omen" I asked, pointing to the shiny orb, "when the moon is like this and there is so much light?"

"Yes, because now the moon is still waxing and rising higher and higher in the sky towards the place occupied by the sun. When it is finally full it will begin to wane, because it wants to be complete like the sun."

"I like that explanation," I told him.

"Also," Chen went on, "where I come from they say that the moon is like a horse that runs straight ahead without looking at the other horse beside him in the halter, so if the other one errs, he won't make the same mistake. It brings good luck to see the moon when it is so pure like tonight."

"I like that even more," I said and confided, "I'm about to go away on a long journey."

"Go now," he said, "while the signs in the sky are still favorable. You will leave and I will go back to the fighting. You see this night does not mean the same for everyone. In the heavens there is peace and stillness but here below we are troubled."

"Well," I murmured, thinking of the murky future and the dangers through which I would travel with my children, "I hope the omen will be good to all of us."

The dog stayed beside us while we talked. Several times, the lonely creature rubbed against Chen's legs and each time he would lean down to pat it.

I had chosen a perilous course of action, but there was no turning back. The signs for what lay ahead, according to Chen's interpretation, were favorable. Hopefully, the spell of the rising moon would last long enough to overshadow my broken heart that I fully intended to leave behind.

Part Three:

BLOOD AND GOLD

CHAPTER 11

**A Prisoner-of-War Camp on the Island of Hazelnuts.
1947.**

It was odd the way memory worked, I thought,
having recalled how I had come to such a
momentous decision to leave Tam. It was now six
years later, and the pain of his betrayal was no
more, replaced in kind by other losses. What I most
remembered was that extraordinary moon and the
melancholy hound that lay at Chen's feet. Tonight
the moon was nothing but a sliver of pale yellow
light—not necessarily a good omen for a woman
preparing to journey to her afterlife. I prayed that
once the bullets entered me, I would die instantly.
And I believed God in His mercy would grant me
this last wish.

For the three or four hours left to my life, I
would still question whether my rash action was to

blame for everything that followed. I had forever been haunted, wondering whether I should have taken more time to think things through and come up with a practical plan—since the misdeeds for which I had been condemned arose from a blind desire to move forward at whatever the cost.

I thought back through the circumstances of our departure from Tuyun, searching for an answer, remembering how I had gone to Lynn and asked if she wanted to come with me as the children's amah. Though she had no idea where Shanghai was, she hadn't asked for an explanation but had said simply, "I will come with you. Here I lost my daughter and everything about this place reminds me of that. Even if my husband comes back from the war, he'll find another wife."

During our packing in the morning, I had reflected a few times that exactly one year had passed since our wooden house at the front had been built. And when Tam had come back in the afternoon, he had commented on the same fact.

Seeing my resolve, his voice had faltered as he said, "I don't want to lose you forever."

Calmly, I'd informed him that I planned on writing to the High Command of his outfit so that he would be able to find the children when he so desired.

"When the war is over," he had ventured, as we all walked toward the military truck and jeep escort waiting to take us to Kweilin, "I'll come back to you and maybe we can start over again."

I had held firm, not even allowing for that possibility. When Tam gave me an envelope with money for the trip and a letter of introduction to the Director of the Central Bank in Shanghai, he had explained that the banking officer was a relative of his mother's and that I would be advanced whatever amounts I needed, which later would be reimbursed by his bank in Canton.

My last words to Tam had been to promise to do everything possible for the children who would no doubt be safer away from the war. "But," I had concluded, "I want you to know that my leaving has nothing to do with my being afraid."

"Of course not," he had said sadly, "you were never afraid of anything, Bianca."

I had watched as Tam said goodbye to the children—embracing Lylongo first, next Jonathan, and finally, baby Jula. Around each of their necks, he had hung a tiny chain that held a little pink elephant—a Chinese symbol of a long and peaceful life. While the truck's engine had revved and everyone but me climbed into the back of it, he had presented me with the statue of the mother elephant.

Everything had been decided. One day had changed the course of all our lives. Tam had spoken his last words to me, just before mounting his horse to ride off. He had said, "There's something I want you to know. I'm never going to come back here to this house. It was ours and will remain so always."

In the prison cell I remembered so vividly the last image of him—Tam taking hold the reins, spurring his horse, and riding off down the hill.

And certainly I hadn't forgotten our harrowing journey to Kweilin—the old Mercedes truck in which we were forced to live for a week, Lynn and the children and I huddled in the back as it careened over bumpy roads across the Kwang-si region. I recalled how we would drive only after sunset until dawn of the following day, with the military escort of four soldiers in a jeep ahead of us signalling when all was clear. We had spent the daylight hours parked in the thick foliage of woods along the way, and had come into contact with passersby. I had been horrified to observe how the population had been worn down by the long years of a war never openly declared, which had only added to the misery of their oppression by wealthy landowners. Farmers tilled a soil riddled with bomb craters. Old men, women and children had peered at us out of windows, attracted by the noise of the truck that could be heard from a long way off in the silence of the countryside.

I had seen their physical starvation, knowledge in their eyes that war would bring more hunger, more bloodshed, more scorn for individual life. Because the people were so desperate, our driver had always stopped a short distance outside each village to avoid the danger of an assault on our truck's provisions. But there had been one instance when we had been just about to set off at night for the next leg of the trip, that we had found ourselves surrounded. We hadn't been able to tell how many eyes were fixed on us in the darkness, but had heard them approaching from all directions. A few had come out into the open, others had hidden among the trees. Wielding shovels and knives, they had continued advancing until the lieutenant in charge of our escort had ordered the soldiers to get out of the jeep and take their positions around the truck. From the back, we had watched as the faces of the mob pressed in on us.

"Stop right there," the officer had shouted, taking out his gun.

"You've got food in that truck," one of the men had said, stepping forward. "We want it."

"We've only got women and children, no food. We're on our way to Kweilin."

Lynn had made the children lie down in the back and had covered them with her body, as I called out, "Look, only we are here. The lieutenant is telling you the truth."

But hunger has a way of distorting human behavior, and the menacing crowd had screamed for satisfaction, demanding that we give them our food. The lieutenant had realized that if he took one shot, the mob would have massacred all of us. Instead he had said softly to the soldier beside him, "Get in the truck and stay there until we've gone." Then he had shouted to the soldier so that the throngs could hear, "You! Throw down a sack of rice." To another soldier, he had cried, "Help him!"

When the drivers of both the jeep and the truck had started their motors and a sack of rice had been thrown down, the lieutenant climbed on the truck and the mob opened up enough to let our convoy pass. We had remained safe, but had there been the slightest mistake, we would have been killed. They probably would have raped Lynn and me and killed the children on the spot, or else left them to die of hunger.

No, I hadn't forgotten that close call, nor how when we were finally a good distance away, Lynn had begun to weep hysterically.

On the other side of the emotional spectrum, I remembered my triumph when we finally arrived at the Kweilin airport—a strip of hard-packed dirt in the middle of a bamboo forest. A Caudron-Bréguet with the name "Twilight of the East" had waited in the only hangar in use for prospective passengers. It belonged to Jimmy, an American pilot who had been living in China for ten years—ever since his company had asked him to fly the route between Shanghai and Nanking and had suspended him there because of the war. Jimmy had informed me that the only other planes that landed there were a few old English Vickers loaded with provisions for the Kuomintang, when and if they had managed to avoid being shot down by the new Mitsubishi Zero fighter planes which then ruled the sky above the front.

Jimmy, a free-spirited sort, had immediately accepted my proposal to fly to Shanghai in return for payment in Hong Kong dollars and had asked me with awe, "Are you really the wife of one of Chiang's officers?" He had also wanted to know if it was going to be a one-way trip or if he was to wait for me to come back. "Ya' see," the friendly

American had explained, "I like to feel that I'm important to someone."

"Right now," I had told him, "you're the most important man in my life."

Perhaps the awful ordeal we had faced had been God's way of helping me take my mind off the heartbreak—the total disillusionment I felt over Tam. At any rate, I had been forced to keep myself in good humor on account of the children and it hadn't been easy—the last two days of the trip had been particularly unbearable. Because it had rained incessantly, the damp had soaked through our clothes and into our bones. Lylongo had caught a fever and the quinine tablets we had given her had sapped my normally vibrant daughter's energies.

"Don't worry, Lylongo," I had told her, stroking her hair, "we're going to a beautiful city with real beds and running water in the tubs." The poor thing had almost forgotten what those modern conveniences were. For that matter, so had I.

It had still been raining when Jimmy, whistling "I'll Go On My Way," had taken Jonathan in his arms and carried him to the plane.

"But who are you?" my son had asked, surprised at being held by such a big fair-haired man. Not knowing Italian, Jimmy hadn't answered but had just smiled back at Jonathan and carried him up the ladder into the plane, allowing him to sit as "co-pilot" in the cockpit. With the rest of us in our seats, the engines had started up and the Twilight of the East had taken off down the runway.

The recollection of overwhelming relief filled my senses these several years later when I thought of what it looked like to gaze down from the plane and see nothing but the vague, distant tops of the bamboo grove. The trip had lasted six hours. It had been an overcast day in May of 1941 and by the time we touched down in Shanghai, I realized that I hadn't once thought of Tam since leaving Tuyun.

So in answer to my questions as to whether I had done wrong by leaving so hurriedly, the response was still no. Even with my life hanging in jeopardy so precariously, I had to face the truth that if I had it to live over again, I wouldn't have done anything differently. The memory of Tam that I cherished was the one in which I had seen him that day long ago, when he ran into the house after his first absence and shouted my name with joy. Ours had been an impetuous, passion-driven love. But after Tam had sated all his hungers, he had gone on, like an adolescent—a young animal—living according to his primal instincts and nothing more. I never regretted loving him, not at the time that I got to Shanghai, and not here and now, as I saw that the sands through the hourglass of my life were almost spilled.

As far as having any regrets about becoming a spy, that was another story altogether.

CHAPTER 12

Shanghai. 1941.

The taxi turned down Bubblingwell Road, leaving behind the gaily-colored and crowded chaos of Shanghai—cars, bicycles, people, a whirlwind of motion. Inside that taxi I felt protected from the evening rain, and from the flux of confusion that streamed by in the street. At the Imperial Hotel, the driver pulled over.

The hotel Director, an elegant and efficient English gentleman, opened my passport and his smile faded. "You came from an area controlled by the Chinese," he said, handing me the document. "I'm sure you realize that we are under Japanese control here."

"And your guests are under Japanese control as well?"

The man forced a curt nod. "Let's just say that family members of one of Chiang Kai-shek's officers are not ideal clients for the moment."

Reaching into the pocket of my mud-covered trousers that I'd worn for the entire journey from Tuyun, I shrugged, telling him, "Oh, I'm sure we will be very comfortable here." I put a wad of Hong Kong dollars on the counter and added, "We'll take a suite. We'll be no trouble to you at all. Surely, you will agree that there is no need to mention anything to the Japanese police. After all, this is a European hotel and you and I are both Europeans, even if there is a war on." How quickly I was learning the ways of the new world I had just entered.

The Director accepted the advance and gave us a two-room suite that opened onto a salon. Trying all the comforts we had gone so long without—the electric lights, the intercom system, the heating, the hot water—was like playing an exquisite game. The porter carried what little baggage we had into the salon while I began filling the tubs in the bathrooms to bathe the children.

There was so much to do to get organized, but for now I wanted nothing more than to plunge into the bath. For someone who had grown up with such material abundance—taking much of it for granted— my two and a half years in China had given me a new respect for even the smallest of creature comforts. Turning off the tap, I remembered all the elaborate preparations there had been in Tuyun just to take a bath: heating the water in a copper pot, having the soldiers pour it in the wooden tub, getting the amah to bring more hot water.

Who, I wondered, as I scrubbed myself in the warm sudsy water, was living now in the little wooden house? For a fleeting second, my stomach gripped with the worry that Tam wouldn't keep his promise and would return with his concubine to the house which had been ours alone. But, no, all that was the past. The past was my enemy, I decided, and forced myself to concentrate on only the situation at hand.

"What's this?" I asked Lynn when I found her on the floor, stretched out on the covers she'd taken from the bed.

"The mattress is too soft," she answered. "It's impossible to sleep on."

"Don't worry, tomorrow we'll have them bring up a mat."

"Thank you." Lynn smiled, saying, "It is all so strange here. Are we really in China?"

"I'm not sure yet," I said, going to the door and checking to see that the children were all tucked safely in their beds, fast asleep.

"There's one more thing," Lynn began, her face registering embarrassment, "I can't understand a word of Mandarin."

I had to laugh. "I know exactly how you feel. The same thing happened to me with the Cantonese." I pledged to start teaching her Mandarin right away. But in the meantime, she and I were both overdue for a good, long sleep.

*   *   *

During those first weeks in Shanghai, I often made my way down Bund Street, the elegant avenue along the Whampoo, where the International Concession was located. It was occupied by nearly one million people—double the population of the French zone and a little more than half of Shanghai's total population. Altogether, three million people lived in Shanghai, making it China's business center with the largest European contingent.

At that time, Westerners in China lived in isolated pockets of the various cities. They were completely self-sufficient and their only contact with the majority of Chinese revolved around those who did business with the international firms; only for such purposes were they allowed into the French and international zones.

Shanghai's work force was the largest in the country. The groups who founded the Communist Party back in 1927 had formed there. They had organized a violent general strike against the British. That same year Chiang Kai-shek had wiped out the labor unions and other Communist groups in the capital of Kiangsu, creating a bitter rift within the Kuomintang.

The Japanese, in hopes of gaining support for their occupation, encouraged the anti-European feeling in the Chinese people. The majority of Chinese wanted the Westerners out. The Japanese succeeded in making the British troops withdraw along with the American soldiers sent by Roosevelt to protect American citizens living in China. At the same time, the Japanese, Italian, German, and French governments agreed to concede their territories and rights to the Nanking government. This in turn led to severe economic restrictions concerning the flow of capital. But in spite of these restrictions, and in spite of the constant threats to the European presence, Shanghai remained the only city in China where Europeans could live and prosper without having to renounce their way of life. And so a complex political and cultural picture was revealed to me as the door of China was opening before my eyes.

*   *   *

In the meantime, however, I had more immediate personal concerns—the well-being of my family which had expanded to include the arrival of my new baby daughter. She was born in Shanghai's Jesuit hospital and I named the exquisite infant

Aloma after a character in a movie I had seen in Italy—a lovely maiden with the blackest eyes and brightest smile who lived on an island in the Pacific.

Aloma was baptized with the surname Tam. Because I had been unable to breast-feed, I'd taken in a wet nurse, who came to live with us at the Imperial Hotel.

Four children—the oldest age five—and two servants now made up our household. After paying four months rent, and clothing and feeding us all, very little of the money Tam had given me was left. We could survive a while longer, but I desperately needed a dependable source of financial support.

With this in mind, I telephoned the man to whom Tam had referred me—the Director of the Central Bank—at his office in Nanking Road, one of the main avenues of the city. That same afternoon, Mr. Young parked his Aston-Martin among the pines along Bubblingwell Road and entered the hotel lobby to greet me.

"I don't know you, Madame, but I have heard a lot about you and it's a pleasure to see you in Shanghai."

We took seats on a plush sofa in the corner of the lobby while I observed that Mr. Young was a rather compelling fellow. Not quite fifty, he was one of those men who remain eternally youthful. Dressed in a blue cotton suit and tie, he gestured occasionally as he spoke, his voice gentle, like his movements. He smoked American cigarettes continuously, exhaling the smoke in wisps and revealing his perfect white teeth, emanating an understated sexuality all the while.

Thanking Young for coming so quickly, I told him only a partial truth—that I had left Tuyun temporarily on account of its having grown too dangerous.

He gazed at me with curiosity, a subtle innuendo to his tone as he spoke. "I suppose that whatever is happening down there is a military secret—that I must content myself with the censored news we get in the Japanese-controlled papers."

"The war is long and will go on for some time, but Tam has faith in Chiang Kai-shek's army."

"And so have we all. Although," he murmured with an alluring smile, "you mustn't say that aloud here. Japanese informers are everywhere, and don't trust the Europeans. But I hope we'll have time to consider you Chinese. You are Chinese?"

Now my voice held innuendo as I answered cryptically, "I'll be here for some time."

We arranged for him to open a credit account for me that would then be replenished by transfer from Tam's accounts in Canton. Suggesting he wanted to show me some of the more exotic sights of Shanghai, Young also invited me to what he called "his restaurant" for dinner that evening.

"There will be time, Mr. Young," I replied, "for us to get to know each other better. But not just yet, I'm afraid."

The next day an errand boy from the Central Bank brought me a checkbook and a receipt for an account opened with a large sum. With the paperwork came a delicate and rare flowering plant, a wanda cerulea, which grows in the damp soil along the banks of the Yangtze River.

That afternoon I wrote and mailed the first of many letters to Tam, enclosing our address, and telling him of Aloma's arrival. For the children's sake, especially Lylongo and Jonathan who were learning to read, I asked that he write to us. But I never got a response—not to that letter, nor to any of the subsequent ones.

I spent the days with my children, passing long hours in the salons and in the hotel's park. Without a response from Tam, I couldn't really be sure how long the unlimited availablity of money would last. Deciding that I would attempt to learn to budget my resources, I moved all of us out of the more expensive Imperial Hotel and took an apartment at the more modestly priced Honan Hotel in the French quarter. Of course, when I had so drastically parted ways with Tam, I hadn't anticipated the very real pressures that limited finances impose on someone trying to rear her children with a semblance of security.

And what was more, I hadn't expected the deep yearning I began to feel for a side to my life that was separate from motherhood. Not even twenty-two years old yet, I couldn't deny the potency of my innate sensual needs and desires. Where once I had suppressed them while waiting for Tam to return from the front, there was no longer any reason to hold myself back. The person to step boldly forward in addressing those needs was none other than the enigmatic Mr. Young, whom I contacted to ask whether the invitation to dinner was still standing.

He had made no mistake in referring to the Shanghai nightspot as his restaurant. It was in fact an exclusive private club which occupied the entire ground floor of one of the largest buildings on Bund Street. Each table was set in a small private room partitioned by graceful painted screens.

Over drinks Young complimented my dress—a strapless black crepe that clung tightly from the bodice all the way to my knees. But his manner was proper and respectful as he went on to say, "I have some news for you, Madame, from Tam."

I put down the porcelain spoon next to the bowl of chicken and corn broth I had just tasted.

"I have received a communication from the commander of his outfit. He has left Tuyun. It is not known when and if he will return."

Taking a breath to steady myself, I said, "It is important that you tell me the truth. What more do you know?"

"I am telling you all that I know. I have been waiting for further news, but there hasn't been any." Young peered into my eyes as if to measure their honesty, adding, "I am sure that you have no other news, either."

"No, I haven't," I retorted. "I've written several letters, but received no answers."

Satisfied, he commented, "Yes, it's very difficult to communicate with officers at the front. That's normal. There's no need to be alarmed. I don't want to believe anything else, but speaking frankly, I must tell you that in the absence of any further guarantee from Tam, his bank in Canton has rejected our last request for a withdrawal from his account. We have taken care of it, of course, but I'm sure you understand that such a situation cannot go on indefinitely."

Actually, Young explained, I had reached the limit of what the bank would advance me on my line of credit.

As I contemplated this unsavory news, the waiter arrived and served us a bountiful dish of creamed Mandarin duck. Unfortunately, I'd lost my appetite.

"There is still one possibility," Young began after putting out his cigarette. "Tam's mother has an account in the same bank in Canton. We could notify her and..."

"Absolutely not," I interrupted him. I didn't want Tam's family to know about my situation, but neither was I about to tell Young that.

"But, you know," he objected, "their business is doing very well."

"Of course, opium will always sell well. But I'd rather not." In these subtle ways, by watching my words and withholding small bits of information—without being conscious of it—I was learning skills that I would soon be putting to use for much more dangerous purposes.

"In that case," he said, "I'm not able to advise
you on a long-term solution. But for the time being,
I have already taken care of the matter."

I smiled quizzically. "With a bank loan or a
private loan?"

"Please don't embarrass me with too many
questions."

"Mr. Young, this matter involves the well being
of my children. I'd like to be informed of what my..."
I paused to search for the right word, "...my
obligations might be."

"No obligations," he assured me. "It is a private
loan, as you put it. But anyone would have done the
same thing. You have seen by now that Shanghai is
an expensive city to live in. Still, you mustn't let
this minor difficulty keep you from enjoying what it
has to offer."

No obligations, he had said, a prelude to a night
of strange and dark sights that he offered to show
me. From his club we took a rickshaw, sitting
beneath its slanted roof, wrapped in a wool blanket
to shelter us from the cool night air, over to the
Pagoda of Dragon Flowers. Before entering the
Buddist temple of the area, we passed a group of
beggars huddled around a fire outside and Young
held my arm as he tossed some coins on the ground.

Inside the temple, the lights from oil lamps
flickered across the long row of Buddhas. Young
paused to lean up against a spiral wooden column
and I walked on ahead. Thinking he meant to go
down one of the corridors, I turned down a narrow
passage lined with Buddhas. At the end of it, a monk
in an orange robe was kneeling in prayer. I turned to
see that Young had disappeared and imagined that
his plan had been to set me free to explore Shanghai
on my own. I gazed back at the monk. A rigidity
gave his thin body a stern and solemn look, his
shoulder blades protruding, his fingers tense, his
eyes staring wide open. Inhaling the thick wafts of

incense and observing the religious ecstasy of the
monk, I felt myself becoming lightheaded as a wave
of dizziness overcame me, almost to the point of
nausea, and I hurried out. Outside on the steps, the
crowd of beggars seemed to be waiting for me.

Suddenly a hand grasped my shoulder.

"Oh," I sighed, relieved to see that Young had
appeared again, "I thought you had left."

"Take my arm," he said. "You are too attractive
to be walking out here by yourself. Don't
underestimate these beggars."

We wandered down to the port, along streets
draped with banners advertising the shops, tea
rooms, gambling houses and all-night bars, many of
them lit with neon signs made in the United States.
A line of beggars had stretched out on the sidewalk
to sleep, according to the city's strict regulations—
always lengthwise on the edge of the sidewalk, so
that pedestrians would not be disturbed.

Colorful paper lanterns painted with flowers,
tigers, and dragons hung above the sidewalks.
Teenage girls sat on the steps of their houses. Others
leaned against the walls, disappearing now and then
to lead some man inside. The men who were leaving
would then go into one of the cheap eating places
that served hot food at all hours.

Stepping into a horse-drawn carriage, Young
asked, "Do you wish to go back to your hotel or
would you like to see more?"

I told him to continue the tour.

"Good," he said, "I have something interesting
to show you." When the carriage stopped a few feet
away from the Catholic mission that was locked up
at that hour with an imposing iron bar, he added,
"It happens here every night. But we must be
patient." He lit a cigarette and began to watch the
mission intently.

"I'm glad you wanted to continue with me," he
whispered with his eyes still fixed on the mission.

"You will never know Shanghai if you remain locked in your hotel. When you come out of your cloister, you will see what it is really like."

Young looked back at me for a moment, satisfied by the eager expression I wore. "But," he cautioned, "you must not make the mistake of the Europeans. They think that they have seen everything and that they have the answer. It is not as easy as that. Now, look."

He nodded toward an old man who had pulled his cart up to the doorway and was placing two bundles on the steps. When he was done, the old man dragged his cart back down the street, its lantern bobbing in the darkness.

Again a wave of nausea passed through me. Those were babies in those bundles, I thought, as the swirl of poverty and desperation weighed heavy in my heart

"Both of them will be saved," Young said quietly, signalling to another rickshaw. "A priest will take them to the orphanage, hoping that they will be adopted by some rich family that has no male children. Or if they are girls, they will become servants somewhere."

We travelled quickly down Fu-Ceu Road. My emotions swung to a happier state—this particular scenery reminded me of Paris, with its brightly colored awnings, its cafes, its restaurants. Small groups of musicians performed out on the streets, playing "A Tisket, A Tasket," "Smoke Gets In Your Eyes," and "Berlin, Berlin." There were multitudes of bars and nightclubs, and an occasional Chinese opera house.

We finally stopped at a cabaret, located in a basement off Nanking Road. To enter it, we passed through a narrow corridor guarded by two muscular Chinese bouncers who accompanied us downstairs to the bar. We were shown to a table and Young ordered a magnum of German champagne, easily and cheaply available in the Japanese occupied zone.

After a few minutes, a young Thai dancer slinked across the stage, her movements syncopated with the orchestra's rhythms. The spotlight narrowed on her as she stripped—slipping off her silk tunic slowly and removing her satin undergarments—until she stood naked on the stage in nothing but her black stiletto heels. She eased back onto a cushioned chaise lounge that was in the center of the stage and pretended to fall asleep, suggesting that what followed was happening to her as if in a dream.

A massive brown bear lumbered on stage, led by a trainer who introduced it to the audience as Igor. The animal's paws were wrapped in a brown gauze and a muzzle was strapped to its mouth. The bear was made to sit on a stool facing the audience. The dream girl then got up and sidled over to the bear. She sat on its legs and took the animal's member in her hand. To the beat of the music she pushed it inside of herself repeatedly, in full view of the audience. The trainer stood to one side, leaving the stage to the two stars, while the spectators, mostly Europeans, applauded wildly.

I turned away. "Can we go now, Mr. Young?"

"Of course," he said accommodatingly and rose to escort me from the lurid exhibition, "if you will grant me the pleasure of your company a little longer before I take you back to your hotel."

He no doubt heard my sarcasm as I asked, "You mean you have other marvels in store for me?"

"Yes. I don't want you to think that Shanghai is only this and nothing more."

The rickshaw made its last stop at a building near Bund Street. Upstairs in the penthouse was a private club, where, Young promised, "We can watch the sun rise over the river and the port. It's almost dawn now."

We sat looking out the window over Shanghai harbor in a small luxurious bedroom suite of the club. The ceiling was inlaid with ebony and gold. The walls were covered with silk; dark silk curtains hung from the windows; and silk cushions were piled on the plush carpet.

Young looked out at the night sky and sipped his vodka, then turned to me.

"You have lived too long in the midst of war to be shocked and frightened by Shanghai. But it's time to forget the war and the dying. You are young and your body desires to live. It desires pleasure." He slid over on the couch, closer to me and his voice was hypnotic as it crooned, "You were married to a Chinese so you know how we make love. We do not hurry like other men. For us, every part of the body has its own special pleasure to be experienced fully. To feel it you must abandon yourself completely to the touch." He continued to gaze admiringly at me and I, still hesitant, leaned against the back of the couch and closed my eyes, trying to think through what possibly was about to happen.

"Ah," he pointed out, "you see, in this moment you are thinking too much, you are not listening fully to your body. But together we will discover many pleasures. Here in this city, there is nothing else, as you have seen tonight. Life lasts but an instant and we are too often forced to do what we do not wish to do."

His words and their rhythm aroused me. "Bianca," he said then, trailing his fingers like feathers over my face and body, "I adore your mouth, so soft, so sensuous, and your breasts, waiting for me, your nipples that I long to kiss, to suck." As he turned me around to unzip my dress, I had already begun to tingle with excitement. Yes, I wanted him and I would not refuse him. He kissed my neck, my ears, his hands exploring my body, caressing it, fondling it in places I had been so longing to have touched. With every movement, he continued to talk, his every word more and more intoxicating as he described how he would eventually make love to me, and how he wanted me to climax by his touch, his hands as smooth and deft as his voice was soft.

"I rubbed myself earlier with a special oil," he whispered. "An aphrodisiac that has made my desire for you more and more intense. And now I will rub you with the oil and with my body, and you will forget everything and the pleasure will last a long, long time, as long as you want it to."

It only took a small amount of the oil, that he stroked over my belly and between my legs, for me to feel that I was succumbing to the pull of some powerful drug. When he took my breast in his mouth, I reached for him, wrapping my legs around him, gasping, and we slipped from the couch onto the silk pillows strewn over the floor.

For hour upon hour, I continued to fulfill every ounce of the desire that I had kept in check for so long, smothering him with the ecstasy he had produced in me. True to his word, Young knew how to give back the pleasure that he took.

He was still asleep when I got up later that morning. Outside the sampans were still tied to the docks, but the newsboys of the Shanghai Telegraph were already racing down the streets on their bicycles, bearing the latest reports: The Japanese had bombed Pearl Harbor. President Roosevelt had declared war on Japan.

CHAPTER 13

Shanghai. 1942-1944.

Not wanting to be wholly dependent on Young, I had begun working as a shop assistant and model at a fashion house run by a French couple, Madame and Monsieur Oury. With the salary they paid me, I was able to continue paying the rent at the Honan Hotel and retain the money from Young in a savings account under my children's name.

The work was stimulating, not at all difficult, and something—given my fondness for couture—to which I was well suited. I came home at the end of the day energized, ready to let the amahs, Lynn and Sue, take a break so that I could spend quality time with the children. Lylongo, who was soon to turn six, especially enjoyed hearing about the beautiful garments that had been purchased that day and the tales of whatever glamorous women had been in as customers. Jonathan, now almost five, was going through a phase where he had hundreds of questions about everything—all of which I tried dutifully and patiently to answer. Holding Jula, who would soon be two years old, in one arm, and Aloma at seven months of age in the other arm, we would gather together until it was time for them to go to bed. Then, after they'd gone to sleep, I would bathe, change my clothes, and step out into the Shanghai night. Once out, I was another person, another woman, whomever I chose to be.

With Young, I was exploring a darker side of desire. Of course, when we went out in public, he behaved himself in a manner that he, and most Chinese, would consider gentlemanly. He provided for me and, in his own way, sheltered me. And he adhered to the custom of not associating with the children of another man.

On those nights we made love often and Young enjoyed talking about it, as if making love and remembering those moments later were the best remedy for the uncertainty of our times. There was something oddly perverse in his way of relating the details of the nights we spent together. And worse, every once in a while he would enjoy describing some of the crudest and most repugnant sexual practices of his people. Afterwards, it seemed that the more atrocious the story he had just told, the more tender his lovemaking was.

I had come to find out that Young was married and had four grown children. For this reason, we always had our assignations in the posh rooms of private clubs. I was always meticulously careful about not having intercourse with him during my fertile time of the month—one of the oldest forms of birth control that, in my experiences, happened to be very successful.

Young didn't smoke opium. Instead, he preferred alcohol and it was rice liquor that removed his inhibitions, inducing him to talk of the sexual deviances of others. He would lie with his head on a cushion, looking up at the ceiling, as if to distance himself from his emotions.

"A group of men," he began one night, "put a woman in a wooden box with a hole at the level of her anus. They set a starving mouse that had been tied to a tiny gold chain at the edge of the hole and as it could smell her flesh, it found its way into the box and entered her anus to feed on her insides. The torture didn't kill the woman, even though the mouse ate at her tissues. They eventually took the woman out and freed the mouse by pulling up on the chain. Then, one by one, the men raped her, forcing themselves where the mouse had just been."

As grotesque as the story had been, I had listened with a morbid curiosity, wondering how he would next please me to make up for what he had subjected me to.

Young got up, had me lie face down on the floor, fondled my buttocks with worship and licked me from behind for a long time until I was uncontrollably filled with desire, my body writhing with want and anticipation for however he planned on fulfilling me. With intensely pleasurable sensations, I felt him slide a greased wooden lingam deep inside me. After he removed it, he pressed himself there, finding no resistance. We climaxed together and I left him exhausted on the bed.

I didn't want to end my sexual odyssey with him, but soon after that I decided I could no longer accept his ongoing financial support. Strangely enough, as I was having these thoughts, he turned up unexpectedly at the Honan Hotel—the only time he had ever come to my apartment. Fortunately, the amahs and the children had just gone down to dinner and I was able to speak with him alone in our sitting room.

He placed an envelope full of money on the desk before he sat down and announced that his oldest daughter was getting married.

"Congratulations," I said. "And this is why you've come to see me?"

"Yes, Bianca. I won't be able to help you anymore. The war has limited my resources and I must see to her needs. In fact, I'll probably have to take a loan in order to arrange a wedding worthy of my family's name."

"But," I said with sincerity, sliding the envelope back to him, "we can still go on seeing each other, I hope."

Young shook his head no at both my suggestion and the return of the money. He put the envelope back in my hands, saying, "We can't go on like this. We have been lovers and have enjoyed a certain style of life together. I can't imagine changing that, but I no longer have the same financial possibilities."

Thinking of our wild excesses and his ample generosity, I told him, "You've done a lot for me and I'll never forget it."

Young bowed, took my hand and kissed it on the palm. He strode to the door and then turned back to me, saying these last words, "You will forget and that will be for the best. Now you must solve your problems, you must help yourself. Our lives change so quickly and we must understand things as they happen. Nothing lasts forever."

* * *

Children are the reasons for many choices we don't dare defend, the justification for everything, the alibi for all my deeds—the good ones and ones I would blush with shame to recall. But I would only have myself to thank for the situation I soon found myself in. Alone I had been sucked into a vortex and now alone I would either find my way out or perish.

"But, Bianca," the woman was saying, "how can I buy that dress after I've seen how exquisite it looks on you?" Her name was Nancy Lee, a charming Europeanized Chinese woman, widow of a western diplomat, well-connected in the political, military, and social worlds of Shanghai. I had never been introduced to her but had seen her in the shop on occasion for several months, ever since the Ourys had put me in charge of sales and running the fashion shows.

I was often complimented on the casual way I wore Chinese clothes. In my work with the Ourys, I had convinced other western women to do the same. These dresses were cut from rich silks reminiscent of the luxury and tradition of the Tsing Dynasty in Manchuria that had ruled China for three centuries. They needed no jewelry, no extra accessories—just a woman who was proud of her body and knew how to carry herself. And in regard to Nancy's question about the particular dress I was modeling for her— an aquamarine silk exactly the color of my eyes that buttoned at the neck and fell to my ankles—I was keen to have her try it on, knowing she would fall in love with it.

"A Chinese dress must be worn with the charm of a Chinese woman," I answered. "It will look wonderful on you. But how do you know my name?"

"Everyone in Shanghai has been talking about the lovely young Italian woman who lives in a hotel with four children and no husband."

"And two amahs!" I laughed. "Come and try the dress on."

In the dressing room, I slipped on a robe and helped her into the dress.

"It's just perfect for you."

"I've also heard your Chinese is as good as your English," Nancy said in an off-handed way as she studied herself in the mirror.

"I also speak fluent French and Italian, of course.

Not that it's much good for anything." I tucked up one of the sleeves. "It will have to be shortened."

"Just the sleeves," she said. "I'm afraid it will have to be let out around the hips." Nancy followed me as I went to ring up the sale and write down the tailoring specifications. "So," she teased, "you model these clothes and they suit you perfectly and the first client who comes along snatches them up?"

"It's my job." I smiled, admitting that she had well detected our sales strategy.

"To look at you no one would ever guess that you've had four children," she uttered with admiration, gazing directly at me from head to toe. "I have never had children, but I've gained weight all the same." As she paid for the dress from a wallet which I couldn't help but notice was full of cash, she asked one more time, "Do you really think it's right for me?"

"It's perfect," I assured her, "just right for you and the elegant social events I'm certain you attend frequently. And it looks lovely with the way you wear your hair up in back. It shows off the embroidery on the collar."

"Please have the alterations done now," she said. "I'll wait in the red room and it would be a pleasure if you joined me for something to drink."

At forty, Nancy was still extremely attractive and continued to hold sway socializing in diplomatic circles, much to the satisfaction of the Japanese officials. With many acquaintances and a well-to-do family, the widow never remarried. She was the leading lady of the most exclusive dinner parties and receptions. At times she must have felt herself the most important woman in Shanghai. But, as I was to learn, she had more social engagements than she could handle on her own.

When I came to sit down with Nancy in the red room, I saw that a waiter had brought two glasses and a bottle of Pernod for us to share.

"I'm sure Monsieur Oury won't mind if we sit here for a few minutes and chat," she said, taking a silver case and a long ivory cigarette holder from her bag.

She lit the cigarette and continued to study me, saying, "You must need a lot of money to support four children. I know that at the moment all you have is your salary from the boutique. For over a year, you have had no message and no money from your husband. You are twenty-four years old and you are alone. Don't ask me how I know all this," she said, waving some smoke away. "Everyone knows everything about everyone else in Shanghai. A woman like you can't hope to remain anonymous. But tell me. Can you possibly make ends meet?"

I betrayed nothing to let her know she had been correct in her assessments, not wanting to allow the truth—that I was indeed concerned about my financial straits—to become public knowledge. Instead, I sipped from the Pernod, saying, "Why do you ask?"

"You are very beautiful, adventurous, and you know many languages. The war can offer many opportunities to a woman of your looks and talents." Nancy paused to see that she had my full attention. "I have a proposition for you. If you will help me with my political and social activities—dinners, meetings with diplomats, receptions, and so on—you'll receive excellent pay and many other benefits. If you accept, we'll begin immediately. Believe me, it's an excellent opportunity."

I glanced about the salon, lowered my voice, and leaned in close to her. "You're asking me to become a spy, aren't you?"

Nancy laughed and continued to talk in a conversational manner. "Don't jump to conclusions, Bianca. I advise you to take my offer at face value. It's not up to me to decide if there will be future developments. No one will ask you to do anything against your will. What do you say?"

Before I could answer or think through the ramifications of this moment—triggered as so many events in my life by the purchase of a dress—she had already lifted her glass in a toast. "Here's to us."

*   *   *

For her encounters, Nancy had rented the whole floor of a large private restaurant on Nanking Road. The guests would sit at a big round table and an array of sumptuous dishes would be served—the very best of Chinese cuisine alternated with Japanese specialties: shrimp tempura, sukiyaki, sushi. There would often be Japanese men, as well as amenable Chinese, British, French, and a few Americans among those invited.

The activities of the evening followed a pattern. My role at these dinners remained the same and I repeated it an infinite number of times. I was to introduce the guests to each other, all of whom were leading figures—regardless of nationality—in the big business of war. They dealt in arms and currency export. Or they were Chinese businessmen who had succeeded in corrupting the already corrupt Japanese government and had managed to secretly obtain contracts for furnishing the troops. Or they were politicians, or Chinese who had fought for the Japanese. Or they were that other special category that flourishes in wartime like flowers in a hot house: business consultants who manage to convince everyone that they are influential and thus end up becoming so.

Nancy and I were the center of attention on those evenings, but I soon became even more popular than her, a fact she seemed to enjoy. At times I felt as if I was back in the old days at the luxurious banquets given for the naval officers of La Spezia by my mother, the Countess, at our home in the Villa Lizza. Admittedly, after that year in

Tuyun and the specter of poverty I had confronted there, I became intoxicated with the power of money and with the prestige and material abundance that was ever increasingly surrounding me. I was like an actress, playing out the role that had been assigned to me, playing it to the hilt with casual daring and nonchalance.

And the script: those conventional formal greetings and small talk formulas uttered with traditional Eastern charm and elegance. The various dishes would be tasted and whisked away by the pretty and young women who were serving. Then came the toasts with kau-peh, sorghum wine, and the little glasses would quickly be refilled. I would drink along with the men so that I too could take part in the relaxed sensual atmosphere that preceded the second phase of the evening, which Nancy had organized to create good public relations among all the guests.

The door to an adjoining room would slide open and we would retire there to smoke opium. The drug was usually prepared by one of the women who had served at the tables, by spreading its dark paste around the end of a stick of sandalwood and warming that over the flame of a lamp. When it turned into a creamy consistency and began to burn, it was placed in the pipe. We did not inhale the bitter smoke, but held it in our mouths so that it was absorbed into our bloodstream through the mucous membrane of the gums. As with the drinking, I would indulge in the opium to better allow myself to perform as temptress and seductress; but not to such an excess that my faculties of observation would be impaired.

The guests would lie with their heads propped on cushioned headrests as Nancy and I kept intimate conversations going—circulating among the men to make sure they were enjoying themselves. The pipe was brought to each guest by one of the girls whose duty it was to satisfy his every whim. They wiped sweat from the men's brows with damp handkerchiefs and fanned them. The girls all dressed and looked alike, with their identical make-up, arched plucked eyebrows, touches of rouge, short shining hair, sparkling eyes. They were graceful, charming, pleasing to the eyes and eager to please, darting about in their tiny slippers, their feet bound in the traditional Chinese manner—a custom begun by a princess with naturally tiny feet who lived around the year 1000. These were the girls from upper class families who hoped that their daughters might become geishas and had begun binding their feet at age five, strapping the toes in such a way that they gradually atrophied.

While we smoked and chatted quietly, listening to the soft music of the ch'in, one of the men would invariably gesture to me, indicating that he desired my full attention. I would lean back on the headrest, take his hand in mine and listen carefully to all he had to say. Inevitably he would confide something he shouldn't have said—secret alliances, code names, strategic locations or routes, those sorts of things. Eventually, I would discreetly rise so that he could follow me off to one of private boudoirs clustered behind the panels of the smoking room. There, as he wished and as he had paid for at great expense, I would be solely his for the remainder of the night.

In this third phase, the pattern was always different, depending on the particular inclinations of the individual man. Sometimes, I would undress him first and rub him down with a scented lotion, then tease him by taking him in my mouth just to the point of climax until he begged for mercy and I would remove my clothing and straddle him. Other times, the man would take the lead—undressing me, fondling and stroking me until my hunger for him was evident. On rarer occasions, a man with voyeuristic tendencies might ask that one of the serving women join with us so that he could watch the erotic unfolding of a young nubile Chinese girl making love with me. But whatever the scenario, one thing remained the same—that a man in a state of heightened arousal loved even more to prove his power by exposing the secrets to which he was privy. If on any of the points he had previously been vague, it would be here that in between my sighing and gasping I would artfully ask further questions. While the man undulated or writhed in ecstasy, he would never fail to give me substantial answers.

One evening it was one of the emperor's officers whispering the names of his Chinese colleagues; the next evening a general from Shanghai confessing of a mission he would soon lead on behalf of the Japanese; or the ambassador from one of the Axis countries telling me about a shipment of weapons he had personally arranged.

In this business of public relations, as Nancy referred to it, a few of the men became regular clients of mine and eventually several of Nancy's clients asked only for me. Perhaps they found me more desirable because of my youth and beauty, though I didn't give it any thought; nor did Nancy, who relished my information-gathering talents. Only later would I realize that I had lost my soul, that good looks were all I truly possessed back then. It would take two more years and my actual arrest for me to understand that in the aftermath of Tam's betrayal, I had turned my anger not at him but at myself and that I had committed to a path of certain destruction. Looking back, I would hardly recognize myself for all the changes that had taken place in me since my arrival in Shanghai.

As in a fairy tale, the illusions of the night faded in the morning. I would leave the restaurant and take a taxi back to the hotel. After looking in on my sleeping children, I would myself collapse into bed.

Later in the day, there would still be no time for introspection as my work took on a more noble nature. Nearly every afternoon the sitting room of the suite we rented was full of people: businessmen whose businesses were threatened, shopkeepers, clerks who wanted promotions, poor people searching for impossible justice. I met with them, listened to them, promised to do what I could for them through my contacts. Whatever they paid me went straight into my children's bank accounts. I later discussed the problems with the influential people I knew and often got what I asked for. My sphere of influence had grown considerably—I was recognized and treated with deference in the most exclusive areas of the city. Nancy valued and trusted me, turning over to me the daily tasks of creating guest lists, writing the invitations, and planning menus as well as entertainment. I eventually had saved enough money to repay my debts to Young, but he refused to accept it.

I bought gifts for the children and some new clothes for myself—small tokens of my victory in the challenge I had accepted that morning when I learned that I was not Tam's only woman.

I wrote to him in detail about the children and asked him for news, but as had been the case all along, I never received an answer. Even so, and even for the fact that I rarely reflected on the emotional inner turmoil that was being suppressed as I so boldly played out my role as a spy and courtesan, I was sure that I would see him again. I felt—I knew on some instinctual level—that Tam was still alive.

* * *

On returning from an exceptionally exhausting night, I got to the apartment to find that Lynn was waiting up for me. She told me that Jonathan had been bitten by a stray dog in a park in the French quarter.

"I disinfected the bite," she said, "but perhaps you should look at it."

Jonathan didn't wake up when I slipped off his pajamas to look at his leg. There was no longer any trace of the bite, not even a scratch, or any redness.

"Lynn," I said, sighing with relief, "thank you for taking precautions and letting me know."

That night I was also relieved to have the evening off so that I could have dinner with my family. Thankfully, Jonathan was in fine spirits, bragging to us about his dangerous adventure with the dog. I couldn't believe how fast time was going by. My son was six years old and Lylongo was seven already. Soon Jula, who like her older sister was outgoing and social, would be four. And the ever beautiful Aloma was going on two-and-a-half.

"When are we going to see Papa?" Jonathan asked, a question he rarely posed.

I started to launch into my regular speech about a soldier's life and about how we all had to have faith that the war would end and their father would surprise them by walking into the very hotel restaurant where we now sat. My words, however, were halted as a waiter approached and handed me a sealed envelope.

An ominous chill ran down my spine, but I opened it with a casual ease and read the handwritten note that had come from Nancy:

> *"A government official in Nanking urgently wants to meet you. If you accept, which I think you must do, the Japanese Embassy will provide a car. We'll make the trip together."*

I slipped the note back in its envelope, then lifted my eyes to meet the curious gazes of Jonathan and Lylongo staring at me from across the table.

CHAPTER 14

The Cities of Nanking, Shanghai, and Canton. 1944.

The Blue River, with its deep waters and wide banks, flows through Nanking, the ancient capital of the South. Between Nanking and Shanghai lies the mighty Yangtze. Following the river's twists and turns, troops and arms had been shipped to Nanking, where the new Chinese puppet government had been proclaimed by the Japanese in July 1941. Wang Ching-wei ruled the area, taking his orders directly from Tokyo.

Nanking was chosen as the capital for the puppet government for several reasons. It occupied a strategic position, from a political and military point of view, in the middle of a vast area. Also, its cultural pre-eminence dated back to China's earliest civilized eras. And prior to the Japanese dominance, Chiang Kai-shek had proclaimed it the capital of Free China. Now, as the Empire of the Rising Sun reached its zenith, the combined efforts of the United States and Commonwealth troops could not defeat the Japanese in an immense geographical zone that reached from the Aleutian Islands to Burma.

Hong Kong, for years the symbol of British power in Asia, fell on Christmas Day, 1941. This was followed by the surrender of Singapore. General MacArthur was unable to defend the Philippines. Manila, Celebes, Borneo, Timor, Java, were all occupied. When the Japanese concentrated their attacks on the Bismarck Archipelago and the Solomon Islands, the Australian government ordered an immediate mobilization of the army. In India, cities and towns were bombarded. Rangoon and Mandalay were in Japanese hands. The road built by the British to connect Burma with Chungking in order to guarantee a flow of supplies to the Kuomintang had been blocked to the South. The network of roads connecting the USSR to the free part of China was too long and in too poor a condition for Stalin to intervene. Meanwhile, three million German soldiers had invaded Russia while an old treaty of alliance with Japan was still in effect.

The only way for the Americans to bring supplies to Chiang Kai-shek's troops was to fly across the *gobba*, the high mountain region between India and China. All the while the Japanese advanced towards the central areas controlled by the Kuomintang. The Communist troops, busily defending their hold on the Yunan, were unable to concentrate on anything else. No army in the Far East could contain the Japanese.

In the midst of all this, Nancy and I arrived in Nanking.

Kesoke Kurata, Special Counsellor to the Minister of Foreign Affairs, was waiting for us in one of the government palace offices.

Kurata was bullish in physique, short and hefty and promising to be lethal in conflicts that were either physical or intellectual. But it was with polite restraint that he welcomed me ceremoniously, saying, "Madame Tam, first let me thank you for everything you have done for us in Shanghai. You have become indispensable to us, especially in keeping tabs on some of our own representatives, who could have otherwise tended to become overly free-wheeling."

I showed no reaction to this whatsoever and refrained from suggesting that most of my information was already known to him through other intelligence sources.

"However," Kurata continued, drawing closer, "I haven't asked you to come all this way merely to thank you. We want to award you the title of Special Advisor to the Nanking government. It is a small reward for what you have done. Hopefully, too, it will be a commitment on your part to continue the work you have already been doing for us. And to help on special missions for which we will ask your assistance from time to time."

I saw a flicker of admiration in Nancy's eyes, a pride in the fact that her protegé had proven so worthy. Warily, I asked Kurata, "What sort of assistance?"

Still containing what I imagined would be a formidable temper, he gestured for us to sit down and said lightly, "Nothing much different from your current work for us. It might involve a bit of travelling between Nanking and Shanghai, a few trips to Hong Kong where we send our officers on leave. You might be useful in organizing social activities for them. Everything paid for by our government. Of course, you will receive a monthly check, which should be more than satisfactory for a woman with four children."

A servant poured cups of a tea that gave off a smoky aroma.

"This tea comes from Burma," he explained, adroitly changing the subject in the manner of someone skilled at deception. "It was brought by the first flight from Rangoon to Nanking. In a few months there will be regular civilian air service throughout all of China."

"Since I've been working with Nancy," I interrupted, allowing myself to take control of the conversation, "I've been free to stop or continue as I wish. Surely that will change if I accept your offer to go to work directly for your government."

His eyes darted to Nancy's and then he made his reply to me. "Yes, that's true but we have a lot to offer." He laughed darkly, saying, "Naturally enough, we expect a lot in return. You needn't think your work for us will go on indefinitely. We only require your help now. For the moment."

My fear rising, I maintained an air of cool as I stated, "You know that I am the wife of a Kuomintang officer. But you must also know from Nancy that I have heard no news from him for several months and know nothing about what is going on along the southwest front."

"Forgive my saying so, but I don't believe you," he said with a kind expression. Then, very sharply, he added, "Please remember that we require your complete cooperation." It must have been obvious that he had penetrated my veneer.

"Bianca is already collaborating," Nancy interjected, "and she knows how to handle every situation..."

"But," I cut her off, anger plainly audible in my aghast, "the major is asking for a lot more, now."

Kurata topped us both as he said emphatically, "And offering a lot more. Your first check is in an envelope on the desk. I know that you have managed to take advantage of the opportunities that have been given to you in Shanghai. You have a chance now to multiply them indefinitely."

I felt the trap closing. It wasn't the lure of money pulling me in, but the potential threat to my life, my children's lives, or even, I wondered, to Tam. The desperation was enough for me to lie and unfortunately to lie badly. I cleared my throat, "Major Kurata, you must realize that Tam never spoke about the war when he came home to me in Tuyun."

He took this in without an initial reaction and walked to the window to look out over the river, studying the ceaseless movement of the boats on the Yangtze. He came back to the desk, lit a cigar, and sat in his armchair.

"You are a Catholic, Madame, and I hope it won't unsettle you if I remind you of one of your Saviour's sayings: 'He who is not with me is against me.' No god has ever spoken more clearly than that."

"The Japanese as Jesus Christ," I said with icy sarcasm, "isn't that exaggerating a bit?"

Kurata sipped his tea. "We will win this war and we will remain in China for a long time. We will remember who helped us, who fought against us, and who did not do for us what they might have done." Suddenly, he stopped talking as a diversionary tactic, so that a forebording silence filled the room. My senses were reeling and I tried to mentally get a perspective on just how much jeopardy I was in.

Given the political climate, one wouldn't call the man sitting across from me a fanatic. Most of the Japanese officers and soldiers were indeed convinced that they would soon be victorious. With the signs and trends at that time in 1944, I probably would have predicted them as the winners as well. They were warriors, fueled even more by the deeply ingrained Shinto religion which had become a state institution as well as a national ethic. It claimed that the Emperor was divine, and this new cult of the Mikado exemplified the indestructible bond between the gods of the past, the present Emperor, and the nation, all of which were worshipped by the Japanese soldiers. Not unlike the Nazi's propaganda, the new order of China was continually propagandized by the press and radio of occupied China. The Japanese openly declared their conviction, instilled in them since ancient times, that their people, their nation, their virile faith, were infinitely superior to Chinese history, culture, and religion. Recent events seemed to the Japanese living proof of this ancient belief.

As though he was reading my mind, Kurata began to speak again. This time with his presumably compassionate voice, he said, "Things are very confused in this moment of history. Nancy is a Chinese woman from one of the oldest Shanghai families. She is vital to our cause: the New China. No one would dare consider her a traitor. Many on the contrary admire her intelligence."

I started to ask him why when he had Nancy's services he would even need me, but again, he addressed my thoughts before I spoke them. "You, Bianca, have one advantage as far as we are concerned. You know something about the art of war. You studied in Turin with your husband and learned many military terms that very few women know. Don't be surprised, we know all about you, it's our business to know about people." He paused enough to lace his demeanor with fearful venom, then continued, "You are thinking that we are asking you to betray your man, rather the man who used to be yours, before he took a lover, and who has not contacted you in a long time. I would not call what we are asking you to do a betrayal. You may refuse, of course. We will obtain this information from someone else and you will lose this opportunity."

"Betrayal is the right word," I said, leaping to my feet, "and I refuse."

Kurata went over to the parrot that was chained to a perch in the corner of the room and fed him a handful of grain, speaking to me with regrets—in effect calming me against my will—as he told me, "You could save many lives. Many Japanese soldiers will die because you refuse to tell us what we ask, and many Chinese soldiers as well. They are determined to go on fighting for a lost cause in order to delay their surrender by a week or a day."

I sat down again in utter confusion, looking once more at Nancy, "Am I really as important as all that? I find it hard to believe."

Kurata opened a drawer of his desk and pulled out a batch of photos. He slapped them down on the desk and singled out one.

"We know that you have seen this man before. When?"

Seeing the last vestiges of my resistance, the Major briskly motioned for Nancy to leave the room.

"I will help your memory," he crooned, as the door was closed behind her. "This is a United States aviation officer, Lee Claire Chennault. How long did he stay in Tuyun?"

Kurata inhaled the smoke of his cigar and let loose a threatening verbal lash with vicious relentlessness in his undertone, seething, "Madame, I have made you a precise offer, but I must warn you that your position as the wife of an army officer is very delicate."

I absorbed the full implications of the threat, realizing that any choice I might have had in the matter had been determined from the moment I'd gone to work for Nancy. Assessing well that he had broken me down, Kurata smiled and articulated his question with relish as he asked, "When did you last see Chennault?"

I blurted the response, "In the spring of 1941." Once spoken, it seemed easy enough to say, but it had, no doubt, been prepared for by a long and bitter line of defeats and compromises. From then on, I answered everything almost by rote, with a deathlike resignation.

"How long did he stay in Tuyun?"

"About three months."

"Was he alone?"

"No."

"What is the code name for his patrol?"

"Flying Tigers, all volunteers."

"Was it an American initiative, or did David Kung have something to do with it?"

"He knew about it, together with the officers of the Kuomintang. They inspected the whole area of the front to decide where to build the landing strips."

Kurata took out a military map of the Kwei-chow.

"Madame, our bombers have just defeated the British and American fleets. They are planning a mass attack on Kwei-chow in a few days. You can save thousands of Kuomintang soldiers' lives if you tell us where the landing strips are. That way we will bombard only the landing sites and spare the troops."

I pointed to the locations on the map that Tam had once shown me.

Kurata leaned back. "My government will not forget the service you have done us."

"Can I go now?" It was all I could manage to say. If it weren't for my children, I would have wanted to die on the spot.

"Of course," he said, placing the envelope in my hands and gripping them at the same time as he added, "But this evening the embassy of the Third Reich is giving a reception to honor the Fuhrer's birthday. Please accept the invitation."

I jerked my hands and the envelope from his clasp, and though I had no intention of attending the reception, I told him I would be there, as long as I could book myself into a local hotel.

"You needn't bother, I have reserved two rooms for you and Nancy at the Hotel Europe. I'll send a car around for you at nine o'clock."

I did not reply to that, knowing I would have to find some other excuse to miss the heinous gathering of Japanese and German officials. Instead, I nodded curtly and turned to leave.

"One other thing, Madame Tam," he said, following behind me. When I turned back to face him, he smiled provocatively, saying, "Nancy had told me you were beautiful. But you are certainly more than that. You are fascinating as well."

*   *   *

The nightmare unfolded. That evening I dressed for the reception, planning to protest at the last minute of being ill, and walked with Nancy down to the car. Just as I opened my mouth with my prepared excuse, we were interrupted by a desperate cry from across the street.

A Chinese girl was shouting and clutching at a Japanese officer, begging him for the money he had promised her for sex. The officer laughed, then ripped his arm away. Everyone had stopped to watch, but no one made a move to intervene. Now on her knees, she clasped her arms around his legs to keep him from walking away, pleading with him all the while for her money. His cap fell off and rolled down the pavement. Suddenly his face became enraged, his eyes glazed and his jaw clenched. He kicked her free of him, stepped back, and drew his sword. She tried to call out but he plunged the blade into her chest. A red stain spread across her dress. He put away his sword, picked up his hat, and walked toward the hotel. I broke from the grip Nancy had on my wrist, ran over to the girl, and tried helplessly to stop the bleeding. People who had watched the killing walked away. Everything around me clouded up as rage, horror, and panic consumed me. "An ambulance," I began shouting, "someone call an ambulance!" No one responded, but it wouldn't have mattered. The girl—who could not have been more than fifteen—was already dead.

I stumbled across the street toward the hotel, walking blindly through the traffic and straight into the path of an oncoming taxi that slammed down on its brakes to avoid hitting me, its ungodly screech echoing in the night. I shoved past Nancy, ran into the lobby and upstairs to my room where I threw myself sobbing onto the bed, my bloodied hands staining the sheets.

I did not answer when Nancy knocked at the door, asking to come in; nor did I attend the reception that I'd never intended to go to anyway. The next morning, still weeping, I folded up the dress I'd been wearing when I'd witnessed the killing—a red silk dress with dark, almost black blood spots on it. I left it folded in the closet and took my bag, called a taxi and went to the station.

After the express train delivered me to Shanghai in the early evening, I entered the apartment in a terrible state, trembling as I greeted the children. Jonathan and Lylongo had never actually seen me cry outwardly and neither of the amahs could understand the reason for my tears.

"Whatever it is," Lynn whispered, "I am sure you will be fine. You are very strong and you always manage."

I took some comfort in her words and in the hot bath that Sue drew for me. After dinner, when I was alone with Aloma, and the children were sleeping in the next room, I started to feel calmer, thinking that the nightmare was over. But I was wrong, it was only beginning.

* * *

"Jonathan," I said to my son the next morning, "you haven't touched a bite of your breakfast."

No response came back from him as Lynn, seeing my concern, tried to give him a piece of toast. Jonathan jerked his head away. Repeated attempts to feed him came to nothing, so I took her place next to him and lifted the glass of orange juice to his lips. He knocked it out of my hand and leaned back in his chair, snarling at me, his eyes glazed and red.

"Jonathan," I cried, "what is it?" I grabbed his arm and he began to writhe and whine, seeming to be oblivious to my presence. In seconds, with a force beyond his six years of age, he had freed himself from my grip and had thrown himself on the floor, his convulsions continuing. His face was flaming red.

"Lynn," I said, "hurry and call a doctor." Fearing Jonathan might hurt himself, I asked a waiter to help me hold him down, as I tried to cool the boy's forehead with a wet napkin. In no time, a Chinese doctor arrived, examined Jonathan and called an ambulance. When it came, I told Lynn to take the children upstairs. Lylongo was crying, protesting that she wanted to stay with her brother.

"Listen to your mother," the doctor said to her, and once he had convinced her, he turned to me with his findings. "Your son has rabies. I'm sending the ambulance to the Pasteur Institute. You must check in immediately with Doctor Kwei."

A few minutes later, I was running down the hallway of the Pasteur Institute, following the nurse who was carrying Jonathan, by now sedated with an injection.

Doctor Kwei, a wirey and youngish man, didn't take long to advise me, "You have brought him to me rather late. The nerve centers have already been attacked."

"But...but..." I stammered, forgetting the incident a few weeks before, "he wasn't bitten."

Kwei shook his head, explaining, "If not, the virus must have entered through some scratch that he got while playing. It has had a long period of incubation and now has spread."

Jonathan was quarantined and I had to look at him from behind a glass window while the doctor injected anti-rabies serum into his abdomen.

I watched all day as the doctor would go in, uncover Jonathan, and plunge the needle into him while two nurses held the boy down. He screamed furiously. Like an uncontrollable obsession, those screams would echo in my head for years afterwards.

I don't remember how much time passed. Hours later the convulsions ceased and his little body took on a recognizable form. This seemed to me a positive sign, a good omen. Only later would I be told that it was the onset of nerve paralysis. After the final injection I was allowed to go and sit next to Jonathan. He was constantly shifting in his sleep and, it appeared to me, trying to wake up. But he was unable to open his eyes. I called to him, murmuring his name—"Jonathan, Jonathan, Mama's here, Mama's here."

The nurse with me kept a close watch on him as his movements slowed down and a pallor spread across his face. His little body arched for a second in one last attempt to expel the evil that had taken hold of it. Then he was still. I brushed the damp hair from his forehead. He was cold so I concluded that it was because his fever had gone down and looked hopefully over at the nurse. Saying nothing, she turned to go get the doctor.

But when the doctor came back, he could do nothing more than join Jonathan's hands together on his chest. My son was gone.

*   *   *

Lynn and I watched as the white coffin was lowered into the earth under the shade of a magnolia tree in the Jesuit Mission cemetery.

When I told her about it, Lylongo seemed to understand that Jonathan, like Jula before him,

Wedding picture of Bianca and General Tam.

Bianca with her four children vacationing in La Spezia.

A young Bianca with her father.

Bianca with her grandparents and cousin.

Bianca's third husband, Erwin Leschziner, with his mother-in-law's second husband.

Bianca with 4th husband, Franco.

would never come back. I stayed with her until she fell asleep. Then I collapsed on my bed, believing with certainty that the death of my only son was a punishment for all my sins.

I prayed for sleep, but when it finally overtook me, it was only with turbulent, fearsome dreams. I dreamt I saw a large building with its door wide open, beckoning me in. I walked slowly up the stairs. The windows were all broken and the wind had blown in piles of leaves, like the bougainvillea of Spezia, into the corners of all the rooms. I went up another flight of steps and found a door on my right. I pushed it open and entered a theater. My mother was the only spectator. She turned to greet me and scolded me for being late. I sat away from her, closer to the exit.

Tam and my children appeared on the dimly lit stage. As they bowed to us, I felt a cold wind blowing behind me and turned to see a window, recognizing it as the window of my childhood home. I looked back at the actors in time to see my mother going up the steps to join them. They all disappeared into the wings without looking back. I tried to get up, but could not move. When I tried to call them, no sound came from my mouth. Tam, my mother, Jula, Jonathan, Lylongo, Aloma—they were gone. The faint light in the theater faded and the only thing visible was a stuffed teddy bear that had been left behind on the stage. The darkness continued to close in around me and I felt myself being sucked into a black cloud.

I awoke gasping for breath and ran to look in on my three girls. They were sleeping peacefully and being watched by Lynn. I stood there with my hand on the door knob, trying to calm myself.

"Can I do anything?" Lynn whispered.

"No." I only mouthed the word and went quickly back to my room, picked up the telephone and asked to make an urgent call to Italy. While I was waiting for the international operator to phone back, I tried to focus my thoughts, to prepare my words and envision some course of action. Young, Nancy, Kurata—they had in a way overpowered me. I had accepted the work with Nancy, and I had compromised myself to the Japanese who might not after all win the war—just that afternoon, news of the American victories had begun to leak through in spite of the censorship.

When Mama's voice answered the telephone, it soothed my pain and calmed my fear. But, still, I was unable to speak and dropped the receiver even as she went on calling my name. It was as it had been in the dream—I opened my mouth but had no voice. However, unlike the dream, I couldn't wake from it because it was really happening.

There was only one person, I resolved, who could help shake me from the madness that had turned real.

I made the arrangements that morning by paying a month's advance to the hotel and giving the amahs their salaries. Then I dictated my will to a lawyer who had been recommended to me by the Italian Embassy. If I should not come back, the lawyer would have to contact my family in Italy and advise them in the event that the children's father did not come forward to claim them within thirty days of my demise.

*   *   *

The French hydroplane slowly made its way across the water of the Blue River. We travelled all day, above the territory of occupied China, and at sunset touched down on the waters of the Si-kiang.

The sights of Canton only brought back more memories of anguish. And perhaps, I wanted to subject myself to them, to punish myself further—to die in the wake of Jonathan's death. Yet the only thing that kept me going was the conviction that, come the wrath of hell, I was going to find Tam.

CHAPTER 15

The cities of Canton, Nanking, and Shanghai. 1944.

"What you are asking me is impossible, Madame Tam," declared Phillipe Simon, the French consul in Canton. "I cannot take the responsibility of authorizing a project which seems to me sheer suicide."

My expression serious, I sat rigidly across from his desk and insisted, "I haven't asked you to do me any favors. I have only asked you to issue me a visa which it is my right to have and your duty to give me."

Middle-aged, Simon had attractive full features and small but very blue eyes. They narrowed with his adamance as he replied, "It is not my duty. Your request is denied."

I sighed with frustration. "Please, why don't you want to help me find my husband?"

He enumerated the reasons—that navigation between Canton and Haiphong had been suspended due to lack of security, that the roads leading to Indochina from the border were controlled by the Japanese, and that every day more and more Chinese territory was being bombed by Japanese fighter planes. He added, somewhat bitingly, that he could not furnish me with a whole military division to accompany me. As an act of conscience, he was refusing to allow me to go to a certain death.

Then, perhaps because he perceived that I would ultimately act with or without his help, Simon softened and assured me that his office would initiate a search for Tam. Stroking his chin and scrutinizing me with those blue eyes, he explained, "Although we are enemies in war, I have excellent and close personal contacts with the Kuomintang government."

"I have already begun the search," I reminded him.

"From Shanghai, of course," he countered, "which is occupied by the Japanese, and not via the diplomatic route. You want to know if your husband is still alive, and I will be able to find that out for you. As I am not very fond of Hitler or his knights in Vichy, I don't know how long I will last, but I have been in China for fifteen years, which is a record in diplomatic circles, especially when governments come and go with the seasons. I know Chiang Kai-shek personally and I used to furnish Madame Soong with all the latest models of French fashion. Political agreements are reached in a variety of ways, Madame."

He took out a pen and a piece of paper, asking me to write down the specifics of Tam's rank, the infantry name he last led, and whatever places I might presume him to be. Simon promised to gain information through his contact at the Kuomintang headquarters, though he warned, "You understand that we cannot ignore the presence of the Nanking government. And of course whatever I have said to you today must be kept in the strictest confidence."

In the gallant style of the French, Simon escorted me out through the Embassy garden toward the main gate, walking me alongside the orange grove of an aviary. In the shade of some loquat trees, two golden pheasants were scratching at the ground, looking for food, and I watched as the French consul stepped over to them, reached into the pocket of his cashmere jacket and held out something to one of them. The pheasant drew closer and snatched it from his hand, its feathers a dazzling display in the light.

The image was sweet, easing the painful constriction around my heart. Surely, with the consulate's help and my own endeavors, Tam would be found.

"It's millet coated with acacia honey," said Simon, straightening up again. "They're crazy about it. Don't look at me as if I were mad. I spend a lot of time in this garden. I don't feel much like going out. Life in Canton offers little of interest to me. And you can't imagine how boring a diplomat's life is: lunches, dinners, parties, receptions. Favors you ask or are asked, and that's all. In a few years, perhaps sooner, I'll retire. It depends on who wins the war. You have to be very shrewd about choosing which side you're on."

I nodded grimly, denying to myself the oppressive wave of guilt that those words conjured. I felt badly for Phillipe Simon—for his apparent loneliness, for feeling powerless in political entanglements above and beyond his choosing. But when he invited me to stay in the apartment of his ex-wife while I awaited word of Tam, I declined.

"Then, will you at least join me for lunch tomorrow?"

"All right," I murmured, trying to muster a tone of gratitude, "I'll see you tomorrow noon at the restaurant of my hotel."

As I opened the door of the taxi, I heard him call my name, "Madame Tam... ." I turned to see him approaching and responded, "Yes, Monsieur Simon?"

"How long do you intend to be in Canton?"

"As long as it takes," I said and took my seat inside the cab. I peered through the window at him and repeated to myself, "As long as it takes."

*   *   *

Though I had never seen much of Canton, I had bad associations with it, given—among other things—its proximity to the place where the first Jula had taken ill and died. But instead of returning directly to the Hotel Victoria, I asked the taxi driver to take me up to the top of the hills overlooking the river and estuary.

We drove to the sacred hill where the Vu-Tse-Len pavilion loomed up toward the sky.

From its terrace, I could actually see the centuries-old walls of the Tartar quarter. Beyond them lay the Chinese city, with its towers, pagodas, and mosques, the highest points of the area.

Canton stretched along the banks of the Pearl River—and across the waters as well, crowded by the many inhabitants of the floating city—and then gradually yielded to the miles of cultivated fields along the river. The extraordinary scenery soothed me. Soon my nightmare would come to an end, I prayed.

The taxi driver had come up with me to the terrace of the Vu-Tse-Len and now waited for me to go back down. There wasn't another soul in sight and I noticed a hungry, eager look on his face. What now, I wondered, numbed beyond caring as he came close.

In seconds, however, I saw that his desire was to show me something he held in a blue velvet bag. He spoke, "I'm sure that a lady like you will appreciate these," and opened the bag, pulling out two gold rings set with jade.

"Beautiful, yes," I said, pretending not to be impressed, "but I can't buy them."

"I'll make you a good price."

"No. I haven't got the money."

"Madame," he went on patiently, "I'm offering you a very good deal. You buy these rings from me and then you go back to Shanghai and sell them for twice the price you paid."

I stared silently as he continued. "Don't you know that the price of gold is very low in Canton? The bank accounts in this city are overflowing. Everyone who works with the English is constantly buying gold to put away. They're afraid they might lose the war, that the Japanese will requisition everything. The price keeps going down. So do you want them or not?"

After having a goldsmith appraise the jade, the driver and I closed the deal. Then I went to the railway station and bought several different Canton and Shanghai newspapers, noting the sizeable difference in the price of gold in the two cities. A master plan revealed itself to me—on my own, without Tam's money or any other man's, I had found a way to support my children and earn my living in China.

I left the hotel early the next morning and rushed to the bank where I asked for a draft to be sent from my account in Shanghai to their affiliate, the Yokohama Bank in Canton. Upon my return to the hotel room, I sat down and wrote a note of apology to Phillipe Simon:

Dear Monsieur Simon,

I deeply regret that I am unable to lunch today as a pressing emergency has called me back to Shanghai. Perhaps we can dine

together soon when I return here to Canton.
In the meantime, please contact me at the
Honan Hotel, should you have any news at
all of my husband.

> *Gratefully yours,*
> *Madame Bianca Tam*

I had told a small lie to Simon—in actuality I
had to wait another two days to get the money from
the bank so that I could buy a modest amount of
gold. But I wasn't inclined to have companionship,
preferring instead to walk the streets of Canton
anonymously—observing other people's lives and
trying to forget about my own. Though I had the
time, I decided not to visit Tam's family. I was
certain they had no idea where he was and I had no
desire to tell his mother how I had been living for
the last few years.

So on I walked for hours both days, my head
covered with a broad brimmed hat, dark sunglasses
masking my empty eyes. There seemed to be a
pounding drum beat within my head, obliterating
my conscience and driving me desperately on.

*   *   *

Lynn was surprised that I had come back so
quickly from Canton. And she was doubly surprised
that despite the failure of my search for Tam, I
seemed to be in a congenial mood. Of course, it was
my new quarry, but I offered no explanations.

The first deal proved to be a success. Gold, of all
things, had come to my rescue at the last minute. It
was easy money—safe, and an excellent return on
what I'd spent in Canton. My next buy, I decided,
would be even bigger and more profitable. But I
needed an outlay of cash. In order to get it and to
travel back and forth between cities with ease, I

would have to resume my work for Nancy and Kurata. As much as I loathed the idea, it was the means to a necessary end. I knew exactly what I had to do and I resolved to move swiftly. The drum beat in my head pounded louder and more urgently. It was my own inner war cry to survive both the possible discovery that Tam was dead and the haunting anguish of Jonathan's death—a death I continued to feel responsible for. Nothing could be allowed to stand in my way, to block me from providing for my three remaining daughters. This aim eclipsed the means. Whereas less than a week before I had declared the absolute necessity of finding Tam—the only man I knew who seemed capable of withstanding the ravages of fate, it was now not my most important mission. What mattered to me now was the gold. It gave me an intoxicated sense of invincibility. I needed no one, I could manage on my own.

With my strategy defined, I hastily wrote to Nancy:

> *Please don't ask me about what happened in Nanking. But I am at your service, if you need me.* —Bianca.

Little did I imagine that such a benign communication would play such a vital role on behalf of the forces that would very soon amass against me.

* * *

A few days later, at my second meeting with Colonel Kurata in Nanking, I was asked to examine some photos of heavy American artillery and to identify the kinds of weapons I had seen in Tuyun.

This interrogation was quite different from the first. I was pleasant, cooperative, not in the least bit nervous as I had previously been. For my gold smuggling activities to succeed, I needed Kurata's trust and knew I had to earn it by playing my role with him convincingly. I readily answered the questions.

"Yes," he said slowly, "I can see you're telling me what you know. But I'm not sure about the reliability of this information because Tam, as you may or may not know, has since left the front line at Kwei-chow. Intelligence sources tell us he went to Chungking to join Chiang Kai-shek's troops and that the General sent Tam into Yunan to combat the Communist troops. This, you can well imagine, enraged Lord Mountbatten who had wanted the Kuomintang's forces to stage a counterattack in the south along with the Burmese reinforcements..."

It was obvious that Kurata was baiting me, as if he was leading up to a revelation of Tam's whereabouts. And, since I'd already answered his questions, I knew that what he wanted in return didn't pertain to the military. But none of his diversionary "secrets" offered new information to me. According to Simon, Tam could be anywhere along the front of the Kuomintang-Nationalist struggle, where it was impossible to communicate or receive information.

I stood without comment and walked close to him, smiling into his bullish face. Plucking my check from his hand, I paused and then said, "Colonel Kurata, you really don't think that I believe Tam could still possibly be alive? If I did, I wouldn't be here."

I didn't linger to watch him sit sullenly back in his chair—deflated in more ways than one.

*   *   *

"I knew you would be back," Phillipe Simon had said to me upon my next trip to Canton, some two months after the first visit. He had led me into his private study at the embassy and had just handed me a dispatch from Chungking:

> *Regarding your request on Major Tam Gian Ciau. Tuyun Command information. Officer missing in action Hukwang front.*

"Missing in action does not mean dead," said Simon, when I looked up at him from reading the dispatch. "They have heard no news in months. But we are still in contact. As soon as I hear anything more, I will let you know. It's not much, but for the moment it's all I can do."

The drum pounded ever louder in my head as all color drained from my face. I couldn't let this state of unknowing debilitate me; I had to keep going.

"I repeat, Madame," the French consul said, taking my hand, "many soldiers of the Kuomintang are in the same situation: they have been reported missing and are most likely Japanese prisoners. Whole battalions have been taken prisoner in Hukwang."

"Thank you for not letting me go out to the front myself," I said softly.

"I would have been a criminal if I had. Tell me, this time are you also planning to rush off again after a meeting with an interesting taxi driver?"

I looked at him in surprise.

"Why make so much mystery about it? I could have sent you to someone at the bank."

The mental pounding abated as I sighed with relief. Then, as we sat down in the Embassy's private dining room, I was even more pleased when I saw the waiter carrying over a platter of lasagne with beef stew and potatoes. It was the first Italian meal I had eaten since coming to China.

"I love Italian food," said Simon, "but my cook refuses to prepare it, being a staunch French nationalist. I had to explain to him that we had a lovely Italian guest. Chivalry alone made him change his mind."

He poured me a glass of Chianti and assessed that I must have been living a difficult life since separating from Tam.

I tried not to sound defensive. "You know what the Chinese say — at high tide the boat rises. I've gotten used to it."

"Your main line of work is the gold trade?"

I was silent, letting him go on.

"In any case, you should take advantage of every opportunity."

"So you know about this—activity?"

"Don't treat me like that, Bianca. You need my help and I'm willing to give it to you. Even in war, being a diplomat has its privileges. You would be a fool not to take advantage of them."

With uncertainty, my brow furrowed, I asked, "How do you mean?"

"It's simple," he began in a diplomatic, reasonable way, "by marrying me, of course."

"Consul," I said, lowering my voice to a whispered accusation, "have you forgotten that I am Major Tam's wife?"

Simon shook his head vehemently but pointed out that because Tam was missing in action, I was—after the time that had already elapsed—free to remarry.

This I interpreted as meaning that Simon either believed or wanted Tam to be dead. The drumbeat resumed. I felt faint. Tam dead? It couldn't be so.

Seeing me so distraught, the consul revised his offer, telling me that in the event of Tam's still being alive I would be free to annul the marriage. "I give you my word of honor that I will not oppose your decision. In the meantime, you must live as comfortably as possible. A French diplomatic passport would be quite useful to you: no checks at the border, the security of our Embassy, and of course my own personal protection. In light of your work with a certain Nancy Lee, such immunity could be vital."

I whispered again, "So you know that I collaborate with the Japanese?"

Simon looked deeply and compassionately into my eyes, saying to the point, "I know that you have three children to provide for all on your own." He took a breath and added, "I also know that I must speak well of our allies in Tokyo."

His ostensible selflessness took me off guard, eerily reminding me of the generosities of Mr. Young before him. I had learned the hard way not to trust the outstretched open palm—especially when it came from a man with desire in his eyes. Help from others always came at a high cost.

On and on went the drumming in my head. I refused his marriage proposal and spent the night alone in the hotel. The next morning I bought more gold and left.

*   *   *

"Let me help you," the man had said on seeing me lugging the canvas bag full of bullion. He had been seated in the Director's waiting room at the Yokohama Bank in Shanghai, where I had come to make my exchange to currency.

As he rose to come to my aid, he smiled, his gold-capped tooth flashing, and introduced himself—Oshima Tanaka, a Japanese businessman who had been living in Shanghai for years.

"Gold, obviously," he said, after we had placed the bag down. I heard a slight lisp as he told me, "I believe we'll have to wait for a while. The Director is not in at the moment."

"I'm in no hurry," I stated and began to walk toward one of the chairs.

He followed and leaned into my ear, saying quietly, "Perhaps we can conclude things earlier. If

I'm not mistaken, you have come here to sell that gold to the bank. Why don't you sell it to me?"

"The bank pays on the spot," I said.

"What makes you think I don't?"

I handed him a note card. "That's the price today in Shanghai."

He scribbled some numbers on the card, then handed it back to me. His eyes darted about before he said, "That's my offer."

"Very well, Mr. Tanaka," I murmured, "you have yourself a deal."

After having the gold weighed downstairs, Tanaka had written out a check and had cashed it for me right at the teller's window. It was a lot of gold and had fetched an excellent price. With an intensified sense of urgency, I had enough money to go that afternoon and enroll Lylongo and Jula in Shanghai's French boarding school. Because they had no friends, and had grown up in the midst of war, never knowing their father, it was my deepest hope that the school would protect them from the atmosphere of death that surrounded us. I sensed an ill wind on the rise, worse even than what had come before, and I wanted them kept as far from my dangerous straits as possible. As for my youngest, Aloma would be well cared for by Lynn. After paying for the steep tuition at the French school, I could no longer afford the other amah Sue, but was able to convince the hotel to take her on their staff.

Two days following our transaction, Tanaka paid me a visit at the hotel to return my bag.

He handed it to me and then plopped down in the armchair next to mine, making himself quite comfortable by crossing his legs casually. That familiar gold tooth flashed as he said, "I spoke to Nancy. She has been waiting for you to come back."

I tried to show no alarm as I smiled, telling him, "I see we have a mutual friend."

"She isn't the only one," he uttered suggestively. He paused for a moment. "Nancy tells me your search for your husband has not been successful."

"True," I said, guarding my real emotions, "the prospects for finding him alive are not good."

Tanaka pretended to pick at a piece of lint on his suit, saying offhandedly, "Did you ask Colonel Kurata about it when you were in Nanking? Major Tam might be our prisoner."

I leapt to my feet, breathlessly blurting out, "Did Nancy send you here to me?"

Tanaka stood as well and took a step toward me. "It's impossible to meet a woman like you without wanting to see her again."

"Yes," I said, no longer hiding my lack of trust, "and my husband's death is an excellent opportunity. You can't imagine how many men have been trying to help me and offer me their service and their advice. You didn't think you were the first?"

"I haven't offered or asked you anything, I don't think," he replied. "Although," his eyes flitted to the wet bar, "a glass of bourbon would be nice."

Obliging him and pouring myself a drink as well, I asked, "Any other requests?"

"Not for me, but yes, Colonel Kurata is very curious about why you seem so certain that your husband is dead. Perhaps you don't really believe him to be."

The drum beat sounded internally once more. Duplicitous games were being played right and left. I saw that my only option to avoid another trap was to hold to my earlier ploy of professing to believe Tam no longer alive. But to do it, I would have to use the truth. I spoke with assurance and rapidity, telling Tanaka, "The High Command in Chungking says that my husband was fighting in Hukwang and that the battle was a disaster. Thousands of men were killed."

"Are you sure that he was there?"

"Probably, even though the British had asked for troops in the south for the war in Burma. But Colonel Kurata already knows this."

Tanaka's lisp was accentuated as he shot a barrage of questions at me. As I had done with his superior, I complied willingly by providing all the information I knew. If there was the slightest suspicion on Tanaka's part that I wasn't collaborating with sincerity, I would be in peril of losing my life.

"How many divisions are there in Tuyun?" he began.

"There were three when I was there."

"The weapons were all American?"

"The most recent, yes. The older ones were British or Russian."

"Does the Kuomintang think that American aid will continue?"

"I heard that General Stilwell came on mission to inspect the troops and protested about the way money was being spent and the way the arms were being used. But I never heard of any threat to cut off the aid."

"And what is Simon's opinion about the battle in Burma?"

It was only here that I hesitated to respond. Startled by his knowledge, my cheeks inadvertently flushed with heat.

Tanaka noted their scarlet hue and took the opportunity to adopt a threatening tone. "Madame, you are an agent of the Nanking government and you have certain obligations which you must fulfill."

I attempted to sound calm and answered his previous question by reporting that Simon believed the Japanese were going to lose Burma. "Simon," I added, "thinks the Chinese will make a comeback once the Americans have succeeded in sending food and ammunition. That's all I know. I only stayed in Canton long enough to buy gold."

"On your next trip," Tanaka said, rising to go and grinning a gold-toothed grin, "try to find out where the consul gets his information." He handed me his business card, demanding that I contact him at his Shanghai address as soon as I came back from Canton.

Showing him to the door, I told him that, obviously, he would have news of my activities through Nancy. "But then again," I concluded, "it won't be difficult for you to find me now that you know where I live."

Tanaka bowed with feigned civility, lisping, "Of course not. You are very well known about town."

CHAPTER 16

The cities of Shanghai and Canton. 1945.

A devil had gotten into my blood. With the war coming to an end, I stepped up my trading.

The tide had turned in the Pacific Theater. The Japanese were being beaten back by the American counter-offensive and by the advance of the two Chinese armies, led respectively by Chiang Kai-shek and Mao Tse-tung.

In June, 1944, American bombers from bases hidden in the Chinese interior had begun heavy bombardment of the Japanese industrial areas: 40,000 tons of bombs were dropped. The Russians had declared war on the Empire and had marched against the Japanese troops in Manchuria. In Cairo, Churchill, Roosevelt, and Chiang Kai-shek had signed a pact, later joined by Stalin, against the Japanese. After Guadalcanal, Guam, Iwo-Jima, and Okinawa, the Allied troops were reconquering the Pacific.

The world that had temporarily offered me a living was collapsing. I operated at a feverish high, trying to put as much money away as possible—even though the price of gold fluctuated dramatically in the midst of the uncertainties and although there were considerable risks. I knew that the sums I deposited might be devalued at any moment, yet I persisted. I also knew that Shanghai might suddenly become a poor market for gold, but that didn't stop me. I clung to the trading—which had once defined my survival—like one hanging to wreckage of a sinking ship. I didn't know what else to do and so I put off leaving—the only thing that would have saved me from future disaster.

Despite the recent progress made by the Kuomintang, there had still been no confirmation as to whether Tam was alive or dead. As the turmoil mounted, I began to lose all hopes of seeing him again. In time, I even managed to convince myself that I would be better off if he were dead. He had betrayed me with another woman, after all; at least that was how I rationalized it, not admitting that I didn't want him to find out who I had become.

And so, needing the protection in the growing crisis, I decided to keep the French consul in Canton to his word. We were married in January, 1945, in a civil ceremony. It was a marriage of convenience, obviously, and as according to the terms he offered we did not cohabitate.

One morning, Phillipe arrived early to the flat he'd given me in Canton. He opened the curtains to let a ray of light into the room, then went into the kitchen and returned with my breakfast on a tray, along with three roses picked from his own garden. They were a bright yellow, like the robe I was wearing, and strangely reminiscent of Tam's first gift to me. I was uneasy enough as it was, cut off from my feelings, and his continual kindness seemed to rattle me even more. I ate the breakfast quickly and then informed him I would be returning to Shanghai that afternoon.

"Bianca," Phillipe said, removing the tray, "why don't you stay in Canton for a while?"

"We agreed that I could live where I wished," I snapped and went to put on my make-up.

"Yes, of course, whatever you want to do. I'm only thinking of your well being. You have worked and earned good money, but to go on working for the Nanking government may not be very wise." With his blue piercing eyes, he stared at my reflection in the mirror, telling me, "You are the wife now of a man who doesn't intend to let you want for anything. And there are excellent girls' boarding schools in Canton."

"I have bad memories of this city," I explained and looked up at him apologetically. "I can't come back and live here."

Phillipe reiterated that the Embassy was now my home and that he would welcome nothing more than for me and my daughters to live there as long as I wished. But it did no good.

I was deaf to the warnings, blind to all the signs. Not even Nancy could convince me of my folly.

"I've come to say good-bye. I'm leaving for London," she announced when she appeared at my hotel on my return to Shanghai. "I don't want to wait until the last moment. The flights are all full."

"Is everyone leaving?" I asked.

Her face, once the toast of the town, was drawn and worried. "After the war ends the vendettas will begin. Better not risk it. Go back to Italy, Bianca. Take your children and leave China for good."

I shrugged, laughing lightly as I said, "They won't do anything to a poor woman on her own."

Nancy replied, "If she is a spy, they will."

"I am not a spy." I glared at her, daring her to contradict me.

She looked at me in silence, studying what must have seemed like madness in my eyes and finally implored me to give her my reasons for staying.

I had none to give her, but went instead into the hallway and took out a white scarf embroidered with purple and gold and put it around my friend's neck. "Goodbye, Nancy, good luck," I uttered. "Thank you for helping me when I was in need."

The world I'd known was coming to an end, and still I didn't try to save myself.

*   *   *

It was August 6, 1945. In the evening, the radio had announced the bombing of Hiroshima. Later that night, Tanaka climbed the steps of my hotel and entered my apartment pensively. He was a far cry from the talkative smiling agent that I'd last seen.

"And where are you escaping to?" I asked him.

Tanaka swallowed and answered slowly, as if he was coming to a realization. "I am not escaping, Madame. I'm going back to my country even if it has been turned into a cemetery. I have a homeland and I mustn't forget that. Besides, to remain here... I don't believe in dying for the sake of an honorable death. I prefer life, no matter what the conditions."

I was surprised to acknowledge such dignity in the man whom I had known only as a spy and a blackmailer. I wished him well and he, like everyone else, urged me to leave China.

First Nancy, then Tanaka, then others. Everyone was getting out, abandoning all the cities of China— the Japanese, the Germans, the Italians, even the French who had supported the Pétain government. Those once self-assured people now trembled at the airline ticket counters, ready to pay any price to get out. They could take only a few things with them on the planes; it would have been useless to try shipping belongings or leaving the country by boat as the waterways were the most dangerous.

All the evacuees came to sell me their clothes, jewels, furniture, and other goods at ridiculously low prices, hoping to raise enough money to flee. Everyone said the same thing to me, "Why don't you leave?" I answered no one, there was no answer— except perhaps the fact that I had been in flight for so many years already. Perhaps I also believed that at twenty-five years old I was a veteran of survival, that I could somehow make the best of the adversity. With that in mind, I carved out what I hoped was a survivor's plan and launched into a frenzy of activity that would prove within a few days to be far more eventful than I'd asked for.

First, I withdrew all my money from the bank, converting it into Hong Kong dollars. I made a quick trip to Canton and bought a large quantity of gold to put into storage until the price went up again.

I rushed back to Shanghai the same day, and managed to secure lodging for Aloma and Lynn at the boarding school where Lylongo and Jula were living. The next morning, I rented a safe deposit box at the Shanghai Bank and gave my lawyer a list of my belongings and the receipt of the amount deposited in my account. It happened to be the same day of the Japanese surrender on board the USS Missouri in Tokyo Bay.

When I embarked the following morning on a trip back to Canton, aboard the Pan American Clipper, I read in the newspaper the soon-to-be immortal words of Emperor Hirohito:

"We bow to time and to destiny. We have decided to forge a road towards peace for all future generations, accepting the unacceptable and suffering that which goes beyond the range of understanding. We bow before the present to safeguard the future."

It was with these words Hirohito justified the surrender, unprecedented in all of Japanese history.

As I got off the boat, I sensed somewhere deep inside me a rumbling. The throbbing in my brain had ceased and now from a truer part of myself, I realized that I too would have to surrender. I couldn't go on as I had been. I decided this was to be my last purchase of gold and I got it at a truly remarkable price.

The bars went straight into Phillipe Simon's personal safe at the French Embassy.

"It will be safe here," he said. "And so will you."

I objected. In three days it would be Jula's birthday and I wanted to be with her.

For the umpteenth time, Phillipe begged me to bring my children and live with him at the Embassy where we would be guaranteed our safety. "Please understand," he murmured, "I know that you don't love me and that you will never give me a child. Accept the help you have been offered until you decide what to do with your life. You need me now and you will be a fool not to accept."

I went over to Phillipe and kissed him, a wave of gratitude nearly bringing tears to my eyes. "But," I warned him, "do you know what it's like to live with three young children?"

He responded joyfully, "I've been waiting all my life to find out."

By simply giving in, I had allowed the nightmare to end. That night I slept peacefully for the first time in a year, dreaming of my family united, happy, safe and secure.

I was even humming the next morning in the car when Phillipe drove me to the airport. It was the crack of dawn and there was no traffic along the streets except for the United States Military Police patrols that now had command of Canton. The car was moving at top speed and the wind blew against my face, refreshing and revitalizing me. Within twenty-four hours I would be back with Lynn and the girls to stay.

In fact, I had left my large suitcase at Phillipe's and was travelling just with a small carry-on bag. Tucked among a change of clothes in it, were two gold bars which I had promised to the director of the Honan Hotel. Even he was trying to secure the future, in any way possible.

Phillipe handed me the bag as I went through passport control. Spotting the Embassy seal on it, the American officer did not venture to open it and waved me on with a quick salute. I almost skipped as I headed for the gate.

"Bianca," Phillipe called, "what time will you be back?"

"The first flight in the morning," I sang back to him, waving and blowing him a kiss.

In wonderful spirits, I climbed the steps to the plane and sat by a window. I couldn't wait to tell my daughters the good news—their mother had finally come to her senses!

I smiled at the steward who was checking to make sure all the passengers were in their seats. Then he closed the door and I noticed the ramp being rolled away from the plane.

Minutes passed and the plane did not move. A few passengers grumbled as the motors were shut off and the control tower's command could be heard ordering the pilot to open the door. Then the ramp was rolled back.

Two American soldiers walked briskly down the aisle and stopped in front of my seat.

"Are you Bianca Tam?" asked one of the soldiers.

"Yes."

He spoke in a monotone. "I am Captain Farrel and this is Lieutenant Gray. Come with us please."

The lieutenant picked up my bag from under the seat and the two officers escorted me off the plane.

Part Four:

DEATH TO THE SPY

CHAPTER 17

The Isle of Hazelnuts. 1947.

The first streak of daylight had come, it was almost the hour of the dawn. If only, I wished, I could see Monsignor Fourquet. The dear man had been with me every step of the way, spearheading the fight for my life. From the beginning, the Monsignor had urged me not to give up my faith. And when I'd asked him why he had chosen to do so much for me, he had said, "My child, the Lord has granted you with a rich and difficult life. I dare to believe that it is His will that you remain alive."

All along I too had dared to hope I would be saved. But with every second ticking by and with every new streak of light, the well of hope had run dry. I took my small, worn Bible in my hands.

"The Lord is my shepherd, I shall not want," I began, reading the psalm aloud and feeling a blanket of peace and renewed strength filling me. I would not weep; I would hold my head high.

Suddenly, I heard footsteps approaching my cell. I wasn't ready yet—there were still more memories I wanted to recount, those that I wanted to take to my grave and those I wanted to purge. Relieved, I listened as the footsteps echoed on down the hall, passing me by. For the last time, I tumbled once more into the past, back to the moment of my arrest and to everything that had led up to my final condemnation.

CHAPTER 18

Canton. 1945.

"You can't do that," I had begun to protest when the American, Captain Farrel, took hold of my bag and started to unzip it.

He had just closed the door of a tiny, barely furnished room, practically no more than a closet. In it were a table and two chairs and a naked light bulb burning harshly overhead.

I pointed to the seal on the bag. Trying my best to remain cool, I reminded him, "It's protected by diplomatic immunity."

"Is that so?" he said, his tone a mixture of sarcasm and scorn.

I attempted to match his intimidation, saying, "That is so, that is the seal of the French Consulate. I am the wife of Phillipe Simon, the French Consul."

"Oh, sure," he drawled, with a cold smile, "if it weren't for the fact that you were already married to Colonel Tam Gian Ciau."

The wind was knocked out of me. In terror, I stammered, "B-b-but, Tam is dead."

"No, ma'am," he said, pausing before he examined the contents of the bag. "They thought he was missing in action until he showed up at the headquarters of his High Command. Tam is alive. I'm sorry about that, but it's true."

He opened the bag wide and held it upside down so that the gold bars thudded onto the table.

Farrel picked one of them up and hissed, "Proof that you've been smuggling gold..."

Though still in a state of shock, I interrupted him, imagining that the situation wasn't as grave as it could have been and said, "But Captain, I merely trade in gold as a businesswoman. I have a family to support."

"Yeah?" He swaggered toward me. "Well, you're charged with smuggling gold for the Japanese." Leering with a combination of lust and disdain in his eyes, he added, "The other two charges, collaboration and high treason, will be backed up by testimony and incontrovertible evidence. That's all, we can go now."

My blood seemed to freeze on the spot and I followed him out of the room. He marched me quickly down a corridor past a large glass window. Through it, I could see an office in which a United States Army officer appeared to be interrogating the man who had tried so valiantly to help me.

"Phillipe!" I called to him through the glass.

Phillipe turned and looked in my direction but made no motion to come to me.

Farrel grabbed my arm and pulled me along, muttering under his breath, "For his sake, pretend you don't know him. The Consul is under suspicion for the same crimes you have been charged with." I went along with his suggestion, realizing that Farrel was actually a decent human being.

A military police van was waiting for us outside the airport entrance. Flanked by two armed guards, I took my seat and the driver sped off.

As we careened through the Canton suburbs, along the banks of the Si-kiang River, I watched the driver make a sharp turn down a narrow street that led into a Chinese quarter I didn't recognize. Now the van moved slowly—there were crowds of people treading alongside us.

The driver was forced to stop in a small square. Angry shouting from outside could be heard—the clamor of the crowds being pushed back by Chinese police. The two guards sitting beside me clutched at their rifles, prepared if necessary to go to the aid of the police. We saw that a path through the throngs of people was being cleared for an army truck that had driven out of the main gate of a large complex of buildings on the other side of the square.

It moved slowly so that everyone in the vicinity could have a good, long look at the man who stood in the back of the truck. He trembled like a caged animal, his eyes wide with bewildered fear, and his hands were tied together behind him around a thick, tall pole. At the top of the pole, a large red sign with black lettering read:

DEATH TO THE SPY

The mob shook their fists at him, yelling curses. Some of them ran up and tried to grab hold of the side of the truck, but were beaten back down by the police. It was almost a game—a crowd furor that the officials were inciting by displaying the condemned man throughout all the streets of the city. After the show was over, the man would be brought to a public execution, a cruel death decreed by quick, inflexible justice that comes at the end of every war.

When the poor devil realized what was awaiting him—that he was the living target for shouts, rocks, bucketfuls of mud and slime—he tried desperately to brace himself with a vestige of dignity, his head down. But he could not resist long and soon collapsed.

"Turn on the siren, and go ahead," Captain Farrel ordered the driver.

I was still visibly shaking when we drove in through a gate and parked along the edge of a square where a group of Chinese soldiers were training. Getting out of the van, Farrel and the two guards led me into one of the many buildings that lined the square. We were met by a high ranking officer of the Nationalist Army.

"Captain Farrel," the American saluted, "of the U.S. Military Police, reporting, Sir. We have arrested Bianca Tam and we sign her over to you, Colonel, as prisoner."

The Chinese officer stood up from behind his desk. "My compliments, Captain," he said. "Good work."

Farrel handed the Colonel my dossier which in turn was placed atop the piles of other folders on the desk. Then to an attendant, the Nationalist Army officer ordered, "Take the prisoner away."

I turned to Farrel, imploring him with my eyes and speaking with haste, "Please don't leave me here with them, Captain. Keep me your prisoner."

"Can't do that," he said, his expression sympathetic but resigned. "The Chinese army is in command here in Canton."

Lurching out of the attendant's hold, I stumbled toward Farrel, crying, "I beg you!"

The next thing I knew, the Colonel and his attendant had pinned my arms behind me and I was being pushed into a hallway—thrown into the grasp of another Chinese soldier who forced me down a spiral staircase to an iron gate. It was opened and then closed behind me. After descending a few more steps, we came to a darkened corridor and then finally stopped just outside a small but heavy wooden door. The soldier beckoned to the approaching warden. A huge, burly man, the warden seemed exceptionally pleased to see me there among his prisoners.

"We needed a woman here," he said gruffly, slipping handcuffs onto my wrists.

He pushed me hard against the door and it slid open. The warden laughed, telling me, "Make yourself comfortable, and try not to get your dress dirty."

The iron key rattled in the lock. There was hard-packed filth under my feet, a rank smell in the air. Trying to adjust my eyes to the dark, it took some time before I could make out the other shapes in the room with me.

Twenty men, maybe more, were lying along the sides of the cell, their hands and feet bound. One man was crawling back to his place after having defecated in the only toilet: a hole in the ground. A dim light filtered down from above through a tiny rat-sized grating in the ceiling—the only exposure to the outer world.

It was worse than any nightmare. I was the only woman and I felt their eyes on me in the dark as I hugged one of the walls, slinking over to the last remaining unoccupied spot. Weak and nauseous, I tried to sit down on the dirt floor, only to see a rat scamper over my feet and disappear into a hole between the bricks. My stomach convulsed and I vomited over and over again, until my head felt as if it would explode.

Afterwards, I lay almost senseless on the ground, gasping. I yearned for a cool hand to soothe my forehead, the way my mother used to do when I was a child. For a second, I began to hallucinate, imagining that I saw her floating angelically into the dungeon.

"Mama," I heard myself whisper and my vision disappeared. Suddenly another kind of madness consumed me as I ran to the cell door, beating it with my fists and screaming at the top of my lungs to the guards to let me out. I was innocent, I shouted, a mother whose children needed her.

The warden opened up, grabbed me by the arm and threw me with all his might down onto the ground, roaring, "Shut your mouth, you filthy spy, or I'll chain your feet as well!"

Unable to stand, I dragged myself along the floor back to my spot against the wall. Just then two guards came in and began scooping rice into wooden bowls that were on a board in the center of the room. The prisoners immediately gulped down their food before the insects could get to it. I stayed where I was and watched as my share was eaten by someone else.

For hours it seemed, I sat as if in a coma—hunched up with my legs pulled into my chest and my handcuffed arms wrapped around myself. At last, I put my head on my knees and began to cry, the first actual tears that had spilled in a long time. At some point, collapsing from infinite exhaustion, I fell asleep.

* * *

God knows how much time had gone by. If it weren't for the pale circle of light that shone down from the grate, it would have been impossible to tell the difference between day and night. I was squinting up at that light when I heard a man's voice calling my name, and a gentle hand shaking me. My head was spinning. I heard someone saying my name over and over. Two arms lifted me and a hand brushed the hair from my face. In a state of utter confusion, I couldn't comprehend what was happening or where I was.

"Bianca, don't you recognize me?" The man asked.

Dully I seemed to recognize his voice. Slowly, breathing deeply to clear the stupor away, I even thought I had seen him before—his dark, intense eyes, his sensual lips, his rugged and proud stance.

"Tam, it's you! It's you!" I threw myself into his arms, weeping uncontrollably, unable to speak for many minutes. Burying my face in his chest, I begged him to take me away, telling him how long I had searched for him, my words tumbling from me with no logical order. "Tam," I choked back the pain, "Jonathan is dead."

He knew, he told me, his voice wavering and then asked me quickly about the girls.

"They're fine, thank God. You haven't seen Aloma yet, but she's beautiful and looks just like you. Oh, Tam, you're alive." For a moment my anguish dissolved as I drank him in with all my senses. But a sudden hard knocking at the door prompted me to recall where I was. "Tam," I whispered hurriedly, "take me away."

He held me tighter before answering, "I'll get you out of here. I promise."

"Now, for God's sake," I raved, "Immediately! I will die here!"

"Listen to me," he said, shaking me by the shoulders, "you must be strong, Bianca. You must be patient. It will take one or two days, three at the most, I swear."

No harm would come to me, he said, as long as I resisted any advances. "You will gain their respect," he murmured, "so you must hold out for a couple of days. I am back now and I will help you. But it's forbidden for me to come in here and my deal with the warden was to sneak in just for a few minutes. I have to go now."

"Wait," I pleaded, having so much to both ask and tell him. "How did you know I was here?"

It was Simon, Tam said, the French Consul, who'd come to find him at his headquarters and who had told him everything.

"You know everything, then?" I wanted desperately to explain the circumstances, to let him understand the motivations.

Yet he surprised me by answering, "Yes, I know everything, but don't worry."

I nodded with a mixture of remorse and relief, telling him that he needed to check on the girls at the French nuns' boarding school in Shanghai. "You'll have to pay for this month," I added, "I don't want them to be sent away."

"They won't be sent away, I promise you."

"And what about me? Will I be saved?"

Tam paused, sighing, and said, "You will be all right."

*   *   *

When the door closed, I prayed in earnest, thanking God. I knew with certainty that the ordeal would soon be resolved. But I would, in fact, soon come to learn that Tam wasn't at all sure of my chances. He would later admit the jeopardy I was in and the difficulty he was up against. What had happened was that as soon as Tam had reached Canton with the South West Army, Simon had informed him of my arrest at the airport. It hadn't been too difficult for him to determine the charges against me from the U.S. Military Police and the counter-espionage of the Kuomintang. The Americans had just undertaken a massive operation in the liberated zones to capture everyone connected with the attack on Pearl Harbor. They had discovered that on December 7, 1941, I was already in Shanghai. As I was the wife of an Allied army officer, working for the Japanese, they assumed I might have been involved. It was insanity—I knew it, and so did Tam. Because the Americans' own intelligence network had been so ineffective, they needed to be able to cast blame on others. In short, they needed me as a political scapegoat.

The Nationalists, following up the anonymous accusation that appeared one day on the desks of their spy bureau, had investigated my gold smuggling activities, as well as my contact with

Japanese agents. They had also investigated my work with Nancy to find out how much and what kind of information we had passed along at the club and during the meetings with Kurata.

The Chinese, considering me a Chinese citizen, accused me of high treason. Tam demanded that the wife of an officer of such a high rank should at least be given some form of preferential treatment. The Colonel in command of the barracks where I was being held prisoner agreed to have me transferred.

*   *   *

I had survived the dungeon for three days when they came to take me to a private cell. They removed my handcuffs, a soldier escorted me out into the courtyard, and there I had seen the blazing light of day for the first time in seventy-two hours. From there, we had gone up the building's central staircase and into a large room that occupied one whole side of the second floor. It was divided into little cubicles separated by thin wooden walls and a curtain. Through the window, I'd noticed a group of Japanese officers—prisoners of war—talking together on the terrace.

"This is your cell. The bathroom is down at the end of the hall for everyone's use," the soldier had said, drawing the curtain. There was a cot, a chair, a table, and a window.

After he had left me, I opened the window and looked out beyond the terrace toward the sights of Canton—daring to believe I would soon be back in a world of freedom.

As I stood there, a Japanese officer stopped a few feet from the curtain and spoke to me. His manner was polite and respectful as he said, "I hope you won't be too uncomfortable here. Is there anything I can get you?"

"Yes," I answered, realizing only in that moment how disheveled I was, "Since you've offered. Have you got some soap and a towel?"

I stayed a long, long time in the shower— emerging from it only when I'd gotten the dirt out from under my fingernails and my hair was untangled.

On the mattress of my cot someone had placed a military shirt and a pair of short pants. At least the outfit was better than the filthy dress I had been wearing for the last three days since being arrested.

*   *   *

"How do you do, Bianca?" The woman had first said when she arrived the next morning at my new cell. I had recognized her immediately even though I had only seen her once, four years before. It was the nurse from Tam's unit in Tuyun—his concubine.

"My name is May," she said, speaking in a soft, nervous voice, "and I have brought you some things you might need."

The meeting was awkward for me as well. Although, how could I resent her? It wasn't her fault that the war had thrown her into a position to become involved with Tam. It now seemed like it had happened in another life.

May placed several packages on the table, explaining, "I've brought you some underwear, a few dresses, something to eat, some toiletries. Everything I could find."

Sitting down on the edge of my cot, I thanked her and offered her a seat.

Shyly, she said, "Tam told me about that horrible place where they put you."

"It's much better," I replied, trying to sound cheerful, "now that they've moved me."

There was another awkward silence which she broke by saying, "I understand that you're Catholic and I thought you might like to have this." She reached into her purse and took out a little prayer book. After thanking her, I saw an expression of alarm in her eyes. "You know," May said tentatively, "I'm a nurse. Would you mind if I examined you?"

She took my pulse, then checked my eyes, ears and throat. She didn't want to worry me, she concluded, but she believed I needed to see a doctor, whom she would send over from the military hospital where she was serving.

While she visited with me, we were forced to make small talk. I distracted myself from the strangeness of our encounter by changing into one of the dresses she'd brought and folding up the military outfit that I'd been wearing.

"I must have looked ridiculous in those men's clothing," I said.

"The green dress is perfect on you," she said. "It brings out the green in your eyes."

Finally, I could no longer avoid asking questions having to do with the real issues at hand. Life was too short for meaningless chatter. "May," I almost blurted out, "are you happy with Tam?"

She nodded, murmuring, "I love him."

"And," I pressed on, "do you have any children?"

"A little boy, and I'm expecting another child." May paused briefly. "Tam knows that you have remarried and he understands why you did it."

I swallowed and asked the most difficult question, "Will he marry you?"

Admittedly, I was a bit relieved to hear that Tam had never asked to marry her, though certainly May wished he would. "Being a wife is one thing," she commented, "but being a concubine is another. A man can have as many concubines as he wants." She was suddenly pensive. "Do you know, Bianca, that they used to require the concubines to die so that they could be buried with their men when the men died? The wife was left alive to care for her children and the children of the others. But," she sighed, "that was a long time ago."

"Yes," I echoed, smiling at her with both sorrow and forgiveness, "that was a long time ago."

* * *

"This is for you," Tam had said when he strode in later that afternoon, handing me a bottle of lavender perfume. "Is it still your favorite?"

He looked notably handsome in a long black lamb's wool coat and he kissed my hand as in the old days.

Dabbing the perfume on my wrist for me, he said, "May told me that you are very weak."

"As you said before, Tam," I responded, "I'll be all right." Then I looked into his eyes and told him how sweet May had been to me.

Tam went on to say that he'd been in contact with the boarding school in Shanghai. Lynn and the girls were well, he related, and the nuns knew nothing about what was happening to me. "I sent them a check for the next month, saying that you won't be able to come back for the moment."

"Tam," I asked seriously, "how long will this moment last?"

He got up, leaned on the window sill, and lit a cigarette. "I spoke to an official of the court where you will be brought to trial. The charges are very serious, especially the counts of spying and high treason." He forced a smile. "I don't want to know if it's true or not, or if you have really done what they claim you did in Shanghai. I'll do everything I can to help you."

"Perhaps," I ventured, "you can imagine why I did what I did."

"I'm not judging you, Bianca. Believe me, since the time that you left Tuyun, I have done a great deal of thinking. I know now that I also had a part in this."

His words weren't coming easily. I sensed that this was his manner of apologizing for the guilt he bore. I asked softly, "Is that why you have come?"

Saying nothing, Tam looked at me squarely and I could tell he was trying to control his emotions. "I don't know," he said, speaking slowly, "when the trial will take place. The longer they take, the better. In the meantime, you must start contacting your family in Italy. I have already notified your mother. She and your father must try to get the Italian Embassy and the Vatican to intervene in your case. Chiang Kai-shek is a Christian, and if some important figure in the Church should take an interest in your case, you just might have a chance. But you must act quickly. Your position is very serious."

He opened his briefcase and put some letter paper and envelopes on the desk, telling me that I would need all the help I could get. "The Chinese are furious with you, especially since you are my wife."

I wanted more than anything to have Tam linger with me, but the Japanese officers who had kindly stepped outside to give us some time alone were now looking up toward the window impatiently. Winter was coming.

We embraced one another briefly and broke away.

As soon as Tam had gone, I sat down and wrote the first letter.

It was addressed to Balinow de Villerose, the Bulgarian lawyer in Shanghai:

> *I hereby give you power of attorney over all the money on account in my bank. And you will be entrusted with sending monthly payments to my daughters' boarding school. Please address any important correspondence to me in care of Colonel Tam at the High Command of the First Army.*

I began writing a second letter to Mama, but the mere effort of writing the first one had completely drained me. For a minute, I put the pen down and, before I knew it, I'd fallen asleep at the desk.

* * *

The Chinese doctor diagnosed a state of physical exhaustion and gave orders to hospitalize me immediately. Only after the staff had guaranteed constant surveillance and my prompt return, would the Colonel allow me to go for treatment at the Jesuit hospital.

Every night I was given an injection to help me sleep until morning and every morning they ran endless tests on me. Within a few days I felt well enough to write to my mother—the first of many letters we would exchange during my imprisonment, and one that was undoubtedly overdue.

Dearest Mama,

I know that Tam has informed you of my situation and has asked you and Papa to use your influence in my behalf. I am only now beginning to recuperate from a physical collapse—no doubt the result of the ordeal I have been through. As I continue to regain my strength, I will write you more and give you more detail. The one thing you must know is that I am innocent. Never doubt it. And never fear, the matter should be resolved in no time.

Your loving daughter, Bianca

My recovery was a mixed blessing. While I was no longer weakened physically, it meant that my stay with the attentive Jesuits was over. Sooner than

I would have liked, an armored jeep came to take me back to the barracks.

*   *   *

It was meal time when I arrived and all the prisoners had gone to the mess. Tam was waiting for me in my cell.

My heart felt light when I saw him, but his news wasn't optimistic. Showing me the summons to appear before the military court, he told me, "The preliminary hearing begins the day after tomorrow. You must defend yourself on your own."

"Will all the judges be from the military?"

"All of them, and all of them Chinese."

I grabbed his hand. "You must promise me one thing, Tam. If they put me in prison for good or if they decide to kill me, you must take care of our daughters. All three of them. They can't lose both mother and father. And even if you have other children, they must come first. Swear it in the name of your father. Swear that you will take care of them and not let them become orphans."

"I swear," he said, clasping my hand.

"Well, then," I exhaled profoundly, "they can do what they want to me."

"No, Bianca. We will fight this together and we must get you the best defense possible."

My eyes widened. The way he had declared that we would fight together made me forget the time and events that had transpired. Here we were together, the two of us, our lives connected as one— despite everything. No, I could read it in his breathing, our extraordinary love had never died.

Tam said nothing, but moved toward me, caressing my face and enclosing me in an intense embrace. He kissed me hungrily and deeply. I did not hold back. I ran my fingers through his hair and held him tight, repeating his name over and over.

We didn't think about where we were, or about the other prisoners, or the people in the barracks. Our passion was everything—and every bit as consuming as it had once been. We abandoned ourselves to our desire, to the moment. Like thieves, we were stealing our pleasure from the indifferences of fate. Every second of the time ticking by was like an enemy threatening to interrupt us. We undressed one another hurriedly, Tam gasping at me with admiration, telling me he had not forgotten my body and how he had yearned for it through the years. I swept my hands over every inch of his skin, storing up the feel of him for all time. We fell onto the bed and he cradled my head in one hand, the other fondling my breasts, my belly and my thighs. As we possessed each other, I dug my nails into his flesh and bit his shoulder, hearing him call my name as he climaxed. At that same second, I too reached the height of my pleasure—moaning and rocking my body to feel his seed enter deep inside me. I knew then and there that I had conceived a child, that once again Tam had given me the gift of life.

For a long time we lay in perfect peace, intertwined in one body. To our dismay, we were forced to pull apart when we heard voices coming from the stairwell down the hall.

Tam quickly dressed. He nodded to me and turned, walking briskly out of my cell.

It was the first time we had made love in many years. And it was to be our last.

CHAPTER 19

Canton and the Isle of Hazelnuts. 1945-1946.

"Bianca Tam," barked the court bailiff. I rose from the bench—the only woman called from among the row of Japanese prisoners—and proceeded into the adjoining room. Because this was a military hearing, I was not allowed the advantage of having a defense lawyer. However, because of their backgrounds as soldiers, there was a chance that the judges would grant more leniency to a woman who had suffered and struggled in the heart of the war. I also perceived, as I was brought to sit and face the seven officers of the Kuomintang waiting to interrogate me, that there was a certain embarrassment on their part at having to judge a woman. There was a small but real chance that the hearing would go in my favor and that within a few hours I would be free.

"Bianca Tam, born in Italy," the clerk droned, "married in 1936 to Tam Gian Ciau, born in Canton, Colonel of the New First Army of the Nationalist Chinese Army. Arrived in China in 1939 with her husband."

The Magistrate asked me, "Do you confirm the statement that has just been read?"

"Yes," I responded, "I do."

The clerk continued, "The accused is charged with contraband activities and political and military espionage, in favor of the enemy, a collaborator with the Japanese from 1941 to 1945."

The questioning began, as one of the judges asked, "Do you confirm that you lived from February 1940 to May 1941 in Tuyun, the war zone of the Kwei-chow?"

"Yes," I began, gauging a sympathetic expression on the Magistrate's face, and knowing that my answer would be very important in my behalf, "I was following my husband."

The judge sitting to the left of the Magistrate, leaned over and whispered something in the other's ear. There was a moment of conferral among the officials that I could not hear and I took this to be a good sign. The Magistrate cleared his throat, asking, "Can you present to the court a document which certifies that you are the wife of Colonel Tam Gian Ciau?"

"Yes," I asserted readily, "I will obtain it from the Vatican where we were married."

An official who had not yet spoken noted, "This document must be authenticated by the court," and then he turned to the Magistrate, who pounded his gavel and announced their ruling, "As the wife of a Chinese citizen you will be considered a Chinese citizen and therefore you have the right to be tried by Canton's Civil Court, and not by the Military Court. The hearing is adjourned." He turned to the bailiff. "The prisoner may go now."

This was a terrible development that immediately rocketed me with shock waves of panic and shame. I could have counted on a military tribunal to consider my Italian heritage. But as a Chinese citizen in a civil trial, I would incur the public wrath—they wanted blood.

Finally reacting to the reality of my peril, I sent an urgent telegram to my mother:

Canton, Nov. 12, 1945

My dearest Mama,

>*Again, please believe that I am innocent. Believe that I have fallen into a trap. Help me, you and your contacts are my only hope of escaping from this nightmare. Charges are very serious. Tam is a General now and could not risk defending me before the officers of his own army, nor the citizens of his country. I think of what will happen to Lylongo, Jula, and Aloma if I am found guilty. Do what you can as quickly as possible.*

>*Your loving daughter, Bianca*

* * *

In the meantime, all I could do was wait and pray, with counsel from no one as to how soon I would go to trial after my marriage certificate was issued from Rome. Even Tam wasn't sure, when he came a week later to let me know my lawyer had responded to my earlier letter. Villerose had acknowledged that the bank had signed my account over to him and that he'd withdrawn the money and had sent it to the children's boarding school. Tam had also received a phone call from my mother saying that she would do all in her power to help me, though no progress had as yet been made.

"The only certainty," Tam warned, "is that you will be moved to a higher security facility. When, I don't know." Then he embraced me and slipped a handful of Hong Kong dollars into my waistband. "You may need this at some point," he said, "but keep it well hidden."

He started to say something, his nostrils flaring as he inhaled deeply. I wanted desperately to tell him that I was pregnant, that within me grew living proof again of our eternal connection. Although I had been accused of crimes that could lead to the death penalty, nothing on earth could have persuaded me not to keep the child. But I refrained from saying anything, choosing to tell him at a more opportune moment. As always, his visit was brief and he abruptly took leave of me.

* * *

Unbeknownst to me at the time, my mother was getting a taste of the difficulty she would continually face in trying to procure intervention on her end. She had received a reply to a plea she had made to the Italian Consul in China:

Nanking, 12/10/45

> *Received your communication. Steps taken with Chinese government in favor of Bianca Tam. Our Embassy will do what it can for her defense. Since she is accused of spying for Japanese we can't do much more for the moment.* —Ambassador Fenoaltea

In his own hand, the ambassador had less officially explained to my mother:

Dear Maria,

We are waiting for the right moment to ask the Chinese Embassy in Rome for help. We must take as long as possible until the zeal for revenge has diminished. We must not forget that a few months ago our two governments, Italy and China, were enemies. —A.F.

*　　*　　*

In the large barracks courtyard in Canton, a few military trucks were idling while the Japanese prisoners filed out. Not knowing where we were being taken, I was the last to climb aboard before the truck took off.

We crossed the city. At the estuary of the Si-kiang River, the prisoners were shuttled on a ferry. Half an hour later we were unloaded on the little Isle of Hazelnuts, where a concentration camp had been built for Japanese prisoners.

I had developed, in the course of the past three months, a toughened exterior. Privately, I had experienced plenty of despair, but I needed my strength—both to endure the battle ahead and to be able to deliver a healthy, strong child into the world. That baby, I was aware, might not have its mother for long.

As we were marched down a street lined with wooden barracks, I kept my eyes straight ahead and came to attention when stopped in the center of a large enclosed area. A soldier informed me that the structure on the end was reserved for me—the only woman among four hundred prisoners.

Another soldier escorted me to my cell, a small but adequate room I would have to myself. He gave me a military salute and started to go.

"Wait," I said, in a timely move, handing him a few dollars. "These are for you. Please tell General Tam at the Command of the New First Army where I have been transferred. But do it immediately."

*   *   *

Meanwhile, outside of my immediate knowledge, a flurry of correspondence had erupted in the wake of inquiries as to the legitimacy of my status as a Chinese citizen. From Rome came the response in the issue of the marriage certificate:

> *Vatican City*
> *February 4, 1946*
> *Secret Archive, Vatican*
>
> *I, Prefect of the Vatican Secret Archive, testify that number 7447 of the Vicariate of Rome corresponds to the certificate attached herewith, reprinted in full.*

From the Chinese Ambassador in Rome came confirmation that no marital rites had been performed on Chinese soil:

> *The Chinese Embassy to the Royal Court of Italy certifies that Mr. Tam Gian Ciau, son of the late Kong and Leung Si, was born in Canton, China, on July 29, 1911 and is a Chinese citizen and has not been married there.*

Had the ruling gone otherwise, there might have been leeway to dispute my being tried as a Chinese citizen. Unfortunately, the Chinese Embassy also declared that a Chinese and a foreigner could marry according to the following rules established by the Civil Code of China:

> *1. The marriage of a Chinese and a foreigner which takes place abroad is valid if it has been celebrated according to the law of that country.*

2. *The Foreign wife becomes a Chinese citizen and the children born of that marriage are Chinese citizens, even though they may be born in a foreign country.*
3. *The foreign-born wife of a Chinese citizen shall follow her husband's condition.*

My mother stoically bore the disappointment that her daughter would face the charges as had previously been decreed and stepped up on using her influence as best she could.

* * *

When Tam heard where I was from the soldier that I'd fortuitously sent, he came at once to see me. With sentinels posted to watch us, we were allowed to walk together along the tree-lined road that ran by the island's shore.

I could tell his heart was heavy, not only in regard to my situation, but also, as he announced, for the fact that his division was leaving for Manchuria. His arm rested on my shoulder and he shook his head, saying, "The worst is to come—the war among ourselves. We are going towards Mudken where we will fight the Communists." He paused, continuing to walk closely beside me, and added, "So once more we will be separated. Not even the victory against our oldest and most hated enemy was able to unite our people." Tam sighed. "After having wanted to go to war, and having fought and won, I had hoped to enjoy peace."

"But, my darling," I reminded him, "sooner or later it will have to end."

"Yes, of course," said Tam. He tried to reassure me, but I saw fatigue and doubt in his eyes as he led me to sit down with him under the shade a thriving hazelnut tree.

I thought of how it had been that summer afternoon so long ago, sitting in the park, the first day we kissed. There was that same calm around us and no sounds other than our voices and the beating of our hearts.

Tam rested his arms on my knees. "I've paid six months advance to the boarding school in Shanghai. If you are released before the time is up, they'll refund you the overpayment." He handed me an envelope of money, again warning me to keep it hidden. "Oh," he said, snapping his fingers as an afterthought, "I almost forgot. I wrote separately to your mother and father to let them know they could no longer send letters to you in care of me, but to send them to the Archbishop of Canton. It seems that the Vatican has begun to take an interest in your case."

Though this was a positive turn, Tam's face bespoke of a pervasive sadness. I knew what it was. He had to leave and he had to disobey his inner will to right what had been wronged between us. First and foremost, Tam was a soldier—subject to the command of his military superiors who superceded the longings he had as a father and a husband.

"Tam," I said urgently, speaking words he needed to hear, "I have no resentment toward you. We loved each other fervently, in the depths of our souls. What we had together cannot be erased, not its beauty, nor its truth."

Because he was set to leave the following day, Tam told me with remorse that he wouldn't be able to go see the children as he'd planned.

"Don't worry," I smiled, "I always told them that their father was a noble knight who was fighting in another part of the world and that when he came back, we would spend every day with him and listen to his wonderful stories."

"And did they believe you?" He asked it as if he needed to believe it for himself.

"They did and so do I," I told him.

His uncertainty, his pain, our poignant tenderness brought tears to my eyes. I blinked them back, wanting only for him to take my strength with him to the battlefield.

Tam lowered his voice to a whisper. "We will see each other again, won't we?"

"Yes," I declared. "We can never lose each other. One of us will always find the other, no matter where we are."

Once again I had the urge to tell him I was pregnant with our child. He hadn't guessed or spotted the change in my body—even though I was already five months along. But, looking as he did, as if he was carrying the weight of the world, I could not bring myself to add more concerns. So I added with a smile, "You see, I'm feeling optimistic."

"Yes, you will be saved," he vowed, "we must believe that absolutely. That is what will happen."

We both turned to see a guard approaching at a distance. Tam helped me to stand up, took my hand and pressed it for a few seconds, and then kissed my lips with his.

He suggested that I not walk back with him, both for the sake of appearance and in light of our emotional turbulence. This was the hardest good-bye we had ever shared and finally, Tam articulated the most difficult question weighing on him. He bit his lip, asking, "Have you forgiven me?"

"I have discovered," I said, "that the person who loves completely forgives completely."

Tam smiled, as if a knot that had been gnawing at him a long, long time was dissolving. He removed his gold chain with the little opal on it from around his neck—his good luck charm. "Here," he murmured, putting it on me, "may it bring you luck."

"No, Tam," I objected, "you need it as much as I do."

But he insisted I keep it, telling me that after seven years of combat, he would rely on his wits and experience to keep him safe. He squeezed my hand one last time and walked away, accompanied by the soldier who had been keeping an eye on us.

I turned to look at the ocean so that he would not see me weeping. These were tears I hadn't shed since my initial incarceration. They were foreboding tears, reflections of my worry that Tam indeed needed his good luck token more than he knew. They were mournful tears too, sad memorials to the losses we had suffered along the way—the death of Jonathan and of the first baby Jula before him. But perhaps I also cried for joy, in gladness for the part of himself that Tam had left inside of me—the secret trophy that I hoped I would hold up to him in victory when he next returned.

* * *

Two months passed without any news reaching me directly. However, in Italy, my mother proceeded slowly but surely.

As far as Mama was concerned, the signature of the Ambassador and the approval of the Minister of Foreign Affairs, together with the seal of the Vatican Archives, were substantive enough for her to go in person to Monsignor Costantini in his office at the Piazza di Spagna. The Prelate showed her the text of the telegram he was sending to his Excellency Forquet, the Archbishop in Canton, whom the Monsignor knew personally.

To His Excellency Archbishop Fourquet
French Catholic Mission, Yat Tak Road:

I beg you to do everything you can for
Bianca Tam, imprisoned by the Kuomintang

government, for whom we are deeply concerned.

> —*Excellency Mons. Celso Costantini
> Propaganda Fide—Roma*

The next time they met, the Monsignor had promising news for my mother.

"Divine Providence is helping your family," began the Monsignor. "Pope Ratti may no longer be at St. Peter's but you know that among the new Cardinals ordained by His Holiness there is a Chinese, his eminence Yue-Pin of Nanking. He will be the first Cardinal in China and has just arrived in Rome in the personal airplane of Chiang Kai-shek."

Mama, as she would later write to me, asked him, "Have you been able to interest Cardinal Yue-Pin in the case?"

The Monsignor replied, "Yes, Countess Maria, his voice will certainly be influential."

My mother, bowing her head in respect, said, "Your Excellency, I beg you not to overlook an essential point—Bianca is innocent."

Yet he explained to her his view on the matter, saying, "You swear she is innocent, but it is not for this reason that we are interested in her case. We are not in service of justice here and do not seek to know if she is innocent or if she has committed any of the alleged crimes. Even if she were guilty, who are we to judge her? We do know, however, that she is the mother of three small children and this is reason enough that she not be condemned to death."

My mother spoke her gratitude, confessing, "I have only you to count on, your Excellency. Our Ambassador in Nanking and the Ministry of Foreign Affairs have taken an interest in the case, but I don't want to delude myself. I know that Italy was allied with Japan and that the Chinese perceive us as an enemy; they have great hostility toward foreigners. Only you can save Bianca."

"Let us hope," concluded the Monsignor, "that we will be worthy of the task to which the Lord has entrusted us."

* * *

The camp leaders had held a meeting with all the Japanese prisoners and had ordered them to maintain a correct line of conduct toward me. Three Japanese officers had been appointed to make sure that none of the men violated my rights in any way.

One of these men was Shakai Yamamoto, a twenty-two year old lieutenant who had been captured after parachuting out of his plane when it had been hit by U.S. anti-aircraft guns.

It was this very attractive, virile young man who had waited for me in the communal laundry room one afternoon to voice his personal concern. Thinking that I would prefer to wash my things—as well as the baby's when the time came—without having to look at the dirty uniforms of four hundred Japanese, he had made me my own wash basin by hollowing out a block of soft stone and connecting a water hose to it.

Yamamoto told me, "This is for your use alone. Anyone else who touches it is looking for trouble." Before I could thank him, he added, "This way I'll know where to find you." With that, he left me, turning to join his two companions waiting nearby.

* * *

As I progressed well into my seventh month of pregnancy, with little communication from those that were trying to help me, my spirits began to flag. My resolve to remain strong, no matter what, was straining simply under the pressure of not knowing—of being powerless in my own behalf.

It was in this mindset, as I wearily returned with the guard from mess one morning, that I saw a tall priest—an imposing and authoritative figure—pacing back and forth in front of my barracks.

"Bianca Tam," he said in a deep, smooth voice as soon as he saw me, "I wanted to meet you before, but your marriage certificate did not reach us from Rome until quite recently. I know that it is very important for you. I've looked it over and it's all in order."

"Finally," I uttered, sighing. "Without it we could do nothing. But who are you, sir?"

"I am Monsignor Fourquet, Archbishop of Canton."

I dared to smile, telling him he had no idea how long I'd been waiting to meet him and asked him to come with me into my barracks cell.

Monsignor Fourquet followed me in and the constant guard took his post outside the door.

"Ah," the tall priest said, noticing my now obvious pregnancy, "I see you have every reason to fight with all your strength to the last."

"The fourth reason," I added quietly, telling the Monsignor that not even Tam knew that there was another child on the way. "Incidentally," I asked with anxiety, "have you heard from him?"

"No, I'm sorry, there has been no word." Fourquet had a large, round open face that invited confidence and evoked warmth. His likewise rounded pale blue eyes seemed meditative and serene. "On a happier note," he said, "I have written the boarding school in Shanghai to make sure that the nuns take special care of your children and the reports are that your daughters are fine."

"Sometimes," I betrayed my fear to him, "I think I will never see them again."

Fourquet gestured for me to sit, though he remained standing. He told me, "You cannot permit yourself to think such thoughts. You must nourish the new life you are carrying and so you have no right to feel discouraged. When General Tam came to see me the day before he left for Manchuria, he gave me a name of a lawyer with an excellent reputation here in Canton. Without waiting for the Italian Embassy's intervention, I have already contacted the lawyer. As per Tam's request, I have also sent the marriage certificate to the Military Court so that your case can officially be transferred to the Civil Court. As we wait, we must prepare your defense. And we must have faith."

I looked askance about the cell, telling him, "The waiting is the hardest part. I've been here seven months, knowing nothing."

"Yes," Fourquet nodded, "the winners need victims but are in no hurry to decide their fate. Then again, are you truly a victim?"

"No, Monsignor. I am guilty."

"Do you know," he said, with no anger in his voice, "that you contributed to the deaths of many Chinese soldiers by passing information to the Japanese?"

Though I could only whisper in response, my voice was clear and steady as I stated, "No one will understand why I did it. For this reason I am prepared to die."

Now he took a seat and leaned toward me, those pale blue eyes of his beseeching mine, "Do not pose limits on the decisions of God and His mercy."

"But I will be judged by men," I exclaimed, "many of them who were once soldiers and others— Chinese citizens who will revile me. Unlike God, they will have no mercy, but will take pleasure condemning me to die a traitor's death."

"Don't think only about human justice. Faith will help you accept the sentence of the Court, whatever it may be."

I confessed to the Monsignor that my life was of no value to me, that it was the lives of my children for which I needed to be responsible. To which he replied,

"Divine Providence will not abandon your children."

These words of wisdom did nothing to console me. "I don't know," I said, my voice shaking, "if you can really understand this anguish—not having any children of your own."

The Archbishop got up and his face stayed calm and loving. "On the contrary," he said, "I feel that I have many children, Bianca. And you are one of them. If you need me, let me know."

The next day a package of things for the baby arrived and I knew who had sent it, even though there was no card or return address.

* * *

When it came near the time to give birth, I wrote again thanking Monsignor Fourquet and asked him to intervene on my behalf by helping me obtain a transfer to the Mission Hospital in Canton.

For days and weeks I waited, without a reply.

Finally, almost on my due date, not one but two letters were delivered to me after being checked by the camp censor.

I opened the one from the Monsignor first:

Dear Bianca,

The military authorities rejected the request I personally put forth to have you transferred to our hospital. They claim that their military hospital is able to offer you the medical care you will need. I will try to guarantee the assistance of one of our best obstetricians. I wanted to tell you this news in person, but I must obtain special permission every time I see you and it is not easy. Please write to me and let me know if you need anything. I will keep you appraised as to the developments of the trial, though we know nothing as yet. Be strong.—
Archbishop of Canton.

I was discouraged, to say the least, but nothing compared to my reaction when I read the brief letter from Balinow de Villerose, my lawyer in Shanghai.

Dear Madame Tam,
 This is to inform you that the Administrative Court of Shanghai has decreed bankruptcy of the Shanghai Bank. Using the power of attorney with which you entrusted me, I have withdrawn your deposits. Unfortunately, the sum deposited has been considerably devalued and in order to provide for the children, I have had to sell part of the gold which you have deposited in the safe deposit box. I will keep you informed.—B.D.V.

That filthy worm, I thought, furiously ripping the letter in many pieces. Tam had paid for the children and Fourquet had obtained the nuns' protection. The lawyer obviously did not let on that he knew all of that and, with the excuse of providing for the children, he was robbing me of what little money I had left. So yes, I now felt myself victimized—by the lack of feeling from the court system, the indifference of the military command who couldn't spare the charity to let me give birth in a normal environment, and ruthless individuals like the lawyer who had helped himself to any future security I could have hoped for. Now my war was with destiny for having made me its target.

*   *   *

"Excuse me, you are wanted in the command office," a soldier had said, coming up to me at the mess hall. It was the day before my due date and it was with difficulty that I put down my tray and followed him. As I stepped into the Commander's

office, all the officers rose to their feet in formal
military attention.

With no expression, good or bad, the
Commander told me a telegram had arrived. My
heart boldly palpitated with joy—could it be news
regarding my release? The Commander handed me
the communication and I eagerly unfolded it. It
read:

From: Officer's Military Camp, Canton
To: Bianca Tam

*We confirm that General Tam Gian Ciau
fell in battle against Communist rebels near
Mudken.* —Command New First Army.

Still clutching the paper with both hands, my
knees buckled and I fell senseless to the floor.

CHAPTER 20

The Isle of Hazelnuts and the City of Canton. 1946-1947.

July, 1946

Dearest Mama and Papa,

Tam is dead, killed in battle. The lawyer from Shanghai has slowly plundered all my savings. Archbishop Fourquet has been denied permission to visit me in prison. As I await temporary transfer to a military hospital to deliver my child, I feel already nothing but emptiness. Perhaps it is foolish to keep this baby who will be born fatherless, with a mother in prison. Perhaps all of my choices have been wrong, but they were made during wartime. You may say that the

*war is over, but not for me. When I think
about the past, about the sudden deaths of
Jula, Jonathan, and now Tam, I feel
completely alone—at the mercy of cold and
faceless entities. The Archbishop tells me to
pray and not give up, but it seems to me that
at this point things are beyond hope and I
have never been this low before. I feel my
own death is very near. I thank you both for
trying to help me, and implore you, in the
likelihood of my death, to care for your
grandchildren as if they were your own.*

Bianca

* * *

I gave birth to a healthy baby boy and named him Jonathan, in memory of his brother. Because I had no breast milk for him, and there was not a single feeding bottle to be found at the military hospital, the nurse brought me a glass of regular milk and a funnel from the kitchen. To feed little Jonathan, I wrapped the end of the funnel in cotton wool, dribbled milk into the funnel and squeezed it drop by drop into his mouth.

In my desolate state, not even the joy of a new life could cheer me. Making matters worse, I had to be moved out of the clean and airy ward in order to make room for three hundred wounded soldiers. The baby and I were put in an unheated closet with a mattress on the floor.

The only relief came when I returned to prison a few days later. After the long hours spent in that miserable cupboard—my barracks cell seemed to me almost like a deluxe hotel. Within the week, there would be more cause for my spirits to rally.

When the Archbishop had come to baptize Jonathan, he had arrived with a man I did not know—a plain, unassuming Chinese fellow. The Monsignor had explained, "For the godfather I have brought with me this kind gentleman, Chang Shu-sak. He is a famous and successful lawyer."

After the ceremony had been performed, the Archbishop wanted to leave us to discuss my case. "Now you must find a way to win the favor of the law or to trick justice on your side," he said, "and I can be of no more help to you."

"But there is one thing which you must promise me, your Excellency," I said as he was leaving. "You must find a nanny for my baby so he can know a face other than my own. Choose someone you can trust and when the trial begins I will give my child to her."

He promised to find someone, and then the door was shut behind him. I turned to Chang Shu, my brow creased with concern, saying, "If you are famous, then you must also be very expensive." I wondered also how this normal-looking man could possibly have earned such an exceptional reputation.

"Usually I am extremely expensive," he said, smiling, "but for your case, my fee will be the publicity I will receive." He took out a newspaper from the pocket of his overcoat and handed it to me. It was a copy of the English daily of Canton, with the front page headlines emblazoned on it:

WAR HERO'S BEAUTIFUL WIFE
ACCUSED OF SPYING

Chang Shu estimated that once the trial had begun, the whole world would be talking about it— the most famous case of the times. To be given the opportunity to handle the defense, he would gladly waive his fee. "But," he stipulated, "if we are to win, you must tell me everything that has happened from the day you left Tuyun to the day of your arrest. You see, unlike the Archbishop who is interested in seeing justice done, what interests me is seeing justice turned to the advantage of my clients."

As he spoke, I saw where his power lay—he had a true gift of persuasion, a dramatic flow to his speech and, obviously, a nimble mind. Perhaps Chang Shu-sak was the answer to my prayers. If not, he was the next best thing. I began to reconstruct to the best of my ability what had happened in the last five years, exposing even the most private personal details to him.

After I finished, my new defense lawyer nodded, saying, "Good, very good. Now, only you and I will ever know what really happened, but if you have kept anything back, you must tell me before the trial opens next month. The more I know, the better I will be able to defend you."

*　　*　　*

August. 1946.

"Don't forget," Chang Shu had begun, preparing me on the day before the trial, "that you are not only a mother, but also an attractive woman. Come dressed in the prison uniform that you wear every day at the camp, but the expression on your face when you walk into that courtroom must show that you are not afraid because you had a hundred good reasons for doing what you did."

For the past four weeks, he had visited me frequently in prison, going over and over the information that would fuel my defense. Finally, he had allowed me to ask a question. "Tell me honestly," I said as we parted, "will we make it through?"

"I can tell you," he declared in his persuasive way, "that we will fight to the end, and even after, if necessary."

The Archbishop had kept his promise and on the morning of the trial the new nanny had come to take Jonathan to a home with her at the Canton Mission. "Love him as if he were your own child," I had told her, slipping the six-week old baby into her arms, "he will have no one else in this world but you."

I had turned from her and my son and walked toward the waiting transport jeep. My eyes focused straight ahead, I had been surprised to feel a light touch on my shoulder and then to see Yamamoto silently hand me a red rosebud. I acknowledged the gesture by tucking it away carefully in my coat pocket.

* * *

The courtroom of the Canton Civil Court was overflowing its maximum capacity with officials, spectators, Chinese journalists and European correspondents. The Judge for the proceedings, a retired military man with a booming voice and ruddy complexion, called for order several times before he was able to officially open the trial. With a semblance of quiet, he stood up, rapped three times with his gavel, ordered the bailiff to have me rise, and read through the list of charges being brought against me.

"Now," said Chang Shu in my ear, "we go to work." The first step of his strategy, as I understood it, was to prove my innocence in my alleged participation in the Japanese attack on Pearl Harbor—the charge we could most reasonably contest.

"Your Honor," my lawyer said, taking the floor, "I call my first witness to the stand, Took Young." From the back of the courtroom, my old friend from Shanghai, the compelling Mr. Young, approached the witness stand. His eyes conveyed a great empathy and understanding as he passed by me—a good sign—and I allowed the confidence I was wearing for affect to actually be felt inside me.

Chang Shu led Mr. Young through the formalities of testifying in court and then asked him the all-important question of how he had come to know me.

The court reporter typed away on the transcribing machine as the following testimonies unfolded:

Mr. Young: I met Bianca Tam in the summer of 1941. Her husband, the deceased General Tam, was related to me through his mother's side of the family. Madame Tam told me that she and her husband had decided that she should come to Shanghai because the situation in Tuyun had grown quite dangerous due to the fighting and she and the children no longer felt safe there. It was her husband who sent her to me because he thought that as director of a bank affiliated with the Central Bank of Shanghai, I might be able to help her if she should come to find herself in financial difficulty. At that time, Madame Tam had four children. We met several times at the bank and at the hotel where she was living.

With an excellent poker face, my lawyer wasn't communicating to me whether he was satisfied or not with this opening testimony. However, as Chang Shu launched into a very direct question pertaining to my innocence, I felt relieved to ascertain that it was going exactly as planned.

Chang Shu: Have you any reason to believe that Mrs. Tam was already in contact with the Nanking government, with the Japanese military, or with espionage agents?

Mr. Young: Absolutely not. She was not entirely well at that time. She had not yet completely recuperated after the birth of her fourth child. Though she talked frequently about needing to find a job to support her family, she was not able to do so until she was well enough physically. Indeed, she later went to work at the fashion boutique of Madame and Monsieur Oury.

Chang Shu: Do you remember when exactly?

Mr. Young: Certainly. Not only do I remember, but I had the date listed in a ledger I kept. At the end of every month I brought her a check, as officer Tam had instructed me. But eventually the financial situation in Shanghai had worsened and I had to inform Madame Tam that the bank would no longer be able to provide for her. It was then that she decided to look for work, at the end of January, 1942.

The Public Prosecutor, a barrel-chested and good looking man, also retired from the military, stood and waived his right to cross-examine the witness. As Young left the stand, I nodded to him, gratitude in my eyes. My battle was off to a good start.

The second witness called was Chester Haley, the manager of the Honan Hotel in Shanghai. I noted to myself the irony of the fact that it was the gold bars I had been carrying back to him that had been found on me when I was first apprehended by the Americans. Chang Shu asked Mr. Haley to recall for the court what he had observed my activities at the hotel to be.

Chester Haley: Madame Tam led a relatively withdrawn life. She spent many hours in the garden of the hotel with her children.

Chang Shu: In those first months of her stay in Shanghai did the defendant receive any visitors or was she often absent for several days at a time?

Chester Haley: The only visitor that I remember ever having seen was Mr. Young, and no, for many months Madame Tam did not leave the city.

Chang Shu: Did she tell you about her new job at the Ourys' fashion boutique?

Chester Haley: Yes, she seemed pleased to have found a job that she enjoyed and with which to support her children.

Chang Shu: And do you remember when she took that job?

Chester Haley: Yes, in February, 1942. If I may say so, it was then that I personally suggested to the owner of the hotel that he offer the Tam family a small reduction in the rate they paid for their rooms because I guessed that she was in economic difficulty.

The Public Prosecutor leapt to his feet, objecting vehemently to Mr. Haley's last comment and suggesting that my economic difficulty was only hearsay. To my great relief, the Judge disagreed. When the Public Prosecutor opted not to cross-examine Mr. Haley, Chang Shu was able to call his last witness for the day—Daniel Oury, the proprietor of the high-fashion boutique called "Elegance," where I'd worked in Shanghai. My lawyer began by asking him to confirm the statements made by the earlier witnesses.

Oury: Yes, I can confirm the information given in the previous testimony. Bianca Tam came into my employ on February 10, 1942.

Chang Shu: What made you decide to take her on?

Oury: Well, she was obviously in need of money. I appreciated her honesty in explaining her situation to me and I wanted to help her out in some way. Later I saw I had made an excellent decision because she was a very capable and hard-working employee.

Chang Shu: Did Mrs. Tam receive any visits from members of the Japanese military or from Japanese civilians while working at your boutique?

Oury: We had many Japanese clients. Women, of course. But I don't remember that Madame Tam showed special attention to any one of them. No, there were no Japanese men or military officers among our clients.

Chang Shu: And when did she leave her position at your boutique?

Oury: In June 1942.

Chang Shu: Do you know why she left?

Oury: She told me she had accepted Nancy Lee's offer to work in public relations. Her pay was much higher than what she received from us and I knew that she had no other source of income.

The Public Prosecutor asked his one question of the day to Monsieur Oury, much to the amusement of the courtroom.

Public Prosecutor: Monsieur Oury, how would you define the "public relations" work Madame Tam did with Nancy Lee?

Oury: To my knowledge, their public relations work was exactly that—public relations.

The court erupted in a smattering of laughter, Chang Shu objected to the question as irrelevant to the charge at hand, and the Judge banged his gavel, decreeing that the last question and answer would not appear on the transcript.

"Sir," the Judge nodded to my lawyer, "do you wish to read a closing statement?"

"I do your Honor," Chang Shu said and approached the bench where the jury had been sitting impassively through the day's proceedings. "Gentlemen," concluded Chang Shu, "it seems evident that these witnesses, a Chinese businessman, an English hotel manager, and a French fashion designer, have sufficiently proved that from May 1941 until June 1942, Mrs. Tam had absolutely no contact with any Japanese spy or military activity or with any country that might be considered an enemy of China. She had come to Shanghai because it had become dangerous for her to remain at the front in Tuyun where there was no doctor to help her with the delivery of the child she was carrying, who was later born in August 1941. She was alone in Shanghai, an unfamiliar city, with the responsibility of four children on her hands. What diabolical impulse could have prompted the defendant to join a Japanese spy ring and to pass information regarding the American fleet at Pearl Harbor, a place in the

Hawaiian Islands, thousands of miles from Shanghai? No, gentlemen, your Honor, not only until December 7, 1941, but for many months thereafter, the only real and pressing concern of this woman was to provide a decent living for her children. It is so evident that I believe that the Americans will have to reconsider and withdraw their accusation, or rather, their suspicion, for it is only unfounded suspicion that Bianca Tam was in any way involved in the Japanese attack on Pearl Harbor."

"So advised," boomed the Judge, who pronounced the trial adjourned until an official standing from the United States government could be handed to the court. For me, this first battle was far from over, but it was a decisive step in my favor—buying me several more months of time in which to prepare for whatever verdict was ultimately to come.

*   *   *

Chang Shu's suggestion that the American government withdraw its charges and the court's decree for a ruling triggered an international flurry of telegrams and meetings, some of which I would later be informed.

August, 1946

To: Countess Maria Peritti
  Via Frisi 18
  Roma Via Swiss Radio

From: Chang Shu-Sak

We ask you and the Count to do everything possible to obtain withdrawal of American charge Bianca Tam collaboration Pearl Harbor.

Through my father's extensive contacts in the Italian military, he was eventually able to enlist the aid of an Admiral who in turn appealed strongly once more to the Ministry of Foreign Affairs:

Nov. 10, 1946

To His Excellency Pietro Nenni
Minister of Foreign Affairs
of the Italian Republic
Rome

Dear Pietro,

If I allow myself to take advantage of our long friendship and of your influential position, it is only to bring to your attention a most sorrowful matter which I beg you to look into personally.
Enclosed here is a dossier of this sad case. I pray that through your intervention something may be done to bring relief to a distressed mother and father, dear friends of mine, who are in deep anguish for their daughter, far away in very grim circumstances.

Yours truly,

P.B.

Following its channels of influence, the Ministry saw fit to go to the American Embassy in Rome, contacting a personal alliance there:

Dec. 15, 1946

To: Franklin Gowen
Embassy of the United States of America
Via Buoncompagni 2
Rome

Dear Franklin,

Allow me to present Countess Maria Peritti who is in urgent need of your advice and help in a very grave matter concerning her daughter. I might also add that the Ministry of Foreign Affairs, and the Minister himself, have taken an interest in the case through the intervention of the Italian Ambassador to Nanking. The Holy See of Rome has also demonstrated a deep concern in this matter.

Thank you for whatever help you may give.

Sincerely,

G.d.B.
Counsellor of the Italian Embassy
of the Holy See of Rome

Just before Christmas, my mother finally succeeded in meeting with Gowen, the Assistant to the Ambassador of the U.S. Embassy in Rome.

"We meet at last," said Gowen. "There are many influential people on your side."

My mother had already sent the Assistant Ambassador a transcript of the testimony given at the time of the trial and pled her own case by espousing how thoroughly convinced she was of my innocence in the American charge.

Gowen had already taken action and told her, "I have requested and received a copy from our Ambassador in China of the arrest report concerning your daughter. The smuggling and espionage charges are backed up by incontestable evidence. But as far as the accusation made by our government is concerned—that your daughter participated in the Japanese attack on Pearl Harbor—so far no proof has emerged from the trial to substantiate that claim." He did add, however, on a less assured note, "I also fought in the war and I know what that battle cost the people of my country. The seventh of December, 1941, will not be forgotten for many years, but it would be wrong if in our zeal to punish the traitors we should also punish those who are not guilty of the crime."

Finally, by mid-January 1947, the Commanding Officer of the U.S. Military Police presented a letter to the court which stated that the United States government had withdrawn charges concerning my alleged participation in the attack on Pearl Harbor as an informer for the Japanese. When Chang Shu arrived at my prison cell to give me the news, I had only a few moments to celebrate the victory before he warned me, "Do not get your hopes up too high, the prosecution will now redouble their efforts to obtain a conviction on the other two charges." He sighed, reminding me that we had no witnesses to refute the testimony of the witnesses the prosecution would be calling and that he would probably opt not to cross-examine.

*   *   *

As the first witness for the prosecution was Colonel Kurata, now a prisoner of war, the amount of military personnel in the courtroom was even greater than it had been back in August. The mood, tense and somber, was altogether different from the almost lively atmosphere I'd first experienced. And though I felt no malice as the bullish Kurata took the stand, I sensed great animosity toward the Japanese officer from the members of the Chinese jury. Still in his controlled, calculated way of speaking, the Colonel described the two occasions on which we met, and the information I had given him. Then, the Public Prosecutor showed the court the receipts of the checks that had been paid to me in exchange for my information and the note I had written to Nancy Lee after returning from Canton:

"Please don't ask me for an explanation of what happened at Nanking. If there's anything you need, let me know."

There was an abrupt gasp from the spectators that resounded in the courtroom. With a tight constriction in my chest, I realized only at that very moment, that Nancy had evidently given the note back to Kurata who had zealously set about unmasking the various members of his network of informers. I wanted to bury my face in my hands, ruing the day that I'd thoughtlessly written the note, but with effort I managed to stare ahead as the prosecution continued with Kurata:

> *Public Prosecutor:* Did the accused provide you with any information which proved useful to the Japanese military?

> *Kurata:* Yes, sir. She helped us to identify the location of the enemy air bases in Kwei-chow and she gave us useful information regarding the kinds of weapons which the Americans and the English had sent to the Kuomintang army.

I leaned over to Chang Shu, whispering, "But Kurata himself told me my information was too dated to be reliable!" My lawyer shook his head, shrugging. There was nothing we could do but sit passively as the questioning went on.

> *Public Prosecutor:* For how long did the accused collaborate with Japanese agents?

> *Kurata:* Until approximately the end of 1944. It was then that our Shanghai agent

Oshima Tanaka met with Madame Tam and received information from her about the placement of the Kuomintang troops in the Southwest.

The day had ended badly for me, but it was only going to get worse. The following morning, a surprise witness for the prosecution was sworn in by the bailiff. It was Wei Hsuan-ch'o, maître d'hotel of the Honan Hotel in Shanghai and—as he revealed to the court and to me for the first time—an informer of the Chinese counter-espionage network. A man who had always been kind to me, he refused to look in my direction as the Public Prosecutor asked him about the aforementioned Oshima Tanaka.

Wei Hsuan: Yes, Oshima Tanaka frequently came to the hotel to visit Madame Tam. I had learned from a teller at her bank that Madame Tam had sold some gold bars to Tanaka, and as a matter of fact, one day Tanaka came to the hotel with a green valise which I recognized as belonging to the defendant because I had often carried it into her room when she returned from her trips to Canton. I knew that Tanaka was a spy and I was able to take a few photos of them together.

With a lavish gesture, the Public Prosecutor presented the photos to the Judge who agreed to accept them as articles of evidence.

Where I had been stunned by Wei Hsuan's contribution to the campaign against me, I felt no shock when the next witness began to testify. His name was Kao Erh-ch'u, a youngish unattractive man whom I recognized at once as having been a waiter at the Blue Dragon Restaurant in Shanghai. Many times, he had made improper advances toward me, which I had repeatedly spurned. Naturally, this opportunity to gain an aspect of revenge had put a smile on Kao's face.

Kao Erh-ch'u: I served at dinners organized for Japanese, German, Italian, and French military officers and civilian officials. Madame Tam was one of the most dedicated hostesses. It was she who most often informed me of the number of guests we had to prepare for and we often decided upon the menu together.

Public Prosecutor: Can you tell us anything about what happened during those dinners?

Kao Erh-ch'u: After dinner, the guests would smoke opium. They paired off into couples and withdrew into the small private rooms where they could stay together undisturbed until dawn.

Public Prosecutor: Do you remember if the accused ever entered those little private rooms, as you call them, with the guests?

Kao Erh-ch'u: Yes. More than once with different men.

The courtroom exploded with a tantalized clamor as journalists shouted questions about what they considered to be a scandalous revelation. The Judge adjourned for the day, promising that the defense would have an opportunity to counter with other witnesses when we next reconvened. That night, I privately gave in to despair, knowing just how damaging the testimonies had been.

In the morning, however, I was composed again and very moved as I watched my friend and once temporary husband, Phillipe Simon, climb onto the stand. Well-versed as he was in diplomatic language, Phillipe testified convincingly that he had never suspected I might be involved in any spy activities and stated that he had been aware of my trafficking in gold. He emphasized that the buying and selling of gold was not illegal then, that I did it only to supplement my income. Seeing that the jury had listened attentively, I permitted myself a grain of optimism. And when Phillipe left the stand, I mouthed the words, "Thank you," to him.

Upon my suggestion to Chang Shu, he then recalled Chester Haley who admitted that the gold bars found in my possession at the moment of arrest had been purchased for him. Unfortunately, his testimony had little sway upon the graver matters at hand.

So it was with a good deal of trepidation that on the next day of the trial, I myself was sworn in and sat to face the courtroom and to respond to the intricate questioning of the prosecution.

Public Prosecutor: Do you confirm the testimony of Colonel Kurata?

B.T.: Yes, I met with him twice in Nanking.

Public Prosecutor: He asked you for military information and you gave it to him. Is that correct?

B.T.: The Colonel told me that he would easily be able to obtain that information elsewhere if I chose not to tell him, and that if I did tell him I might save the lives of many soldiers.

Public Prosecutor: Do you also confirm the testimony of Wei Hsuan-ch'o in which he stated that you also passed information to the Japanese agent Oshima Tanaka?

B.T.: Yes, that is what happened.

Public Prosecutor: And the work for Nancy Lee?

B.T.: Yes, that too.

Public Prosecutor: Didn't the salary you received from the Oury's allow you and your children a relatively comfortable existence?

I paused for a moment, stifling a flash of anger. My lawyer had adamantly instructed me not to appear combative on the stand.

B.T.: Yes, we were able to make ends meet, with a bit left over.

Public Prosecutor: If so, what need was there then to go to work for Nancy Lee and later, for the Nanking government? Perhaps ambition and greed were your prime motivation?

There was a death-like stillness in the courtroom, as all eyes focused anxiously on me, waiting to see my reaction to such an accusation. I looked directly into the questioner's eyes and gave my reply.

B.T.: Love, sir, is never greedy.

Public Prosecutor: And it never occurred to you that you were committing treason?

B.T.: Reasoning about it was a luxury which wasn't afforded to me at the time. My life, my children's lives, and possibly my husband's life were all under threat. Furthermore, the information I had dated back several years—in strategic terms, it was relatively unimportant.

Public Prosecutor: But it was first-hand information.

B.T.: Yes, I told him only what I had personally seen.

Public Prosecutor: And it never occurred to you to ask yourself what the duties of the wife of an officer of the Kuomintang were?

B.T.: Yes, sir, it did occur to me. I thought about it a lot and it seemed to me that my first duty was to provide for our children.

Public Prosecutor: Even if that meant becoming a spy?

B.T.: I never killed anyone.

Public Prosecutor: But the information you gave Tanaka and Kurata contributed to the deaths of many men.

There was another eruption of disorder as my lawyer stood to object to the inconclusive statement of the prosecution and the Judge's echoing voice ordered silence. Overruling Chang Shu's objection, the Judge turned to me and instructed me to respond. I swallowed and spoke with difficulty, though there was simultaneously defiance on my face.

B.T.: I realize that I am guilty as you say. I do not wish to justify my actions, nor do I expect to be understood.

Two guards accompanied me back to my place and Chang Shu, who had chosen not to cross-examine me, instead rose to call our last witness—the amah Lynn Te-kuei, my devoted servant and friend. He began by addressing the matter of the gold.

Lynn Te-kuei: Yes, I knew that she frequently went to Canton to buy gold. I knew because she was always happy when she could put money away for her children. She worked hard to have enough money to enroll the little girls in the French school in Shanghai run by nuns. I also knew that she went to Canton to try to find her husband, who she hadn't heard from in many months. She became very depressed after the death of her son Jonathan and said that fate was against her but that she would do anything possible to make sure that her children would have a better life. I know how much she loves her children and I know that she is a kind woman and a good person."

The record would later show that at this point Lynn was unable to continue, overcome by a flood of tears. As I watched her being helped down, I saluted her with my eyes for her sincerity and courage. I was aware of a silent wave of sympathy for me coming from the Chinese citizen spectators as well as the foreign press. Bringing Lynn up as the last witness had been an excellent strategic decision on the part of Chang Shu in his attempt to obtain the lightest sentence possible for me.

The Public Prosecutor was outraged, knowing that this emotion could not be allowed to stand in the way of his obtaining the death sentence that he so ardently desired as my punishment. The wiry man sprang from his chair, interrupting the silence to begin his final plea.

"Now that the moment has come," said the Public Prosecutor with grand animation and severity, "we must try to determine to what extent, to what degree, Bianca Tam is guilty of the crimes with which she is charged. The American government has withdrawn their accusation and buying and selling gold is certainly not a crime punishable by death." Then he turned and stalked toward me, directing his words as he intoned, "But you, Bianca Tam, we have heard many authoritative testimonies which show beyond the shadow of a doubt that you betrayed both the man you claim to have loved and his country, of which you are a citizen. The information that you passed brought about the deaths of thousands of Chinese soldiers and strengthened the position of our enemy, the Japanese. I understand your concern to provide your children with a comfortable existence, but how many men lost their lives in order to guarantee greater comfort to four children? The Japanese are also human beings, the defendant declared, hoping that by saying so she might justify her actions. Yes, it's true, she saved the lives of the enemy who invaded and occupied China for years, but there can be no doubt that she also exterminated many of our own men. Did other women, Chinese wives and mothers, act thus, as the defendant did, in those long, terrible years of the war? Women who subsisted in conditions of extreme difficulty, much less comfortable than the rooms of the Honan Hotel of Shanghai, women who certainly never dreamed of the delights of the little private rooms of the restaurant where Bianca Tam not only betrayed the values and the country of her husband, but also her love for him. A woman who has offered herself to many men for one night of pleasure, can she be a good mother? What kind of example has she set for her children by her actions? We have been given sufficient evidence to prove that Bianca Tam is an unscrupulous and immoral woman, ready to sacrifice all moral principle in order to satisfy her carnal desires and her greed for money and position. But we cannot allow her to justify her unspeakable actions by simply saying she needed money. Money is not a god before whom we must prostrate ourselves, abandoning our most cherished values. No."

The Public Prosecutor paused, breathing deeply, and turned from me to take in the entire courtroom— the spectators, the jury, and the Judge. His black beady eyes glinted in the last rays of the afternoon light that fell through the courtroom window as he concluded, "Bianca Tam is guilty of high treason and we cannot pardon her for this crime. Nor can we betray those who have suffered and who have come here to this courtroom in search of justice. Your Honor, gentlemen of the court, in full conscience I ask that you find the defendant guilty as charged and that she be put before a firing squad and shot to death in punishment for her crimes."

His words had fallen upon my ears like gunfire itself. All the hope that had been mustered during Lynn's testimony had totally fled. Turning to glance at Chang Shu, I could not imagine how even with his persuasive manner, he would be able to turn the tide in my favor. Watching him now rise to face the court, I noted that his face appeared to be tired and his stance tentative.

But in that same moment, as he opened his mouth to speak, he immediately captivated every listening ear. His voice was calm and controlled. Unlike the prosecution, Chang Shu had not a trace of melodrama, yet in the anticipation of his argument, one could have heard a pin being dropped.

Chang Shu began, "Before leaving for the front in Manchuria, where he fell in battle, General Tam came to see me and entrusted me with a letter which he begged me to read at his wife's trial before the court withdrew to decide the verdict. In honoring his request, I did not introduce it earlier, nor did the defendant herself have knowledge of it. I assure you my intention is not to create a surprise effect, as the Public Prosecutor is surely about to protest."

In that second, the Prosecutor had indeed already jumped up to object, but saw at once his effort would go to naught and sullenly sat again.

Chang Shu continued only after a beat. "I wish only to comply with General Tam's request, and I believe that everyone here will agree that the request of a war hero like General Tam demands our respect. Perhaps if I had read it before the Public Prosecutor's last speech, he might have softened the harsh tone of his invective against Madame Tam, a woman he does not know, nor the many hardships she has incurred at such a tender age." Pausing for a second, Chang Shu took a moment to gaze around the courtroom, filling his lungs as he did and when he spoke, it was with force. "Certainly, none of us know her as well as the man who wrote the following letter."

Chang Shu put on his glasses and informed the court that the letter had been written in May, 1946. He then read it verbatim:

Dear Bianca,

More than anyone else I should feel outraged and betrayed by your actions in recent years—if you are guilty as they say. I have meditated a long time about what happened after you left Tuyun, after you had discovered that your husband, the man you had followed to a foreign land, who you had followed all the way to the front, already had another woman. At that time, I did not understand your reaction. But I realize now what was behind everything you did. And for this I am responsible for having abandoned you for so long, without any news of me, with the responsibility of four children to care for. When we were living together, you were an excellent mother. I know well that has not and will not change. I am at fault for having deserted you. It is a serious mistake on my part that I cannot erase, but I hope that you may find comfort in knowing that

*I have always loved you deeply and that
nothing you may have done could ever
change my love for you. Be strong and
don't forget me.*

Tam

Chang Shu paused for a second. The only sound
to be heard in the courtroom was that of a few
spectators weeping quietly. It was an act of God that
I myself did not weep for the effect of Tam's letter
had filled me with the most profound emotion I had
ever felt in my life. From this moment forward,
regardless of the decision of the court, it mattered
not. I had already received the only true pardon I
cared about—Tam's.

When he spoke again, Chang Shu's eyes were
riveted on the judge as he stated, "This woman has
already paid for her crimes. If destiny does exist,
then it is destiny that has punished her for her
crimes, robbing her of her loved ones. Human justice
has kept her far from her children in a concentration
camp for almost two years. He who had most reason
to be angered, to seek justice—he who was
betrayed—has forgiven her. Who are we then, all of
us, not to grant her pardon? Do we really believe
that punishment or death can help someone? Bianca
Tam? Her children? The memory of her husband—
General Tam? Our country? I don't believe so. 'If thy
brother offends thee, forgive him. And if he
trespasses against thee seven times in a day and
seven times in a day turns again to thee saying I
repent, thou shalt forgive him.' Gentlemen, the war
is over. Give us with your decision an example of
mercy and of true freedom. In times of peace we
need forgiveness, not revenge."

The President of the court asked me if I wished
to speak. "No, your honor," I replied. "It has all
been said."

He turned to the Judge, who banged his gavel once and said, "Gentlemen of the jury, we will now move to private chambers and determine what the sentence will be." The gavel struck again and his voice boomed, "This court is adjourned. Proceedings are concluded."

I stood up and two guards escorted me out of the courtroom.

CHAPTER 21

The Isle of Hazelnuts. January to April, 1947.

Monsignor Fourquet brought the news to me in
my cell. The Archbishop said nothing, but opened his
arms to embrace me. As he did so, I knew at once
what had been decided. I wept briefly, then was still.

"Do they know when?" I asked.

"No date has been fixed yet."

I told the Monsignor that though I had turned
myself over to the power of God, I did not feel
ready to die.

"Good," he exhaled, "because the fight is just
beginning." With this, he showed me the morning's
headlines from newspapers throughout China. Not a
single one defended the court's decision. "This will
help you appeal for a pardon, and we must try
everything possible. Here and in Rome."

"Rome didn't do much," I said hesitantly.

"But now our Holy Father has honored me by calling me to Rome to continue my humble mission."

"So you're leaving me, then?" I murmured.

"Perhaps it is Divine Providence that has prompted my transfer to Rome. I will do everything I can for you. Your task is not to despair. The sentence cannot be carried out until the appeal for a pardon has been rejected. Months will pass, and as I have always said, time is on our side. Write to me in Rome and I will keep you informed every step of the way."

I pledged my undying gratitude to the Archbishop, whether or not he would be successful—which I had to doubt. "And convey the same to Chang Shu." I added, "Have you spoken to him yet?"

"It was he who informed me. You know, he never believed they would find you innocent, but he is still counting on a pardon. He had no idea that public opinion would take sides with you in such a strong way. Even the U.S. and British papers are divided."

As he left, vowing to uphold the duty he claimed God required him to do, I felt a new kind of loneliness—my rock of spiritual support would no longer be there to guide me.

He climbed into the jeep that had brought him to my barracks. As it drove away, I followed the Monsignor with my eyes until he disappeared beyond the camp wall.

*   *   *

The next day, Monsignor Fourquet wrote to my mother and father.

January, 1947

Dear Count and Countess Peritti:

The Holy Father has granted our prayer and has agreed to see me.

*What can I say to His Holiness about
your daughter?*

*Bianca herself admits to having
committed most of the crimes she has been
accused of. She also admits to having lived
a very scandalous life. But there are many
reasons why Bianca should go on living:
your great sorrow, respect for your devout
family, the fate of four children who have
already lost their father. And there may
still be another reason—a much more
profound one. I believe that the Lord, if
one of His humble servants may indeed
attempt an interpretation of His will,
wants Bianca to go on living so that she
may be led to an understanding of her
actions—to pass these spiritual tests into
an enlightened future.*

*It must also be noted that your
daughter's case has aroused keen, vast public
opinion on her side. Of course it is very
unlikely that Chiang Kai-shek will pardon a
woman who has betrayed a high-ranking
officer in his army.*

*But the impact of a gesture of clemency
must not be underestimated in a moment
when the Chinese Communist army, through
repeated military success, is increasing its
hold on the Chinese population—and at the
same time in a moment when the Church is
particularly interested in spreading the
word of the Gospel in such an immense
country. This is evident from the recent
ordaining of the first Chinese cardinal, His
Eminence Yue-Pin. Perhaps all this will
offer Chiang Kai-shek—who is Christian—
the opportunity of proving himself to be a
much more magnanimous ruler than the
cruel and merciless figure that his
adversaries accuse him of being.*

*Let us wait and hope and never cease
praying for the Lord to have mercy on
your Bianca.*

Mons. Antoine Fourquet

*   *   *

The weeks had passed slowly. Every ten days the camp director allowed me to go out for a few hours to see my son. The military escort accompanied me to the Mission home, waited for me, and then took me back to the prison at sunset. Those encounters served only to remind me of the strange gap between Jonathan, who was just beginning to live, and myself, who was about to die. In reality, at twenty-seven years old, I was still young, but I felt weathered and beaten down—feeling every passion dwindle away in both mind and body.

One day after lunch—which like all my meals took place alone in my cell—I had walked toward the hazelnut groves, up to the top of the promontory that afforded a view of Canton beyond the river. The wind had brought with it the sounds of ship sirens and foghorns intermingled with the voices of fishermen crossing the river in their junks.

Suddenly I had heard the notes of a waltz from a harmonica and turned around to see Yamamoto playing it. He smiled, revealing the pearl white of his teeth, and the wind tore through his black straight hair. He'd learned the waltz from German pilots when he was imprisoned with them, he told me, taking a few steps in my direction.

I admired his good looks as one did a beautiful painting, but numbed as I was, they could not stir me. Nevertheless, I made polite conversation, asking whether he knew how to dance the waltz as well.

"Of course," Yamamoto replied. "I dance it every night with General Shoten. He is a marvelous partner, since nothing better can be had. But no one dares to invite you to our little parties of condemned men."

I reminded him, "You are prisoners, not traitors. You won't be put to death."

"No," he corrected me, "most of us will be judged as war criminals guilty of massacres of the Chinese people."

"Even you?"

"I bombarded a farming village where our Command said a Kuomintang base was hidden. And then I was shot down by the Chinese."

"At least you didn't meet the fate of the Kamikaze pilots."

He spoke philosophically, "When you fight you know you might die and often death is more dignified than a mediocre life." Yamamoto leaned against one of the trees, appearing to be hardly more than a boy. His face was sorrowful as he said, "My rose didn't bring you luck."

"It was beautiful," I said without any sadness of my own, "and it lasted several days before it wilted."

"Bianca," he whispered intently, "you won't die, you will be saved. I dreamed I fell in love with you and I suffered because one morning a white boat came to get you. I shouted your name but my voice did not come out and you looked at me and waved goodbye. That is what will happen."

He gestured for me to sit down under the tree with him and I could not refuse. Like a playful child he plucked a blade of grass, and made it whistle between his teeth. But like a wizened sage, he told me, "If we have to die we must live every second left as fully as we can. Accepting our destiny, we will become stronger. A great Samurai said that when you cannot choose between living and dying, it is better to die, and do everything as if it were being done for the very last time."

Then quickly he told me of a tournament being held that evening, inviting me to come. Without an answer from me, he said, "But don't let anyone know I was here with you today."

I watched him stand and run from the grove, remembering a time not long ago when I had been free to respond to the call of human desires. It seemed like a very long time ago.

Yamamoto had not told me that he was one of the contestants. Bare chested, wearing only a pair of cotton boxing shorts, he entered the makeshift ring at the bell before the last round.

The other officers, sitting cross-legged on the ground or leaning on the wall, watched the fight. Yamamoto danced around his opponent with short, rapid steps. Agile and alert, careful to avoid being taken by surprise, he waited for the right moment to throw the other officer to the ground. But to Yamamoto's youth and vigor, the other man countered with much more experience and an uncanny ability to foresee his opponent's moves. The handsome young contender and the older officer scrutinized each other thoroughly—at times entwined hand and foot, other times keeping back, with no clear advantage on either side. The backing of the onlookers seemed to be divided, but the greater part, all of them more or less Yamamoto's age, were rooting for the young man. When Yamamoto turned to see that I had come after all, he was momentarily distracted and his adversary took hold of his wrist and threw him over his shoulder. But before being pinned in defeat, Yamamoto darted aside with a contraction of his muscles and went for his opponent. Locked together, they fell to the ground. Yamamoto immobilized him and held him down with all his strength until the referee announced the young fighter the winner.

As he bent his head so they could crown him with a laurel wreath someone must have made, I saw his body shining with sweat, his muscles still quivering, his lips swollen from the blows he had received, his hair full of dirt from the floor of the ring, and his eyes mad with joy.

It had been a long time since I had seen such a desire to live.

He looked at me, his naked chest dripping wet and still heaving with exhaustion and emotion. He mouthed his words without sound so no one else could hear, "I did it for you."

*   *   *

The bugle had just played taps when Yamamoto snuck through the small window of my barracks cell.

He had gained entrance with a clever ploy— throwing a rose through the opening of the window and catching me by surprise. I had told him he was crazy, that the guards were posted in the corridor and that others were on their rounds outside.

"Exactly," he'd said, "if you let me in I'll be safe. Or do you want me to get caught?"

Once inside my cell, he lay down on the floor, out of reach of the halo of light cast by the oil lamp. "Blow it out," he whispered, "they'll think you're asleep."

I did and sat down at the foot of the bed. A faint light shone in from outside.

"Bianca," he murmured low, "you mustn't avoid me any more. Promise me. I can't live without you."

Bit by bit, my passions were reawakening, but I whispered back still cynically, "And how much longer will they let us live?"

"No," he exclaimed in a hushed tone, "I'll decide the moment to leave this world. No one else has the right to decide that for me. I do not accept the surrender of our noble Emperor. I have been captured and defeated and I can't change what will happen. But I can decide when it will happen."

He took out a tiny box from the inner pocket of his jacket, opened it, and took out a black tablet. "Cyanide. You die instantly. Death is something much too noble to be left in the hands of your enemies."

"How long have you had those?"

"Since my first mission," Yamamoto told me, only his eyes showing from the thin streak of light coming in. "Every Japanese soldier carries them— they are preferable to being killed by the enemy. Think of the humiliation of being brought before the firing squad, the waiting, the last night, the satisfaction of those who have your life in their power—a life which should never belong to them."

As he spoke of the very fate that I knew awaited me, I begged him, "Leave me one of those tablets. I'll need it."

"You won't die, Bianca," he swore. "They won't be able to kill you and this will be your victory. My victory will be dying when I choose. In this way, we have not been defeated and that is what binds us together. It is stronger than the decisions made by men."

A powerful warmth flooded into me as I realized that this young handsome creature was a part of my destiny—part of the lessons being laid out for me. He was silent for a moment, as if he could read my mind.

He peered into my eyes as he said, "Yes, I love everything about you, Bianca—your life, your children, your betrayal, everything you have done and everything you will do. I love your beauty—it has become even more splendid here in this place we are forced to live in."

He took my hand and kissed it. Then he gently helped me to floor, caressed and kissed my face.

"No, not here," I said. "Let's go outside."

We slipped out through the window and walked hastily toward the hazelnut trees. Together we fell on the ground. While kissing, we undressed each other.

The first time was very quick—we had been holding back our desire for too long. But knowing that no one would search for us until the dawn, we made up for it as the night wore on.

"Now we'll make up for all the time we have lost," said Yamamoto. "Come here on top of me. Take me inside you, but don't move. We will make it last. Do you feel it? Everything is still, there is only us, here. No one can take this away from us. Please, more, as long as we love, we're alive."

He gripped my hips and pulled me to him. For a long time he kept moving inside me, each rhythmic stroke a stolen eternity of amazing pleasure.

Yamamoto and I saw each other every night but agreed to greet each other, whenever we met during the day, with the same formality that I reserved for the other officers. There might have been grave consequences for him were we to be found out— especially because I was the only woman among four hundred men who had been forbidden to approach me.

But at night our passion overcame all obstacles. There in the woods on the hill, the highest point of the island, or in the barracks if the north wind from Canton was blowing, we went on loving each other as we had done the first night.

"Have you ever noticed," said Yamamoto one night in the dark while we were lying on the floor of my room, "that the fishing junks sometimes come very close to the island? I've been told that you can bribe them." He went on to describe an escape plan for the two of us that he had devised.

"It's impossible. There are sentinels everywhere—inside and outside the fence—and there are police patrols all along the river."

He objected, saying that despite the risk, a few had successfully escaped. "Once I cared nothing for my freedom. But now that we are together, Bianca, it matters again. Don't you see?"

"Yes, I see," I agreed. "But that has happened here and would never have occurred if we were free. I don't want to be tied to a man. I would never have done this if it weren't for the fact that I have been condemned to death: we love each other because we must die."

There it was—the hard, ever-present truth of our situation.

* * *

March, 1947

Dear Mama,

Please don't ask me to explain my silence since my last letter of such utter hopelessness. In spite of the court's decision, I write to tell you and Papa not to despair, for I have given up despairing. I have suffered, I have cried, I have refused to accept this death sentence—but now I am serene, waiting for the day to come.

I haven't written to the children for a while. Lylongo and Jula are able to read and I think they would like to have news of me. But just as I must get used to the idea of losing them, perhaps it would be better if they forgot me.

There is one thing I must again beg you to do for me—please swear that you will not abandon them. Please come with Papa and your new companion to China to get all four of them and take them with you back to Italy. Let them grow up in our land and give them everything they need for their security and well-being. They will be orphans, but they will have a grandmother who will save them.

I do not ask to be pardoned. I know you have done everything possible to save me. At least you can save four lives, the lives of my children, your grandchildren. Knowing that you will do this for me—and I know you will—will free me from the gravest worry that troubles me and will help me face my destiny more calmly. I know that if I have sinned, I must pay for my crimes.

Bianca

I was to learn later that the following exchange had also occurred in those days:

To: Mons. Antonio Riberi
Apostolic Delegate
Peking, China

Your Excellency:

Fourquet has informed us of Bianca Tam's case and of the request for pardon set forth by her lawyer and by her family—very devout Catholics.

His Holiness wishes that the Chinese Church should take a direct interest in this case, in the person of yourself and Cardinal Yue-Pin, who is familiar with the case. An act of clemency obtained through the intervention of Catholic authorities could be very beneficial to the cause of the faith in that country.

The High Pontiff would be very content if things could be resolved in such a way.

Sincerely,

Mons. Celso Constantini, Rome

Cardinal Yue-Pin then received an appeal to act from the Apostolic Delegate:

> *Your Eminence,*
> *Our long-standing association seems to be the reason why Mons. Constantini of the Propaganda Fide has chosen my modest person as go-between for you to obtain the aim which it seems His Holiness holds dear to his heart. It is a difficult case and poses serious problems to our conscience. We enclose the letter we have received from Rome and pray that the Lord will help us and advise us.*— Antonio Riberi

*   *   *

April, 1947.

When my lawyer Chang Shu received the notice that the court had completed its review of all appeals for a pardon, he arrived immediately. Unless a miracle took place within the next twenty-four hours, the sentence would stand. My execution would take place the next day at ten in the morning.

"What kind of miracle?" I asked with a burning knot in my throat.

"Sit down," he said in a voice just above a whisper.

With all the time I had spent resigning myself to this inevitability, I could not fathom its proximity. Less than twenty-four hours to live? It could not be!

Speaking slowly and deliberately, Chang Shu reminded me of what I knew—that this was a troubled time for China and my case had become entwined with complex power games at the highest level.

Yes, there was a dim but possible note for hope—for a "miracle"—in that General Chiang Kai-shek and Cardinal Yue-Pin, Bishop of Nanking, had met. They had discussed the Catholic Church's future support of the Kuomintang troops in the civil war against the Communists. This could come from the Church, Yue-Pin intimated, by way of helping to improve the Nationalists' communication network via the many missions in China that were under the jurisdiction of the Catholic Church. Chiang Kai-shek was indeed also looking for moral support—being a Methodist—along with the political and military support furnished by the other powers who had continued to equip his army. He was well aware that the prestige of the Nationalist troops had received a great blow.

General Wedemeyer, sent personally by President Truman, had openly criticized the Nationalist government's corruption and military inefficiency. The government was unable to begin rebuilding the country and control inflation. It had confiscated gold, silver, and currency owned by private individuals—in the manner that I too had been deprived of my valuables. As far as the ordinary Chinese were concerned, the Kuomintang no longer enjoyed the mandate of heaven and every day Mao's army pushed northward with repeated success.

My lawyer told me that the meeting between the General and the Cardinal—which took place in the same palace that had housed Wang-Ching Wei's Japanese government—was ostensibly an attempt to create solidarity between the Kuomintang and the Church, insofar as Pope Pius XII had decided to excommunicate the Communists.

Among these pressing and crucial questions, Cardinal Yue-Pin had skillfully slipped in my request for a pardon. It was Yue-Pin himself who wrote the letter to my lawyer Chang Shu to inform him that whatever Chiang Kai-shek ultimately decided would bring my tortuous case to a close— either way. Yue-Pin related that Chiang Kai-shek felt a great hostility toward the woman who had betrayed the most brilliant young officer of the Kuomintang, whom he had known personally, General Tam. Chiang Kai-shek had expressed his firm belief that any act of pardon in my case would have a demoralizing influence on his officers, who would feel that their commander was unable to defend the honor and memory of his soldiers. To which the Cardinal reminded the General that the accused's family would donate a generous sum to his cause should she be pardoned. This money could be put to use for the public good, if Chiang Kai-shek consented to perform this act of clemency in a case that was by now a public matter. Above all, a demonstration of mercy at the moment of civil war, on behalf of a Western Catholic woman, would be a humanitarian act of vast consequence.

In short, Chang Shu said, just before leaving my cell, my very life depended on many broad and conflicting political issues. My "miracle," he said, was in the hands of Chiang Kai-shek. He promised that if anything happened during the night, he would alert me at once.

I had asked one last question, whispering, "Will you be there tomorrow when I go before the firing squad?"

He hadn't answered directly. Instead, he had said, "Even though I am a realist, I still sometimes believe in miracles."

*   *   *

That night, right before my long journey into memory had begun, I met Yamamoto in the hazelnut wood. My young lover knew nothing of my now-decided fate. He did not know that he would never see me again, nor that he had been wrong about my being saved. I chose to tell him nothing.

In that moment of abandonment we experienced all the pleasure of which we were capable. I gave him my body, my life, wildly desiring that some part of me would go on living in him after I was dead. I felt, for one last time, the pure, indominatable joy of giving and receiving. For those enraptured few hours, I felt completely alive, with profound clarity, dignity, and regret.

*   *   *

And so, as you have heard, I had spent the rest of the night alone in my barracks cell, reliving everything that had led me to this final place. The candle of my life, as destiny had decreed, was all but burned out. Soon—chosen for reasons I dared not comprehend to be marked by fate—I would be annihilated, or perhaps, reborn.

You who have travelled with me into the past, who have heard my story, would you condemn me to die? Or, as I have pled my own case, would you grant me a stay of mercy? When I began retelling my saga, I warned that my guilt was born of my passion and youth. And as I have reflected on my actions, it has occured to me that so few of us—especially when we are young—are allowed the time to truly contemplate what we do and what we have done.

Having been reared as I was, I never had the time to really grow up. So much had happened to me in such a rapid, short amount of time. Maybe, I speculated, this night of reminescence had been God's last gift, His way of allowing me to finally come into my adulthood.

As though to confirm these thoughts, the birds outside started to sing again. And as the dark cover of the sky gave way to the dawn, I tried to decipher what the bird songs signified. They were sad, sweet, serene melodies—ambiguous, like our lives and our awesome desire to live.

I closed my eyes and bowed my head in prayer. When I opened them, I saw that morning had come.

Moments later, an officer of the court arrived to get me. He informed me that a short hearing would be held prior to my execution. Chiang Kai-shek, it seemed, had not come through. Instead, he wanted to make a public example of my punishment.

Even so, it would delay my death for another thirty minutes. For this, I chose to be grateful.

CHAPTER 22

Canton. 1947.

The courtroom was even more crowded than it had been during the trial. The atmosphere reeked of a euphoric bloodthirstiness and the animated movements of almost everyone reminded me of buzzards and vultures waiting for a carcass to be laid out.

But, as the newspapers would later depict, I entered the room resolutely—dressed as before in my grey prison uniform—not frightened or trembling, but poised and calm. Chang Shu, on the other hand, sat down next to me as if he himself was the one who would soon be going to his death. I saw that his hands were shaking and I took them in my hands, clasping them firmly and mouthing the words, "I'm ready."

The Judge requested silence and began to read, his ever powerful voice echoing throughout the courtroom. "Regarding the request for pardon presented to the court on behalf of his client Bianca Tam by her lawyer Chang Shu-sak, and in consequence of the intervention of the President of the Government of the Republic of China, his Excellency General Chiang Kai-shek..."

My lawyer let out an audible gasp, just before it was echoed throughout the entire courtroom. It had happened! The miracle had taken place! Chang Shu turned to me, his ghostly white complexion changing at once to a brilliant rosy glow. He had already understood, seconds before I could even register what was happening, and he had ceased to listen to the remainder of what was being said. I saw the profound and surprised happiness in his face and understood as well. I suddenly felt dizzy and could not myself make out the rest of what the Judge was saying. At once, I felt a hard mass dissolve inside me, and then a feeling of lightness, of freshness, come over me. I covered my face with my hands and cried for joy, the first time I had cried openly in the courtroom. In quick succession the past two years went through my mind—the long days of imprisonment, the humiliation, the depravity, and alongside that I felt the lifeforce that had kept me going, grow again in what seemed a limitless capacity.

And then came those few magic words that every condemned person yearns above all to hear:

"The accused is pardoned and granted liberty on the condition that she leave the territory of the Republic of China within sixty days."

"You are free, Madame, you have won," boomed the judge, turning in my direction.

The courtroom went wild, as reporters trying to get my first statements on this phenomenal turnaround climbed over the barriers and gathered around me. Only after rigorous action on the part of the police was order restored.

Chang Shu came over to me, put his arms around my waist and helped me to my feet. Though my legs were unsteady, I was able to walk with him through the exit reserved for defendants. It was a sunny morning; the smell of earth mixed with the scent of flowers in the air. We drove across Canton in his car, went aboard the ferry and returned for a few minutes to the Isle of Hazelnuts. I walked quickly now, followed by Chang Shu who had to run to keep up with me.

"Here," he said, when he did catch up, and handed me an envelope full of currency that came enclosed with a note from Phillipe Simon, my kind, temporary husband.

"I could only give it to you after the sentence had passed," said Chang Shu. "All your things are at my house. Phillipe Simon saw to that before he left. He was called back to France and is no longer the French Consul in Canton." He paused and seemed embarrassed. Then he handed me a package he had hidden under his jacket. "And this is a little something from me. I don't want you to leave China dressed in a prison uniform."

It was a white cotton dress with stockings and a pair of shoes.

I kissed Chang on the cheek.

"If I am free I owe it to you," I exclaimed. "I hope you feel a small fraction of my joy."

"Of course, I feel important." He smiled with the wise and ceremonious air of the Chinese. "But only by reflection: you are the sun and I the moon."

I hurriedly began gathering my few belongings. "Wait for me here," said Chang, rushing to the door. "I must go and see about your dismissal papers, which in a case of pardon, are issued immediately."

At that moment Yamamoto came in. He was pale as a sheet and his eyes were glazed.

I embraced him and caressed his neck with my fingers—the way I used to do with my children when they were sad.

"I knew all along this time would come," he said softly. "I am happy for you, Bianca Tam."

He was a young man, almost a boy, that the war had uprooted from his home and had cast down again in a desolate land.

I swore to him, "This moment will come for you, too."

He shook his head. "It won't come. But at least one of us will go on living. You will live, and part of me will go on living inside you."

Holding back the tears, I begged him to not even think such thoughts. Then I took a piece of paper, wrote my address in Italy on it, and slipped it into his pocket. As I did, Yamamoto took my hand and kissed it, holding it to his lips for several seconds. Afterwards, he placed something in my hand, closing my fingers around it. So doing, he said, "I have never regretted captivity since loving you."

Yamamoto rushed out without looking back.

When I opened my hand, I saw a tiny gold ring with his name engraved on it and tearfully slipped it on my finger.

*   *   *

Together with Chang Shu, I took the last ferry and crossed the river to Canton.

I immediately went to the Mission to pick up my son, and felt a pang of anguish to discover that Jonathan did not recognize me. In time, I resolved, the scars of the nightmare would disappear—as long as my little family was reunited.

In the car, with Jonathan on my lap, I looked out through the window at the city passing me by.

"Canton has always brought me bad luck," I said to Chang Shu.

"But this is the last time, Bianca Tam. Your clipper leaves for Shanghai in four hours."

Part Five:

BLUE SILK

CHAPTER 23

Shanghai. 1947.

It seemed to me that a long, harrowing chapter—
one that had begun the moment I had met Tam and
had agreed to share his opium tea and all that his
life of peril entailed—would have come to a close.
But I was soon to discover that this was not so, that
one can not so simply shut the door on all that has
come before. Like the rivers that lead circuitously to
the sea, the events of our lives lead in strange
patterns to other events and only slowly over time
can we begin to fathom the purpose and the true
destination of the journey.

Out of the nightmare that had quite nearly
taken my life, I had learned a great deal—about the
consequences of my decisions and actions, and
some of the intricacies of the thing we call love. In
many ways I had changed, or so I believed, and re-
entered a life of freedom thinking I was prepared

to face the difficulties ahead. Although, I couldn't imagine they would be that difficult, considering what I had already been through. I would soon be proven very wrong.

If I had changed, the once international Shanghai had literally transformed and was barely recognizable to me. The Japanese had left. One year after the surrender, nearly three million had returned to their homeland, thanks to the help of the United States and their civilian air lines. The Europeans were also leaving forever those cities in which they had resided for more than fifty years. Canton and Shanghai were hurriedly abandoned and the various legations of foreign countries began to resemble small armed and heavily manned forts rather than embassies. No one knew what Mao's plans were, but they knew that the Communists would take control of all economic and commercial activity, the principle means of income for the Europeans in China. Fraught with the escalating conflicts between followers of the government and those who were rallying behind the cause of Mao Tse-tung, a volatile political climate was evident everywhere and it had absolutely no room for outsiders.

It was in this "new" Shanghai that I met Erwin Leschziner—whom destiny provided for me to learn my greatest lesson about love. And I suppose it was also fate that had us meet in a high-fashion boutique where I was trying on a dress.

Erwin was a handsome man—with greying hair, an aristocratic nose, a chiseled jaw line, and sparkling, sly eyes—who did not show his forty-seven years. He was a successful wholesaler in fabric and the owner of several boutiques in Shanghai. This placed him in the "foreign capitalist" category, a group which did not have a promising future in the New China.

As I would later learn, his wife Inge—a lovely, ethereal, and psychologically fragile girl from Bavarian high society—had committed suicide. Many of his relatives—parents, brothers, sisters, and others—had disappeared at Dachau and Auschwitz during the Holocaust. I would also come to know that he had no friends in China and lived alone in a suite at the Cathay Hotel, created by Sir Victor Sassoon in Art Nouveau style and later transformed into the "Hotel of Peace."

"It suits you marvelously and I am sure you are the only woman who can wear it," said Erwin as I was arguing with the shop girl who was telling me that the dress had already been promised to the wife of the British military attaché.

He introduced himself and added, "You are right in wanting that dress for yourself, madame."

I was both flattered and pleased by his attention, hoping that I wouldn't have to let such a beautiful work of art slip out of my hands. It was a magnificent dress of blue Thai silk, inlaid with scarlet, mauve, and forest green flowers. It evoked admiration, in the way that I have always loved the beautiful things that the human hand creates in competition with nature—an inclination even furthered by my long stay in China.

"Mrs. Bianca Tam is absolutely right, Soo," Erwin said to the salesgirl. "Welcome back to Shanghai and congratulations on your victory. Here at the shop we were all on your side, weren't we Soo? Don't worry about Mrs. Bruce. I'll speak to her myself and she'll be happy to give up the dress."

"Are you the owner?" I asked, skipping the preliminaries. "I've come a couple of times to your shop, but I've never seen you."

"The third time brought us both luck."

I asked him whether the rumors about him were true—that he was said to be the best designer in Shanghai, but also the most expensive.

"Not as far as you're concerned, Madame Tam. He took my hand and kissed it. "This dress is for you. Please accept it as a modest gift in honor of your liberation."

I was wary of taking such a gesture too seriously, so I thanked him and then changed the subject. Alluding to the lavish presentation and the many garments in the shop, I commented, "It looks like you are the only person who is not in a hurry to leave Shanghai."

"You on the other hand must leave," he replied.

"I must leave and I want to leave. China has taken too much out of me."

"Will you return to Italy?"

I forced a smile. "Well, I must introduce my famous children to their grandmother."

For a moment Erwin's smile faded as he told me, "If Mussolini had not copied Hitler and begun persecuting the Jews, I would have certainly chosen Italy as my home."

"Why not do so now? That is, unless you'd rather stay here and design dresses for the wives of the Communist leaders."

"Well, the temptation is strong," he said, laughing and stroking his chin. "It would certainly be an amusing challenge. I'm not sure where I'll go, but I believe I must resign myself to leaving this city which I have loved very much. Today a whole world is coming to an end. Unlike you, I am grateful to China. This country accepted and protected me from the devastation of the war, which I only experienced from a distance."

There was a quality about Erwin that immediately made him familiar to me, as though I'd known him before. I could tell, without having yet heard the details, that he had a deep sadness in his past. At the same time his grace and charm made one desire his company. Because of this, though I had explicitly refused to attend any social functions in Shanghai, I accepted his invitation to a luncheon he was giving in his hotel the following day.

While readying to leave China, I was living with my children and Lynn in a comfortable hotel in the International Concession. Fortunately, Chang Shu had managed to get back at least a part of my money and valuables which Villerose had tried to finagle. Together with the money given to me by my ex-husband Phillipe and some money from my family, I would be able to make it through the weeks ahead until we took the British Overseas Aircraft Company flight back to Europe. But I still had no idea how we would live once we got there.

An uncertain future—four children, an impoverished family, and a war-torn country, as my mother informed me. To make matters a bit more complicated, I was not prepared for the necessary transition I had to go through. Nor was I at all forewarned about the varied ways that others might react to me and how their reactions might make me feel.

But the minute I walked into the Cathay Hotel wearing the dress which Erwin had given me, I began to get an early taste. I realized, as everyone turned to stare at me, that the dress suited me after all. Blushing at their compliments, I also realized that their fascination wasn't only with my appearance. Throughout the lunch I obliged the guests—answering their barrage of questions to satisfy their curiosity about my life. Indeed, Chang Shu's prediction had been correct—I had become the most talked about woman in post-war China.

Love, espionage, prison, the trial, the death sentence, the pardon—a whirling and fateful circle—and there I was in my Thai dress. Life often exalts what it first attempts to destroy.

That was the first of many social occasions during which I was continually scrutinized, as if under a magnifying glass, and made the target of smiles, of loaded comments, of gossip. At first, I'll admit that I enjoyed this certain notoriety. But soon enough, I would grow tired of it, appearing less and less in public, until finally I would feel as though I was being tormented.

*   *   *

Erwin was discreet, a true gentleman. Now and then he took me to dinner, or invited me to go for long walks, or to the theater. He was always punctual, understanding and protective.

On the way home one evening, not long before my scheduled departure from China, I had an idea. "Erwin," I suggested, "it's still quite early. Why don't you come and meet my family?"

We had grown very close in the short weeks and it seemed natural to ask.

"Here are my jewels," I said in my suite, introducing my children Lylongo, Jula, Aloma, and little Jonathan—aged ten, six, five, and one, respectively. All of them were growing up to be exotic and beautiful—their mixed racial parentage bringing out distinctive characteristics. Erwin commented that Lylongo's eyes were extraordinary: deep green, slanting upwards, not sad, but rather serious. Already she had the quality that I had been forced to learn: self-defense.

I left the children with the amah and went to sit with Erwin in the hotel lobby. "It's a far cry from the splendors of the Cathay Hotel," I began.

"I'll come back with you to Europe," he said, taking my hand and holding it tenderly.

His unexpected intimacy had in reality been prepared by all the days we had spent together up until that moment. I did not know how to act, what to say, how to respond to that warm voice and that gentle hand that now pressed mine. I was at a turning point once again, which destiny had mysteriously presented to me.

"You can't live alone," he said. "That's obvious. Unless you want to close yourself away in the house with your mother and meditate on your past sins. If you want to start a new life, you need a man beside you to help. You need a husband."

"I've already heard this story from my ex-husband Phillipe," I quipped, pulling away.

Erwin was far from discouraged, telling me, "He was absolutely right. And today it's even more true."

"It's not as desperate as all that," I said.

He continued as if he hadn't heard the objection in my tone, smiling and looking at me with his twinkling eyes. "You're in a very difficult position, Bianca. As long as you remain in China, you can act the role created for you by the trial and the newspapers. But once you're back in Italy, your fame will be worthless—you'll just be a widow with four children. Yes, one who was pardoned, but who was judged guilty after all."

I was infuriated and told him he was being both arrogant and rude. I asked, "What gives you the right to judge?"

Erwin took my harsh words and replied softly, "You know that what I've said is true. Think about it. For the moment you are enjoying your freedom and your children, and you are content, but this time will end. I love you Bianca and I want to help you."

I had come to a momentous realization and sat down as though thunderstruck, murmuring, "No man has ever really helped me."

"Then I'll be the first. I'm asking you to marry me, here in Shanghai, before we leave."

I stood up. I sat down again. I stood once more. My head was spinning. I was torn between passive acceptance and pride, docility and rebellion. "Give me time to think about it, Erwin." I nodded goodbye to him and went up to my room. The next morning I sent back the beautiful Thai dress to his shop without a note.

He answered in kind by sending me a bouquet of white roses with a note saying he would call on me that evening after dinner.

I could only laugh when he arrived as he said he would, on time and elegantly dressed as usual. Somehow, I had to find a way to get him to take "no" for an answer. Without saying a word, we walked together down to the lobby.

"Look, Erwin," I began rather coldly, "if I haven't been a good mother, I will certainly be a terrible wife. Tam is dead and I am a widow and I intend to remain so. I will never do again what I did for my first husband. I'm sorry, Erwin, your marriage proposal has come too late."

He was more resolved and assured than anyone I had ever met, as he said calmly, "I'm not asking you to marry me and grant me all the rights and privileges of a husband. You will still be able to do anything you like. We don't even have to live together."

But I had been this route before with the French Consul and knew that it could not work. I confronted Erwin, "Then why do you want me to marry you?"

"I am completely alone," he uttered wistfully. "The idea of helping you and offering you the protection you need fills me with happiness. I am old enough and rich enough for people to respect me. Believe me, that respect could be very useful to you."

"That's not a good reason to get married, to be useful to someone according to a plan." I didn't know why I was bothering to continue the conversation, yet somehow neither Erwin nor I had gotten up to walk away.

He next tried to convince me by promising that, if I desired, I could have the marriage annulled once I had returned to Europe. Erwin also reminded me that I had expressed my concern about supporting myself and the children in Italy. "Well," he added, "you will likewise have to prove to your family and all the others who defended you and helped you that they weren't wrong about you. It won't be easy to convince them that a twenty-seven year old woman has the right to live as a free-spirit, just as she likes."

"That's the last thing on my mind right now."

"It ought to be the first," he insisted. "The rest is what you need me for."

I looked at him with curiosity.

Erwin explained that it was his desire to see that my children were enrolled in a boarding school. For me to bring them up on my own was wholly unrealistic, he said. "Your affection and desire to protect them along with your feeling of guilt will inevitably lead to a suffocating over-protectiveness. They can never forget what they have seen, whatever part of the world they live in. Your duty is to provide them with a good education. But all your love will not make up for the absence of a father, and they would certainly get used to the presence of another man at your side. I want to be that man."

"Everything you say is, in its own way, true, Erwin. The mother of these children really doesn't know how she is going to make her living or what she'll do with herself."

I was giving in, slowly, to the need for security, to a trustfulness, to Erwin's benevolent plan.

In that place where everyone was running away, where everyone's future was in doubt, I had to resolve my situation at the core; I couldn't become another exile, this time in my home country. Even if the haste with which I made my decision predisposed me toward another failure, I had to risk the course of my life, to find it once more.

"I sincerely hope," he said, eerily reading my thoughts, "that we will be able to overcome our doubts as well as the uncertainties which await us in Europe."

A stillness that precipitates the moment of decision had come over me as I sighed and asked him, "Erwin, do you remember what they said at the trial about me—that I was a woman without scruples who would do anything for money?"

"You don't have to worry about money now. Fashion is a well-paying business, and it will continue to be so now that the war is over."

"I'm still an unscrupulous woman."

"Go on," he said smiling. "Now you're playing the part of the fallen woman. You are, however, different from other women and this is your great appeal. An appeal that can't be passed up." And then he paused, kissing both my hands tenderly, and said, "Go ahead and be unscrupulous, then, with me."

* * *

The Chinese consider the seventh day of the seventh moon a lucky day. On that night, according to legend, two stars, Shepherd and Weaver, today known as Altaia and Vega, joined together and journeyed through the abyss of the Milky Way.

We chose that holiday—the only holiday before our departure—to celebrate our wedding.

Erwin was waiting for me in the hall of the municipal building of Shanghai—where the table was draped with the red and gold silk banner displaying the traditional colors of China. I arrived with Lynn and the hotel doorman, who served as my witnesses. Erwin brought two friends of his from the fashion business, a Czech and a Pole, both Jews, as his witnesses.

Ours was a marriage of mutual understanding, decided by two people who barely knew each other. Under Chinese law—for I was still a Chinese citizen—I took on Erwin's status as a displaced person. This would help me to obtain new documents with my new name.

Erwin beamed while the articles of the marriage code were read aloud regarding the duties of the father towards the children's future. He had wanted a child by his first wife, Inge, and now he found himself with four children that he really did want to consider his own, hoping that the distance they had already shown to him would soon turn to affection.

We avoided all publicity about the marriage and the four witnesses were the only guests at the lunch which Erwin gave at the Cathay Mansion. He had even managed to find some German champagne (not very easy to come by after the Japanese exodus) and with that we ended our traditional Chinese meal.

In the afternoon we moved into his hotel. Lynn and the children were given rooms on a separate floor, while he and I occupied a suite of two separate bedrooms with a salon.

When I went to my room I found an exquisitely beautiful camphor-lined chest, an antique dating from the eighteenth century, magnificently carved by Manchurian craftsmen with scenes from the life of Confucius. I marvelled at the detail which became more rich and intricate the more I studied it. Erwin had filled the chest with kimonos, robes, silk and cotton fabrics. It was his wedding gift to his bride, that in two weeks, would return with me to Italy.

As planned, Erwin would join me later at Mama's villa in Spezia, where I intended to stay for a long time. Assuming that I would want to leave alone and have time to reacquaint myself with my mother, he delayed his own departure, saying that he had some business to attend to in Shanghai and that he would not be able to leave so soon.

Those were our plans, but we had made no decisions as to what to do after he had joined me in Italy.

"It's a magnificent gift, Erwin," I said, eyeing the chest. I was both touched by his generosity and astonished at its beauty.

"Have you had a look inside?"

"Yes, but it will take me several days to go through it all. I want you to tell me everything about each item. All I know is that they are extraordinarily lovely and that many of them must be antiques."

"Yes," he said, "I will tell you everything, whenever you want." But first, he reminded me, we were due to go out for dinner.

As we were driving down Nanking Road, and memories overcame me, I pointed out to Erwin a three-story building decorated with colored lanterns. "That's where Nancy organized her encounters," I said.

"Aren't you curious to see what it looks like now?" he asked, and he immediately told the driver to stop and let us out.

Upon his insistence, we were seated at a table on the same floor where Nancy had held her banquets. I bristled, telling him, "I'll be leaving Shanghai soon. It wasn't really necessary for me to see this place again."

He beckoned the waiter and said to me cryptically, "This is where your spy story begins. Better to come back here than to pretend it never happened."

I told the waiter to bring me a bottle of rice brandy—usually had at the end of the meal—along with a pot of jasmine tea. Then, realizing he'd intended to bring me here in the first place, I asked Erwin if he was going to take me to visit all the places that were part of my illustrious past. Drinking several glasses of brandy, one after the other, I felt myself growing belligerent toward him, not understanding why, yet not restraining myself. "Erwin, you wanted to see this place," I baited him, keeping my voice low, soft, and inviting. "And do you also want to see what happened afterwards, between me and the other guests?"

"Stop it," he tried to hush me, "you're drunk."

"Sorry to disappoint you," I hissed. "Nancy is gone, the Japanese are gone, Bianca is no longer a widow. She has found herself a good husband and has to act like a nice little wife, or else Erwin Leschziner will withdraw his protection."

He refused to fight with me, saying that he would never have married me had I been any different than I was.

"You like whores, then?" I said, raising my voice.

"I like you," he said, still treating me kindly, though I was being unkind.

"Because you think I'm a whore," I challenged. "A whore with four children, however. Are they enough or do you want some of your own as well?" Not giving him a moment to respond to my hostility, I went on, telling him, "Don't think they'll treat you like a father. You aren't Tam. It's very strange. Tam never did a thing for me, but I loved him very much, and you're helping me in every way. You're absolutely right when you say that I need a husband, so you help me, but I don't love you. We know each other, we go out together, we're married, but we haven't even slept together and you haven't even asked me to go to bed with you."

"I would never force myself on you," he said, angering and confusing me even more.

Whispering seductively now, I reminded him that I enjoyed being taken by a man, being utterly desired. Having become a Chinese woman in many ways, I told him he should realize that Chinese women serve and obey their men in everything.

"You are not a subservient woman," he retorted, now a slight edge of command in his voice.

"In bed, I am," I crooned, sliding my tongue along my lips. "Look. This is where it happened. There, behind the sliding door. We would go in there and the hat-check girl, who used to be the lover of the Secretary of the Japanese Embassy, would prepare the pipe and pass it around to everyone and fan us whenever we got too hot. Then she would make love to him. It took me awhile to get started, but eventually they were all quite satisfied. Oh, don't think that there were all that many men. But they grew attached to me and wouldn't let go. They even became jealous."

The only emotion he showed came through in a subtle flush of his cheeks as he asked, "How many of them were there?"

"Erwin, you're jealous, too. You're jealous of my past." I felt the truth of my words as I pounded the table with my fist, "You'll never let me be free as you promised. But I've already told you—I'll never be yours, or anybody else's. Never again."

Suddenly I stopped, interrupted by a stray memory. I said nothing, but Erwin could read in my eyes what I was thinking.

"You're thinking about Yamamoto," he said. "Aren't you? He's dead. He killed himself by taking cyanide the night before he was to be brought in front of a firing squad. I sent a telegram to the camp in Canton and they answered me a few days ago."

"He wasn't pardoned, then," I murmured. "He was such a handsome boy. And he was right. Better to leave this world than live as a prisoner or with a constant feeling of guilt or as I do, unfree to feel my own emotions. He had the guts to end it."

With no outward jealousy, he asked, "Did you love Yamamoto?"

"I was in prison and he was a young man who was going to die." Unable to weep for Yamamoto, I reflected aloud, "It seems strange, but all the men I really love, die. And when I married Phillipe, I was immediately arrested and he was sent back to France. I am condemned to a solitary life. I must bring bad luck."

"It's not true for me," he said in a low but sure tone.

My earlier aggression now gave way to dejection. "This must be my punishment. To give myself to men who are then taken away from me. Unable to belong to anyone and belonging to whoever wants me. That's how it happened with you. Perhaps only because you were the first man to come along when I returned to Shanghai."

"Perhaps there are other reasons," he said, rising, as if he knew something I did not. I threw back my last glass of brandy and followed him out of the place of the past.

On the silent walk back to the hotel, I tried to collect myself, trying to use my experience to understand what in fact Erwin wanted from me. I had never been in a position not to be intensely desired by a man and his seeming indifference in this regard wounded my pride and made me feel unable to rely on my powers of enchantment—these being perhaps the only qualities of which I was sure in myself. I was also deeply attracted to him physically, further frustrating the situation.

When we got back to our suite, I turned to him and confronted the issue, saying, "Erwin, I still have not felt from you whether you want me or not."

"I want you very much, Bianca."

Dutifully I approached him, took his hands in mine, and kissed him for a long time. I knelt before him, and still he seemed distant, even as I undressed him and took him in my mouth.

Before dawn I returned to my room, having felt little while with him, and even less afterwards.

*   *   *

History, they say, has a way of repeating itself. Where once I lived a double-life as dutiful mother and spy, I now took on another divided existence.

I considered myself in two different ways: with Erwin—the only man I allowed to know the truth—I thought of myself as guilty, with self-loathing, ready to pay for my crimes, convinced that this was the only possibility of redeeming myself and of guaranteeing a future. But when I was with other people, I was proud and outgoing—seeing myself as a young, admired woman who had come through the war, had passed through prison and the death sentence—untouched and unashamed.

As the talk of the town, I received an abundance of social invitations during my last ten days in Shanghai, often from officers and diplomats who did not know of my marriage. For the most part, I preferred not to accept, out of respect to Erwin. But when we did attend these functions, I played my role to the hilt—just as I once did when I had gone to work with Nancy.

As soon as I would enter a salon, Erwin usually at my side, I would immediately feel the curiosity and attention of everyone in the room and I did little to avoid their fascination. It made me happy for the moment, like a teenage girl who wants to be sought by all the boys. Circulating among the guests, my head held high—as if to say proudly, 'here I am, Bianca Tam,' I felt an odd need to be appreciated, which even the publicity during the trial had not extinguished.

At the last of these such events, a reception at the British Embassy, Erwin had left me to mingle and had gone off to take advantage of the presence of the Embassy attachés to ask about passports for displaced persons. From a distance, he continued to observe me throughout the party.

A woman who lets herself be desired becomes desired. How well I knew this, as a throng of men encircled me, each vying for a private moment. I appealed to men my own age, men much older, married men—all of whom considered me a woman who needed protection. I understood that some desired me because the thought of helping me made them powerful; others wanted me because I was known to have been with many men and they thought they could easily have me.

The most insistent of all the guests was an attaché from the Italian Embassy, who had come alone to the reception. He was more or less Erwin's age and his position at the Embassy, in reality quite mediocre, must have given him an exaggerated sense of self-importance and he managed somehow to pull me aside to converse alone with him. He eyed me ironically, making subtle jabs about my scarlet past, all leading up to the point that I needed a man like him to make things right.

Apparently annoyed by this, Erwin made his way over to us, but remained just behind me, listening in on our conversation.

"I know," the Italian attaché was saying, "that your sentence requires you to leave China, as I myself will do soon. I suppose you've already thought about how you will be received in Italy. Many Italian social circles are still rather bound to traditional values." His voice was laced with sarcastic innuendo.

"So," I replied, "you're saying that I'll have to put up with the scorn of others."

"I'm just saying that it will be difficult for a woman who is alone."

"She is not alone," Erwin interrupted, stepping forward.

The attaché regarded him with feigned calmness. "I don't believe I know you."

"And you won't. Leave the lady alone and don't bother her anymore. Not here or in Italy."

All the other guests were staring at us.

"You're a complete idiot," snorted the attaché.

Erwin grabbed him by the collar. "You disgusting little runt, stay out of my way." Erwin pushed him a few feet backwards.

Though furious, the attaché did not react.

Erwin took my arm and pulled me away. Then he stopped, turned to face me, and spoke passionately, "You're free to do as you like, but not to let yourself be insulted. Let's go. We're going back to the hotel. Don't worry, your image isn't damaged. On the contrary, you'll be admired even more. You're hardly out of prison and you've already found a man willing to beat someone up on account of you."

He took me by the arm and we left. Without a word we went up to his room at the Cathay and made love. This time he was the one who desired me, and I gave myself to him completely.

"It excites me to see that other men desire you," he confessed afterwards. "And to watch your pleasure when you feel that you are being courted."

That night we slept together, the first time we had done so.

*   *   *

As part of the preparations to leave, I had helped Erwin in his shop with his inventory—deciding what clothes he should take with him for his business in Europe. The rest would be left to Soo and the other workers.

His business acumen was impressive. During the first exodus which had occurred in the latter part of the war, he had deposited a large sum of money in an American bank, foreseeing that the situation in Shanghai would grow much worse. Unlike others, he had not gone bankrupt and his money, in dollars, had not been devalued. To Erwin's credit, the future would be bright for Soo and the others who took over the shop and who would later succeed in avoiding the damage done to private enterprise by the Maoists coming to power. The shop—once called "Old Bond Street"—would survive for quite a while under a new name. And perhaps, though I wouldn't know for sure, it is still there today on Nanking Road.

Erwin had transferred his money to a bank in Munich—the city that had once been his home. He had made the decision, since he would be returning to Europe, that it was time to go back and visit. He knew that his whole family had been killed, but he still had an important friend whom he was concerned about. Erwin had told me that Axel had been a great comfort to him after Inge's death. He was younger than Erwin and thanks to his work at the Ministry of Culture, Axel had managed to spend the war years in the city without having to leave for the front or to join any special Nazi organization, with the exception of the obligatory membership in the Nazi party.

In 1939, when Erwin had escaped to Shanghai, he had asked Axel to go with him. But Axel had reacted like many other Germans and had declined, saying that although he was not a Nazi, he didn't wish to abandon his homeland at the beginning of a war. Unlike the Jews and other victims, he had not been persecuted or forced into exile and he could not have imagined, as many could not, the atrocities that the Nazis would later perform.

*   *   *

As my time in China drew to a swift close, the most pressing separation facing me was leaving behind my long-time servant and friend Lynn. It had been my decision not to take her back to Italy, a hard decision made for several reasons. It had been partly because she represented the anguish of my past—a past I wanted to obliterate. But more importantly, I felt she had devoted the entirety of her life for the last six years to me, and it was time to return that life to her so her future would not be one of servitude.

At first, although she had understood my reasoning, she reacted fearfully, not knowing how she would make her way in the world. She could not return to Tuyun where she no longer had roots and she also worried that she would have trouble finding a job in Shanghai. "People may remember that I worked for you," she had said, "and they will say that you were a spy and that I helped you."

I had calmed her, explaining, "All the people who knew you are gone. Don't be afraid, you're young. Don't think about the past, because life must go on."

But words had not been enough to fully assure either of us and finally I had thought of a perfect solution—which Erwin happily supported. He had given Lynn enough money to buy a share in his shop and enter into the cooperative with Soo and the other girls, who in fact had been having a hard time raising all the money they needed. It had been my last gift to our much loved amah who had become my only real friend out of the eight years I'd spent in China.

*　　*　　*

It was no longer the Japanese who roamed the streets of Shanghai looking for a good time, but Allied soldiers and Nationalist officers. The city and its inhabitants had two distinct realities. The workers of the factories and of the port had reorganized their labor unions, which created an inner front that favored the Communist advance. This new force of workers was the first center of gravity for the new political power of the Communists that now swept across China, conquering other major cities.

In 1948 and 1949 they would move down to command the central areas and the eastern coast—eventually capturing the region of Canton and the southwest. By May of 1949, Mao would have entered Shanghai and in the months that would follow, his army would go on to conquer the whole Yangtze River valley. Hankow, Wuchang, and Hanyang all would fall. Within months after that, the entire country would attain what many would consider the most stable and authoritative government since the Manchu Emperors of the seventeenth and eighteenth centuries.

After the violence committed by the Japanese army and the massacres of the deepening civil war, the Communist troops would maintain a scrupulously correct line of behavior in the conquered areas. They would not pillage, steal, or rape the civilians. On the contrary, they would organize parties with music and dancing in order to communicate their few and easily understandable goals to the people: end war forever, give China back to the Chinese, abolish poverty and illiteracy, establish a government of the people. As happens in the great revolutions, their message would be clear, essential and straightforward. Undoubtedly, they would be supported by the vast majority of the population as a force which would have then come to give them peace, liberating them from both internal and external oppression.

At the time that Nanking would fall, Chiang Kai-shek would transfer the seat of his government to Chungking for the second time, after withdrawing from the Presidency of the Nationalist government. He would not re-assume this title until March 1950, after having gone into exile on Formosa.

At the time of my departure from China, the Nationalist forces were still more numerous and better equipped than the Communist Army, but were probably worn down by the war with the Japanese that had begun back in 1937. They were certainly less disciplined and united than the Communists. Whole battalions and their officers were beginning to pass over to the Maoists' side. In

Yunan, Mao had known how to wait out the war, bearing up under the accusation that he had placed his own interest and that of his army before the needs of the Nation. But now he was enjoying the fruits of those long years of preparation and within three years following the defeat of the Japanese, he would conquer an immense and divided country. On October 1, 1949, he would proclaim it the Republic of China and would be its elected President.

*   *   *

Obviously, I did not know with foresight of the specifics to come in China's history. But I sensed deeply that around me China's past was already colliding with the flood of massive change to come. And on the evening before our departure, I felt very sad. I asked Erwin to come out with me and we went for a walk along the Bund. The sampans were docking along the banks for the night, tying themselves one to the other.

"When I first arrived," I said to him, "I didn't ask myself if it was forever and I don't want to ask myself the same question now—whether I'll stay in Italy for good."

"We're in the same position," he said, gently linking his arm through mine. "We must both start a new life and it's better not to be alone in such circumstances."

"I have never wanted to be alone," I admitted.

I looked out at the Whampoo. The sun was setting there where the river widened, in a summer display of pink, blue, scarlet, and violet.

The truth of what I was feeling hit me. "I'm afraid, Erwin," I uttered. "I've never been truly afraid, not even when the Japanese bombarded Tuyun or when I was waiting to go to the firing squad. But now that I am free and alive, I'm scared."

He turned to face me, saying, "Your fear will last just the time of the voyage. Once you've arrived in Italy, you'll forget it. And you'll find your strength again."

"You know, I always felt in control, that somehow by making drastic decisions and acting boldly I had mastered fate. But now I feel as if I've never really decided anything for myself."

"Very few people," he responded, looking back at the river, "manage to live without having to choose. Living the life that has been given to you is enough."

I smiled sadly and turned one last time to look at the river and to feel the wind blow on my face.

*   *   *

Erwin brought Lynn with him to see us off at the airport. He gave each of the children a gold four-leaf clover—to bring good luck for the trip and for their new life.

I embraced Lynn, who in turn embraced the children one by one. Then she led them to the passport control, leaving me alone with Erwin.

"So we'll be seeing you in Spezia," I said.

"I'll call you before coming. As soon as I get to Italy."

"Why don't you just surprise us instead?" We shook hands firmly. "Goodbye, Erwin," I said and went to join the children.

Erwin watched me from a distance as we climbed aboard the plane. I looked back to see him standing perfectly still, not even waving, just before I disappeared from his view.

Once we were airborne I looked down through the window. From up there the only thing visible was the twisting course of the Yangtze River.

CHAPTER 24

Europe. 1947-1959.

The war that had raged across Europe had taken a heavy toll in Italy. I had left behind me the city of Shanghai crowded with Allied soldiers and as I came out of the train station in Rome, I saw still more Allied forces. But the feeling in China, when I departed, was one of great uncertainty.

By contrast, I found the spirit in my homeland exalting.

Although Italy had lost the war and its army had been quickly dispersed in a matter of hours—a fact which revealed to the world the cowardice and inefficiency of the Italian commanders—the best of its leaders had been involved in a political and military project that would annul the monarchy and prove to the world that the country was ready to work for its own redemption. Poverty abounded—the Nazi retaliation and Allied bombardments had left their mark. Still, one felt a great pride, a strong wish to reconstruct, and a keen optimism on all levels of society. The war was over.

This was the atmosphere in which I began my new life in Spezia, where my mother had since returned to our ancestral home. Everything to me was both automatically familiar and yet wholly changed. Our Villa Lizza had been emptied of its luxurious furnishings, which had been sold during the course of the war. Most of the valuables were gone—the antique English furniture, the collections of silver and china, priceless Renaissance paintings by Genoese artists, even one by Giandomenico Piola that had so fascinated me as a child: a sensual scene of Queen Esther kneeling before the Emperor.

The rooms still had great charm, in spite of the commonplace furniture that had been placed here and there to fill up the empty spaces.

But the gardens had been the most damaged. The dwarf palms near the steps of the entrance had dried up, the flower beds were overgrown with weeds, the lemon-house had fallen in and the azalea vases had all been broken. The gardener and the other two servants had been dismissed at the beginning of the war since my mother could no longer afford to keep them in her service.

Mama, however, didn't complain. She felt she had sold her belongings at a good price and took pride in making do. This little corner of the country with its abandoned garden and its glimpse of the sea was her whole universe. That was, until I arrived with the children, and added a cheerful touch of confusion to her daily routine.

She had aged visibly. She hid her wrinkles with make-up and changed her clothes constantly—in the morning, for a walk, for tea, for formal occasions. In this rather poignant way, it was as if she was reliving the elegance of the past—as if everything was still as it once had been and nothing had happened. All this, including a strain on an already distant relationship with my father—who still resided elsewhere—filled me with a sense of not belonging; of being a stranger in one's own home.

Erwin wrote me frequently and with each letter that arrived, Mama expressed disapproval, not understanding why such a new husband would be travelling around Europe instead of rushing to be with me and the children. Believing she would never understand, I chose not to tell her about the pact of reciprocal freedom that I had made with him.

Then finally, one lovely September day, Erwin arrived at Villa Lizza.

I had come in from my swim and was drying off on the rocks in the warm autumn sun when suddenly I felt a shadow fall across my face. With my hand, I shielded my eyes from the sun and saw immediately that it was him—he had kept his promise to surprise me. He reached down to me and lifted me from the ground in an embrace.

Before he could get a word out edgewise, I begged him, "Erwin, can we go away from here soon?"

"Whenever you want," he said, caressing me.

As we walked hand in hand along the beach together, I asked him whether he'd met my mother on his way in.

"Yes," he laughed, "I had quite an interrogation from her." My mother, it seems, had drilled Erwin about his intentions and our plans. But all in all, he thought he had assuaged Mama's concerns and had impressed her.

"Are you well?" he asked. "You look it. Have you gotten some rest?"

"If I go on staying here I won't ever do anything else in my life except rest!" I exclaimed, laughing. But then in a wistful voice, I told him, "I was born here, and I have many wonderful memories of this place which I don't want to spoil. It's not because of my mother, but the neighbors, I can't bear the

nosiness of our neighbors and acquaintances here. I
am not treated well, and though I could stand it, it's
awful for the children."

Then and there, the two of us made a plan to go
to Switzerland. Erwin convinced me, saying, "The
Beau Soleil is there—the best boarding school in
Europe and the headmistress is a friend of mine. I
think it will be good for the children to be far away
from Italy—far from the malicious gossip of other
children and their parents. We can go and visit so
that you can see that you're leaving the children in
good hands. Then we'll go to Munich for a few days."

"And then?"

Erwin told me the garments he had exported
from Shanghai had now arrived in Florence, where
he had already begun to get his fashion design
business started. So, he said, "We'll settle in
Florence where you will be Mrs. Leschziner, just like
it says in your passport. No one knows you in
Florence. You'll be protected there."

"Erwin," I murmured, stopping us in our tracks,
"I don't know yet if I love you, but I know that I
need you."

"I never doubted that."

"And that's enough for you?"

"For the moment, yes. And that's not meant as a
threat," he added.

We went into the villa holding hands.

*   *   *

I couldn't go on living there. My mother, who
had been so loving during my adolescence and who
had been a source of strength and support during
my trial in China, now seemed to turn against me,
demanding to know why I had not done things a
certain way. Why hadn't I come back to Italy
immediately after I had discovered Tam's
unfaithfulness? And why had I accepted the brutal

and bitter consequences of being completely alone when she was there to help me for the asking? These were the questions and reproaches that she posed to me without cease. My mother, who was used to fighting for the freedom to express her feelings after the sad experience with my father, had understood my desire to remain in China, but she did not accept what happened later.

"I have always helped you in every way I could," Mama had reminded me, "and when the telegram arrived from the lawyer announcing that you had been pardoned, I was so overjoyed that I fainted. But don't ask me to justify or overlook your actions, because I can't."

I had replied that I never expected her to and pleaded, "Mama, I know that I owe my life to you. And I know that perhaps you will never be able to love me again as you did in the past. But for the future, whenever and wherever we are together, I beg you never to speak about what happened. It's the only thing I ask of you."

She had agreed to my request and had in turn made me promise to ask her for help if ever I needed it. "Remember," she had ended the discussion, "this house is always your home."

*   *   *

I was discovering that living seemed harder than escaping death. Erwin saw, too, the evidence of what sort of reception had been shown to me and the children when we celebrated Lylongo's tenth birthday at the villa. My mother had invited all the children of the neighborhood and not one of the guests came. In spite of the gifts and the pretended gaiety, the party was a disaster. As a result, we chose to leave Spezia even earlier than planned.

After Erwin hired a young governess to help Mama look after Jonathan in Spezia, the rest of us took the sleeping car for Lausanne. Our little family spent a few fun-filled days, staying in a lovely hotel in the old part of the city, and then, despite that the academic year at the Beau Soleil had already begun, we were able to enroll the girls.

As soon as we said good-bye, unfortunately, my spirits plummeted and I began to second-guess the decision for them to grow up at such a distance from me. Eventually, I would resolve that it had been the right thing to do, both because of their later success in the world and also because they had been protected from being ashamed of their mother's past. They understood, of course, that I was not an ordinary woman—but they also must have understood that I had done everything possible to give them a normal life.

But the biggest difficulty was that I would come to resent Erwin, who had influenced me in the decision to send them away to school. His reasoning would benefit the children, yet it also drove a wedge between the two of us—a woman can never completely forgive a man who separates her from her children.

*   *   *

In 1947, Munich was little more than a heap of rubble. Yet what struck Erwin most was not the destruction, but the emptiness. Nothing was where it once had been. There were only traces of a vanished world. And along with the buildings, the people had disappeared. Nearly all the people Erwin had known were gone.

I could see the pain and grief he felt in confronting his past—a grief that all the few Jewish survivors felt after the horror had ended. After two days Erwin couldn't take it anymore and chose to cut the visit short.

He announced this to me at breakfast on the third day, as we sat in the restaurant of our hotel, the Bayerischer Hof, one of the few hotels in the city that, though visibly damaged, had reopened. As he seldom did, he began to talk more openly about the events of his past.

"After Inge's death and before my exile from Germany," he said, as his eyes appeared to be filling with memories, "I was not completely alone. For a long time I was unable to forget her or to forget the last words she addressed to me in her suicide note. She blamed herself for not being able to give me what I needed, but it was not her fault. Our misunderstandings and my rejection of her did not depend on her. Only her death allowed me to discover the truth." Erwin broke off and I encouraged him to continue.

"I've already mentioned Axel to you," he said. "When we met he was eighteen—fifteen years younger than me. He was a student and was extremely handsome. Together we discovered intimacy and passion which I had never known. We separated only when the Nazi laws required me to leave the country. He did not want to leave the university and he had no idea what was going to happen. In all these years we haven't forgotten each other and we have kept in touch. He was the one who kept me informed about my family." Erwin cleared his throat. With what seemed like relief, he said that he'd already written Axel about me and that he wanted to go see him.

Though I suggested that perhaps he would prefer to go without me, Erwin actually wanted me to come along. And, understanding a bit more about him now, I agreed to go.

Axel lived in a block of city-owned apartments at the edge of town. As we went up the stairs we could hear someone playing the Carmen overture— playing it badly—on an out-of-tune piano.

He was blond, had very blue innocent looking eyes and was barely past thirty. What most caught my attention, however, was the constant trembling of his hand—the sign of someone who has received a severe shock and hasn't yet begun to cope.

Erwin had seemed quite nervous earlier, but now face-to-face with Axel he had regained his composure.

Axel poured us glasses of a liqueur that had an unpleasant taste. He apologized about the shabby apartment, saying, "It's not a very comfortable place here." Then he added, "There's nothing comfortable in Germany today."

A young man appeared in the doorway to the other room. He was dark-haired and he wore his shirt open at the chest.

Trying to control his emotion, Axel said, "We'll be moving out of here soon. Some friends at the Ministry will help me find a better arrangement. Those few of us who remained faithful deserve help, don't you think?"

"If faithfulness is a virtue," said Erwin.

The other young man standing in the doorway turned without saying a word to us and closed the door. We heard the opening bars of the Carmen overture being played on the piano. Then he hit a wrong note and stopped.

"Do you find me changed, Erwin?" Axel included me in the conversation, though he didn't have a great deal of choice. He shook his head, sighing. "You have no idea what we've been through. You can't imagine what it is to pass from victory to defeat, and experience misery and terror and spend days buried in the bomb shelters out of fear. Every sound of falling bombs, every loud noise or harsh wind, and I felt the end was near. I used to think, 'Now I'll go out and be hit by shrapnel.' It's good to die when death comes as a liberation."

I thought of Yamamoto, my young lover—of his innocent face, of his obstinacy, of that innocence too soon lost. But Axel hadn't died and his pain made me realize how many victims of the past there were. I squeezed Erwin's arm and he saw that I was overcome.

"Axel," Erwin said, standing up, "It's time for us to go."

"Wait a moment," said Axel and he hurried into the other room. When he returned, he handed Erwin a large envelope. "Take this. These are all the documents you need to obtain an indemnity since you have lost all your relatives and your shop was expropriated. It is your right."

"Good luck, Axel," said Erwin in his warm, encouraging way.

"We'll need it."

Going back down the stairs we heard once again the opening bars of the Carmen overture on the piano.

*　　*　　*

After returning to Italy, we had settled in Florence where Erwin had launched his new fashion business, basing it in the fifth floor of a building at Piazza Santa Trinita. We lived together and I helped him with his projects. Though Florence was still in the process of rebuilding itself, there was also room for the good life—for refined social activities and aesthetically pleasing surroundings. But in spite of our deep fondness and creative collaboration, it seemed that fate had doomed me to sabotage the stability I had found with Erwin.

I was haunted by the past, restless and suffocated by its ever presence inside of me. When I looked at Erwin, seeing beyond his kind, benevolent role, I saw a man also riddled by torturous memories. It was our bond, for he too saw through me as a witness to my past—to the side of myself I wanted not only to hide but to bury for good. It was that which pulled us together and that which pushed me away.

Taking advantage of our pact of equal freedom, I often came home late at night after parties I had attended with new friends, mostly young men my own age. At thirty-one, I was no longer the wild innocent, but I had become even more resistant of having anyone control me. Several times I introduced Erwin to the young men who momentarily dazzled me and comforted my restlessness. One of them was Gino, descendant of a noble Florentine family, who with his pale blue eyes and thick black hair, small mouth and perfect teeth, was indeed a reincarnation of a youthful Renaissance nobleman.

In retrospect, I would realize that flaunting men like Gino was my capricious and destructive way of testing the limits of Erwin's love—making him jealous and reminding him of his past; a weapon I somehow felt he wielded against me. My other weapon, my physical charms that had conquered many a man, had been rendered useless with Erwin. I had confronted him with this once, claiming that his very sporadic advances proved he did not find me beautiful or appealing enough.

He had objected, saying, of course, he found me beautiful—to him the most beautiful woman in the world. "Though in objective terms there are other women more physically beautiful than you," he had also said. "My love isn't based on this, but on the beauty of your spirit, on what shows through when you walk into a room and everyone turns in your direction. It is not the face and figure of the century that attracts them, but a quality you own that seems to come from another world, a hypnotic source of energy." He had been speaking with great emotion, concluding, "This is what I love, the person, the woman, not the pretty outer shell."

But perhaps I had been unable to accept feeling worthy of this and I had countered, "No. You love me for two reasons: because you think you can defend and protect me and because you think I understand you. I am the only person that you care for, the only one left. But I am not the right person for you."

Erwin had reminded me, "I have never asked you for anything and I have helped you solve your problems."

It was all too true. But finally, unable to bear my dependence any longer, I demanded that he let me go. "You don't want a wife," I began, "you want a daughter. Remember, though, I grew up without a father and I have been free all my life and I have been with many men. Perhaps you wouldn't have asked me to marry you if there weren't so many things you had to forgive me for. A good father accepts everything, understands everything. But as long as I am with you I'll never be able to forget China, prison, betrayal, and all that has happened."

Unmoved by what I had said, he remained firm, unwilling to give up even one inch of the territory he had conquered, of the rights he had acquired. "It was your life," he said.

"Well, I want another life," I shouted, "and I can have another life without you." Seeing he was impervious, I searched for the words that would sting the most and said coldly, "In the beginning, I really thought I could grow to love you. But I was wrong."

Erwin did not answer. He fell into an armchair and covered his face with his hands.

"You'll be happier when I am gone," I said calmly.

"Where do you want to go?"

I described my plan to him, my desire to go to Paris and work in fashion there with his acquaintance, Christian Dior, whom I asked that he contact to make the arrangements. I had already found out that Dior was hiring new staff at his atelier on Avenue Montaigne and that he was becoming the most important name in fashion in post-war France.

Erwin finally did as I had asked, forgiving my abandoning him with an almost embarrassing selflessness. However, he had warned me, "Bianca, running away from me won't rid you of the past. One day you must stop running and face it."

On the day before my going to Paris, Erwin announced that he had a favor to ask of me in return for recommending me so highly to Dior. We walked down to a popular café, the Red Jacket, and sat down at a little table in the square. It was a cold clear morning in January.

"I don't know," he said, speaking very quietly, "if you want to ask me for a divorce or not."

I shrugged, saying, "I haven't really thought about it yet."

"You know that I will not oppose your decision when you do decide to go through with it. But there is one thing I ask of you. If you agree, please let me know what's happening to you—what you are doing, who you are with. I want you to leave me a little space in your life. You'll have your new life, but I beg you not to disappear completely and to go on existing in my life."

He was leaving me free. Erwin, whose past was a ruin of death and destruction had seen me as a symbol of life and vitality, a symbol of courage and daring to confront life and the uncertain future. He had offered me his protection—his way of loving. Now he was making his exit and his maturity kept him from falling into despair. He wanted to leave a subtle tie between us so that he would not feel useless. My eyes filled with tears and I leaned over to kiss his cheek.

"Whenever you're in difficulty, you know you can count on me," he said, before we rose to take our last stroll together.

He was sure, he told me, that we would meet again and I agreed. Deep down, I believed that fate would never totally cut me off from a man whom it had brought me together with in the first place.

* * *

Cultured, refined, with an expert eye for design, Christian Dior was a gentleman, the first requirement for a fashion designer. Whoever worked for him was quickly charmed by the way he managed to draw the best from his employees and by the respect and esteem he showed to his colleagues.

He was immediately pleased with the way I welcomed and advised his clients who came to me—especially those who refused to purchase anything unless I had seen it on them.

Dior complimented me often and was very much interested in my opinions. He noted that my years in China had refined my taste to a developed aesthetic sense, both demanding and delicate, with a love for little exotic touches that created a sense of appealing mystery.

Paris, where I knew no one, opened its arms to me and made me believe the haunted existence was over. Even though my legal name was still Bianca Leschziner, I introduced myself as Bianca Tam and found myself at the center of the world of haute couture.

Dior celebrated my looks, saying that I had the flexibility and open abandonment he most sought in his models. In the evening, when work was finished, we would go up to the top floor of the building where his atelier was housed, up to the penthouse where Christian created his fashions.

One of the young designers of the atelier would come with us. Up there, suspended among the rooftops, with a splendid view of the city lights, often with the music of Chopin playing in the background, Dior had me pose nude while he tried out the various garments he had created from fabrics chosen with me in mind. While the young designer sketched, Dior would walk away to study me from a distance, then return and rearrange the folds of the fabric draped about me.

At one point, he said to me, "The beauty of the male body is an absolute. We all know it—the discus thrower, Apoxyòmenos, and so on—that will always remain the same, for no civilization will be able to replace the canons of beauty which have been so firmly established. But the beauty of the woman is multiform, in constant transformation, yet faithful to an ideal—within reach, yet inexpressible, elusive, physical. My idea of the beauty of a woman is to see her completely open, self-abandoned, offering herself, waiting for someone who will make her come alive and transform her."

Another time, while we were preparing for the winter fashion show designs, we tried a heavy black wool fabric on me. I expressed my doubts.

"But this isn't the color of death," said Dior. "That's why the Chinese choose white for the color of mourning, because death is not dark. The beginning of a long voyage cannot be dark and sad. Black is the color of waiting, it covers the shape of the body while it is at rest and then when the body moves, black reveals those forms. It is the color of desire. A woman who dresses in black must know that it is her body that gives life to that color—to tantalize and make herself endlessly desirable. Black is your color, Bianca."

The day came when he asked me to be not only his inspiration but his collaborator as well, putting me in charge of introducing his work in Italy.

It was a happy arrangement. The Dior shows I organized were a great financial success and soon became important events in the life of the beau monde of Milan and Rome.

Rome in those years, so obsessed with the pursuits of pleasure, seemed the perfect setting for me to enter Italian high society without the stigma of my past. I became the friend of actress Linda Christian, after having met her at one of the fashion shows. How well I would later remember both her shyness and her drive, her love affair with Tyrone Power, which ended with a splendid marriage ceremony in the church of Santa Francesca Romana. I met Prince Ruspoli, who was elegant, charming, extraordinarily intelligent. I met many people—aristocrats, adventurers, actors, leading ladies and extras in that wild merry-go-round of the Roman dolce vita that was even more hypocritical, crazy, and cruel than the world described in Fellini's film.

All the same, even though I was enormously busy with work as well as a consuming social life, an old loneliness crept back into my being. Like ghosts knocking at the gate of conscious awareness, the past had not yet truly allowed me my freedom.

*   *   *

It was at the Gallia in Milan where I had organized a show that would yield a decisive encounter. I was attired in a black wool suit which Dior had chosen for me. The sophisticated look was accented by a rich green hat and multi-colored feather plume.

The festivities had gone on all night and it was nearly dawn when I asked the clerk at the desk for the key to my room. He handed it to me along with a note:

> *I have been waiting all night to drink a glass of champagne alone with you.*—Franco.

I looked up and saw a young man standing before me—tall and refined, with mesmerizing dark eyes.

As we drank, I found that he was extremely forward and likewise irresistible. Though I tried to insist that I was not looking for a suitor, he pledged, "I won't give up—not with a woman who attracts me as much as you do."

"It must happen often," I said.

"Not at all," he replied. Pointing to his wedding ring, he explained, "I am completely free. I was married, I have two children and I have been living separated from my wife for two years, if you want to know."

"Sometimes it's necessary to free oneself from the past, don't you think?"

"Yes, I agree. We married young, overestimating the strength of our love." Without pausing, he asked whether I had ever been married.

"Yes," I answered briefly. "I am a widow and I have four children—all in boarding school."

"But you are very young."

Laughing, I told him I would be forty before I knew it. He laughed as well, letting me know that we were the same age and observing that we both were taken to be much younger than we really were. And then, upon his invitation, I followed him to his car and soon found myself beholding a stupendous sunrise at a vista near the Abbey of Chiaravalle.

As the day's first light slanted against the red brick towers of the Abbey, Franco confessed that this was his solitary place where he came to reflect—I was the first woman to share its beauty with him. With that, he began to kiss me, a kiss that lasted all the way back to my hotel and through the morning hours in which we made love.

"I'll never leave you, Bianca," said Franco, before we fell asleep in each other's arms awash in the broad light of day.

CHAPTER 25

Rome. 1959-1985.

In no time, Franco had decided to follow me back to Paris, where we had resided in my suite at the Hotel Ritz and together we had enjoyed the immense pleasures of our passionate romance. As I had always done in my life, I was throwing caution to the wind—not certain where he and I were headed—but existing for the moment.

I had told him everything about my life in detail and he had listened, asking no questions, doubting nothing.

I'd said, "I wanted you to know so that you wouldn't think I was something other than what I really am."

"What do you think you are?" he'd asked.

My response had been this: "I am my past."

He said he was not jealous of Erwin and that it

was not love which bound me to him, but the shared memory of our time spent in Shanghai. It was a relationship, he pointed out, that I had chosen to terminate. Like all men, Franco could not understand that the experiences of the past remain fixed in a woman's soul for a long, long time. It troubled him nonetheless and he explicitly asked me never to contact Erwin again.

* * *

The time had come for me to spread my wings and fly, professionally speaking, and I had given my notice to Christian Dior. When I told him that my intentions were to launch my own fashion business in Rome, he had tried to dissuade me, confessing that he did not want to lose me. But eventually, he gave my project his blessings and he even threw in some of the trade secrets that had helped him prosper.

But once in Rome, unforeseen circumstances presented us with an unfortunate obstacle: lack of money.

Franco's wife had accepted his request to annul their marriage, but in return had requested a huge sum of money which Franco had immediately given her. He still had his business, but while he was away with me in Paris, his partner had mishandled matters. The man had gone bankrupt, forcing Franco to cover the deficit. In the end, Franco was forced to sell everything he had in order to pay off his debts.

After paying for my children's requirements, what little was left of my savings allowed us to pay the rent on an apartment and not much else. Without question, I had faced poverty before and had gone to excessive means to prevent it. In addition to its necessity as a form of security, money gives one options—such as my desire to open my own business. Of course, too much wealth can be a psychological burden and a barrier to self-reliance. But on a basic level, I had discovered that I was one of those people who required enough of it to enjoy a certain style of life, over and above mere survival. As my history had portrayed to me, I was even attracted to gold itself, to the image of solidity and to the good luck that gold can bring; but also to the dangerous consequences of that attraction. Now, once again, it was time for me to take action and I resolved not to repeat old mistakes.

We selected the location for a shop in Via Veneto. My domain was to be the selection of the fashions and sales; Franco would handle the administrative side of the business. As to the lack of funds, I gathered my courage and wrote secretly to Erwin.

I informed him of our situation and asked for his help, relating that I would be visiting the children in Lausanne at Christmas time. I suggested that if he wished, he could meet me in Florence, where we could speak more in detail about my plans.

Erwin responded that he would rather not see me. He had finally found peace with himself and was afraid that seeing me again would probably upset him. But he did not disappoint my request for help. To our house in Rome he sent a huge trunk filled with some of the most beautiful clothes in his collection, along with some bolts of precious fabrics he had just received from China. He informed me that he had managed to maintain business contacts in China and was one of the few merchants in Europe who carried these splendid fabrics in his shops.

I told Franco that the clothes and the fabric were part of Erwin's wedding present.

Soon Erwin opened an account in my name in a bank in Rome, providing me with a very large sum of money. Knowing this would be damaging to Franco's pride, I told him that the money had come from a trust fund put aside by my mother.

Erwin asked only one thing in return—that I call the shop "Raphael." It was years later before I understood the significance of that name. As I would come to know, it was the archangel Raphael who had freed Sarah from the devil, thus allowing her to make a happy marriage.

*   *   *

Life with Franco passed quietly, with no surprises. We were happy living together and reaped abundant success in our business enterprise.

He showered me with tenderness and affection. I repaid him with complete fidelity, along with a wise irony won from an existence that had been full of many varied experiences.

Every year on the seventh day of the seventh moon, Erwin sent me a greeting card to our shop address in Via Veneto, including some brief news of himself. He still had his shop and his atelier and he was living alone in a room at the Red Door Hotel.

I wrote him back and told him about the children, who had finished school and were starting life as adults; about Franco and myself and our successful business; about my mother's death, which had been a peaceful passing, despite the inevitable grief and problems of old age.

One day a delivery man brought me a package. Inside was an antique Chinese chess set, hand-carved in ivory, dating from the Manchu dynasty and similar to the one I had lost on the trip from China back to Italy several years earlier. Erwin had sent it from China.

It was the last news I had of him.

*   *   *

My union with Franco lasted twenty-five years. More than twenty years after the birth of my first child by Tam, I gave birth to two more children who grew up in our house in Rome.

Then, in 1983, Franco became ill with a tumor. He understood its ramifications, but did not want to be hospitalized. And so for two years, I cared for him at home.

"I don't want to leave you, not even for one night," he had said.

A few days later, he died at home.

I remained alone, sold the shop, and concentrated my energies on the concerns of my six children. All of my sons would marry and would find themselves running successful businesses of their own; my daughters too would marry and devote themselves as mothers. All six of them would emerge distinctly self-reliant and independent.

If being a mother and getting my children started in life was my calling, I can say that I fulfilled it.

But I had never learned how to live alone. And I felt strongly that I did not want to consider my life over. I had to concern myself with the future, which is much more pressing than thinking of the past. Bit by bit, the past had ceased to haunt me, leaving instead its lessons—most of them about love and about the mandate of living life fully.

Erwin had once told me that very few people are able to live out what fate has bestowed upon them. If anything, perhaps that is the secret inherent in the tale that began with Tam and his opium tea. In whatever form, everyone is given his or her own opium tea—a door to adventure and experience and learning. Many people have judged my life as extraordinary. If that is indeed so, it stems from the fact that I have walked through the door.

There was only one person I felt I needed to see to complete my understanding of destiny's special plan for me. As he had once promised to help me in whatever I needed, I set off to Florence to find

Erwin. But the atelier was no longer in his name and he no longer lived at the Red Door.

I was unable to find out anything more about him.

EPILOGUE

One morning while reading through one of the Rome newspapers, I came across an article reporting the death of the great fashion designer, Erwin Leschziner. He had died of an attack of apoplexy and was found drawn up in an armchair in front of the window of his room on the second floor of the Savoy Hotel.

As I read the obituary, I realized that this same window looked straight into my flat. I asked the hotel porter how long Mr. Leschziner had been staying there and was told that he had been a guest at the hotel for about a month.

One month. Erwin had observed me for one month.

If it was his wish to be the last, then he had succeeded.

After Tam, after Yamamoto, after Franco, he had won the race by waiting out the years. But why had he not come forward to receive the prize?

I'll never know the answer to that question. But it's certain that Erwin chose if not the moment, then at least the circumstances of his departure from this world—there at the window overlooking my home, where he could see the camphor chest he had given me many years ago as a wedding present. It was proof, if he needed it, that part of him had remained with me for all those years of our separation.

Life resembles the course of a giant river— arising from its source with no more than a trickle, drawing its tributaries, growing and rushing on in a tumult. But towards the end of the journey it grows calm again, and solemn, and it yearns to reach the boundless peace of the sea.

I offer these pages as a gift to a man to whom I am deeply indebted for his love and understanding.

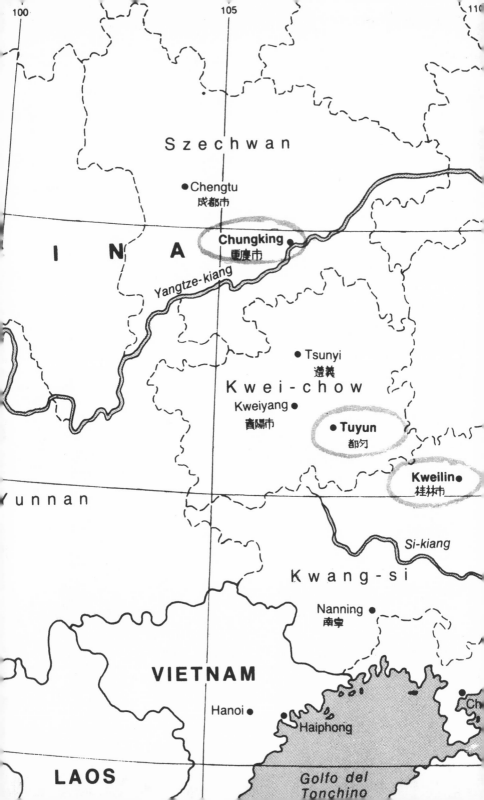